Ronald Dworkin

CW01513167

Ronald Dworkin occupies a distinctive
phy. In public life, he is a regular contr
and other widely read journals. In philosophy, he has written important and
influential works on many of the most prominent issues in legal and political
philosophy. In both cases, his interventions have in part shaped the debates
he joined. His opposition to Robert Bork's nomination for the United States
Supreme Court gave new centrality to debates about the public role of judges
and the role of original intent in constitutional interpretation. His writings in
legal philosophy have reoriented the modern debate about legal positivism and
natural law. In political philosophy, he has shaped the ways in which people
debate the nature of equality; he has spawned a substantial literature about the
relation between luck and responsibility in distributive justice; he has reframed
debates about the sanctity of life. His work has also been the focus of many
recent discussions of both democracy and the rule of law. This volume contains
new essays on Dworkin's key contributions by writers who have themselves
made important interventions in the debates.

Arthur Ripstein is professor of law and philosophy at the University of Toronto.
An associate editor of *Philosophy & Public Affairs*, he is the author of *Equality,
Responsibility and the Law* and co-editor of *Practical Rationality and Preference*
and *Law & Morality*.

Contemporary Philosophy in Focus

Contemporary Philosophy in Focus offers a series of introductory volumes to many of the dominant philosophical thinkers of the current age. Each volume consists of newly commissioned essays that cover major contributions of a preeminent philosopher in a systematic and accessible manner. Comparable in scope and rationale to the highly successful series **Cambridge Companions to Philosophy,** the volumes do not presuppose that readers are already intimately familiar with the details of each philosopher's work. They thus combine exposition and critical analysis in a manner that will appeal to students of philosophy and to professionals as well as to students across the humanities and social sciences.

FORTHCOMING VOLUMES:

Jerry Fodor edited by Tim Crane
Saul Kripke edited by Alan Berger
David Lewis edited by Theodore Sider and Dean Zimmermann
Alvin Plantinga edited by Dean-Peter Baker
Bernard Williams edited by Alan Thomas

PUBLISHED VOLUMES:

Stanley Cavell edited by Richard Eldridge
Paul Churchland edited by Brian L. Keeley
Donald Davidson edited by Kirk Ludwig
Daniel Dennett edited by Andrew Brook and Don Ross
Thomas Kuhn edited by Thomas Nickles
Alasdair MacIntyre edited by Mark Murphy
Hilary Putnam edited by Yemina Ben-Menahem
Richard Rorty edited by Charles Guignon and David Hiley
John Searle edited by Barry Smith
Charles Taylor edited by Ruth Abbey

Ronald Dworkin

Edited by

ARTHUR RIPSTEIN
University of Toronto

CAMBRIDGE UNIVERSITY PRESS
Cambridge, New York, Melbourne, Madrid, Cape Town, Singapore, São Paulo

Cambridge University Press
32 Avenue of the Americas, New York, NY 10013-2473, USA

www.cambridge.org
Information on this title: www.cambridge.org/9780521664127

© Cambridge University Press 2007

First published 2007

Printed in the United States of America

A catalog record for this publication is available from the British Library.

Library of Congress Cataloging in Publication Data
Ronald Dworkin / edited by Arthur Ripstein.
   p.   cm. – (Contemporary philosophy in focus)
Includes bibliographical references and index.
ISBN-13: 978-0-521-66289-5 (hardback)
ISBN-10: 0-521-66289-3 (hardback)
ISBN-13: 978-0-521-66412-7 (pbk.)
ISBN-10: 0-521-66412-8 (pbk.)
1. Dworkin, Ronald.   2. Law – Philosophy.   3. Law – United States – Philosophy.
I. Ripstein, Arthur.   II. Title.   III. Series.
K230.D92.R66   2007
340′.1 – dc22   2006038179

ISBN   978-0-521-66289-5 hardback
ISBN   978-0-521-66412-7 paperback

Contents

Contributors

DAVID DYZENHAUS is a professor of law and philosophy at the University of Toronto. His most recent publication, *The Constitution of Law: Legality in a Time of Emergency* (Cambridge, 2006), is a revised version of the JC Smuts Lectures given to the Faculty of Law of Cambridge University in 2005.

JAMES E. FLEMING is Leonard F. Manning Distinguished Professor of Law at Fordham University School of Law. He is author of *Securing Constitutional Democracy: The Case of Autonomy* (University of Chicago Press, 2006), coauthor of *American Constitutional Interpretation* (3rd ed., Foundation Press, 2003), and coauthor of *Constitutional Interpretation: The Basic Questions* (Oxford University Press, 2007). He also has published a number of articles in law reviews and books, and he is Faculty Moderator of *Fordham Law Review*. During the 1999–2000 year, he was a Faculty Fellow in Ethics at the Harvard University Center for Ethics and the Professions.

SANFORD LEVINSON is the W. St. John Garwood and W. St. John Garwood Jr. Centennial Chair in Law at the University of Texas Law School and a professor of government at the University of Texas at Austin. He has also visited at the Harvard, Yale, NYU, Boston University, Hebrew University, and Central European University schools of law. Among his many publications are *Constitutional Faith* (Princeton, 1988), *Wrestling with Diversity* (Duke, 2003), and *Our Undemocratic Constitution: Where the US Constitution Goes Wrong (and How We the People Can Correct It)* (Oxford, 2006). He was elected to the American Academy of Arts and Sciences in 2001.

ARTHUR RIPSTEIN is a professor of law and philosophy at the University of Toronto. He was a Laurance S. Rockefeller Visiting Fellow at Princeton in 1995–1996 and held a Connaught fellowship in the spring term of 2000. In addition to numerous articles in legal theory and political philosophy, he is the author of *Equality, Responsibility and the Law* (Cambridge, 1999) and coeditor of *Law and Morality* (Toronto, 1996, 2nd ed., 2001) and *Practical*

Rationality and Preference (Cambridge, 2001). He is currently writing a book on Kant's legal and political philosophy. He is an associate editor of *Philosophy & Public Affairs*.

SCOTT J. SHAPIRO is professor of law and professor of philosophy at the University of Michigan, Ann Arbor. In 2001–2002, he was a visiting professor at Yale Law School and the following year a Fellow at the Center for Advanced Study in the Behavioral Sciences. He is the editor (with Jules Coleman) of the *Oxford Handbook of Jurisprudence and Legal Philosophy* and is a member of the advisory board of *Legal Theory*. He is currently writing a book that aims to defend a positivistic conception of law by drawing on recent work in the philosophy of action, in particular the theory of shared agency.

BENJAMIN C. ZIPURSKY is the James H. Quinn Chair of Legal Ethics at Fordham Law School, where he has taught since 1995. He is the author (with John C. P. Goldberg and Anthony Sebok) of *Tort Law: Responsibilities and Redress* (Aspen, 2004) and numerous articles and book chapters in torts, jurisprudence, and constitutional law. Professor Zipursky has taught as a visitor at the University of Pittsburgh School of Law and New York University Department of Philosophy.

Introduction: Anti-Archimedeanism

ARTHUR RIPSTEIN

I said I thought that legal philosophy should be interesting. He jumped on
me. "Don't you see?" he replied. "That's your trouble." I am guilty of his
charge.

– Ronald Dworkin

Ronald Dworkin occupies a distinctive place in both public life and philosophy. In public life, he is a regular contributor to *The New York Review of
Books* and other widely read journals. In philosophy he has written important and influential works on many of the most prominent issues in legal
and political philosophy. In both cases, his interventions have in part shaped
the debates he joined. His opposition to Robert Bork's nomination for the
United States Supreme Court gave new centrality to debates about the public role of judges and the role of original intent in constitutional interpretation. His writings in legal philosophy have reoriented the modern debate
about legal positivism and natural law. In political philosophy he has shaped
the ways in which people debate the nature of equality; he has spawned a
substantial literature about the relation between luck and responsibility in
distributive justice; he has reframed debates about the sanctity of life. His
work has been the focus of many recent discussions of both democracy and
the rule of law.[1]

Dworkin's public and philosophical voices are closely connected. He
criticizes Robert Bork for his deficient views about the relation between
law and morality, the proper conception of democracy, and the philosophy
of language. During the Vietnam War, he used his general account of the
relation between law and morality to explain the relation between draft
resistance, civil disobedience, and the rule of law. His account of equality
of resources frames his interventions in public debates about health insurance. His understanding of debates about the sanctity of life engaged with
both public debates and more abstract questions about the relation between
political and personal morality. Dworkin also played a significant role in
facilitating the first contact between prominent South African lawyers and

1

the African National Congress. He concluded a lecture in 1984 by saying "You may find it odd that the lawyers' contest about styles of adjudication finally turns in the way I claim on ideals of community, that volumes of philosophy speak in the fall of every judge's gavel. It may be odd, but I'm sure it's true, and even a little thrilling."[2]

EARLY PHILOSOPHICAL DEVELOPMENT

A journalist who recently wrote about Dworkin described him as regarding biographical questions as "odd and trivial."[3] His life attracts a certain amount of interest, in part because of his remarkable ability to give clear and polished lectures in complete paragraphs, without depending on any text or written notes, and without any apparent expenditure of effort. People who have dined with him wonder whether his famed discussion of the person with a taste for plover's eggs is more than a philosopher's example. Dworkin has no doubt had an interesting life, but the aim of this book is to engage with his ideas. In the light of his own views about the relations between authors and the texts they write, it seems appropriate to keep this biographical section even briefer than is standard in books in this series.[4]

Dworkin was born in Providence, Rhode Island, in 1931, one of three children. He attended Harvard on a scholarship, studying philosophy, and went on to Oxford as a Rhodes Scholar. Dworkin was by all accounts an outstanding student at Oxford. H. L. A. Hart, who was then the University Professor of Jurisprudence at Oxford and widely regarded as among the most important legal philosophers of the twentieth century, was a reader for his final examinations and surreptitiously kept a copy of Dworkin's papers for himself.[5] Hart later intervened to have Dworkin appointed as his successor to the Chair in Jurisprudence.[6]

At Oxford, Dworkin's interests shifted from philosophy to law, and after completing his degree he attended Harvard Law School. In an interview in the NYU Law School alumni magazine, he describes law school at Harvard at the time as easy for anyone "reasonably adept at moving arguments around."[7] He then clerked with Judge Learned Hand of the United States Court of Appeal. Hand was by then semi-retired and directed Dworkin to read and comment on the Holmes Lectures which he was to give at Harvard Law School the following year.

After clerking, Dworkin practiced law for several years with Sullivan and Cromwell in New York City before accepting a teaching position at Yale Law School. At Yale he taught basic courses, and he also taught a course together with Robert Bork. In 1969 he accepted the position of Professor of Jurisprudence at Oxford, succeeding Hart. In 1975 he moved half of his appointment to NYU Law School.

Hart and Hand were each significant influences on Dworkin's intellectual development. In each case, he reacted against their views, and his considered responses to them will emerge in different ways in some of the essays in this book. The general direction of the reactions can be described fairly briefly. Hart defended the position in legal philosophy known as legal positivism, according to which law and morality are fundamentally distinct. By this Hart did not mean to deny that law and morality frequently overlap, but rather to claim that they were conceptually distinct, so that questions about what the law is on a particular matter are always conceptually distinct from questions about what the law should be. The difference between what the law is and what it should be is, of course, familiar to anyone who has ever been morally dissatisfied with particular laws, but Hart elevates this intuitive distinction to a broader philosophical account of law. For Hart, the separation between questions of what the law is and what it should be reveals a deeper distinction. Hart regards questions of what he calls "critical morality" – the morality by which we think we should decide what to do and assess the actions of others – as substantive, so that the answers to them depend on the content of morality. Law, on Hart's understanding, is fundamentally different, because questions about whether something is legally required are answered in a different way, by looking to the sources of a law, such as legislative decisions or judicial precedents, rather than to the law's moral merits. In this respect, legal rules are more like the rules of a game, such as chess, than like moral rules, because any legal question can be answered by considering the authoritative sources. Those sources may sometimes be unclear or even inconsistent. If they are, on Hart's account, a judge or other decision maker has no law to apply, and so can be understood only as making new law.

Dworkin ultimately rejects all aspects of Hart's approach. He rejects Hart's positivism, he rejects the idea that the law on a particular question can be identified exclusively by its sources, he rejects the idea that the law has gaps in it, and, most important, he rejects the very idea of the sort of conceptual analysis of law that Hart claimed to provide. The rejection of this approach to legal philosophy is among the most prominent features running through all of Dworkin's work. In rejecting Hart's account of the nature of law, Dworkin, at least in part, rejects the question that it is supposed to answer. At the same time, he denies that the rejection of those questions means that he has simply changed the subject. Instead, he argues that the question that Hart took himself to be answering is really a version of the question that he, Dworkin, provides a better answer to. For Dworkin, questions about law are always questions about the moral justification of political power, and any answer to those questions that purports to be about something else must be interpreted as an oblique answer to that moral question.

Dworkin also reacted against the ideas of Learned Hand. Hand is now most remembered in the legal academy for several of his decisions in the law of tort, which have given inspiration to economic analyses of tort law. Dworkin's response was to a different aspect of his work, captured in the Holmes Lectures that Hand presented at Harvard Law School the year after Dworkin clerked for him. Hand was deeply critical of judicial review of legislation, which he regarded as antidemocratic. His views about judicial review led him to advocate judicial restraint and deference to legislative intent. Those aspects of Hand's view of the judicial role are well-represented in the contemporary American judiciary. More striking was his readiness to explicitly acknowledge the implications of this view for the United States Supreme Court landmark decision in the case of *Brown v. Board of Education*, which called for the end of segregation in schools.[8] Against the dominant academic trend, Hand thought that *Brown* was wrongly decided. Dworkin's grounds for rejecting Hand's arguments have remained a central theme of his writings on the American Constitution. They also inform his broader views about the nature of law and legal interpretation. For Hand, the moral language that frames constitutional provisions does not give citizens enforceable claims against the state. For Dworkin, that same moral language is pivotal to the constitution as a whole. This language is not simply a hortatory preface to its legal provisions, but the legally mandated tools for interpreting the other parts.

The third important influence that Dworkin has acknowledged is the great political philosopher John Rawls. Rawls is widely credited with bringing the ideas of freedom and equality together in modern political philosophy and for the reintegration of normative political philosophy. Dworkin openly endorses many aspects of Rawls's approach to political philosophy and constitutional law, writing in a "Confession" at the end of an essay on Rawls and the law "some of you will have noticed a certain congruence between the positions in legal theory I say Rawls's arguments support and those I have myself tried to defend, and you may think this is no accident. So I offer you a confession, but with no apology ... each of us has his or her own Immanuel Kant, and from now on we will struggle, each of us, for the benediction of John Rawls."[9] At the same time, Dworkin also reacts against Rawls, in particular against his view that political philosophy is sharply distinct from the ethical questions that each of us must answer in deciding how to live our lives. As a consequence, he also rejects Rawls's conclusions about the nature of public reason and the types of argument that are acceptable parts of public debate. If political morality and personal morality are continuous, no line can be drawn between those parts of moral argument that are acceptable parts of public discourse and those that are not.

SOME KEY THEMES

Dworkin is a difficult person to write about in general terms, in part because he is still working actively on all of the questions that are taken up in this book. Indeed, he has already responded in print to a draft version of one of the chapters included here, and, as this book goes to press, he is working on another book that will bring together the central themes of all of his work.

The details of Dworkin's achievements and interventions are considered in the various chapters of this collection. My aim in this brief introduction is to say something about the relations between them and the underlying themes that they share, and to situate those themes in relation to recent developments in philosophy more generally. Underlying all of Dworkin's work is a particular understanding of the nature and role of practical philosophy. This distinctive view of practical philosophy is expressed in virtually every question that he seeks to address. Dworkin engages with many seemingly technical issues in legal and political philosophy, but he always does so in a way that frames them so that they are continuous with public debates. His tools are unmistakably those of a philosopher – drawing distinctions between various seemingly similar questions, and working through the implications of hypothetical examples.

ANTI-ARCHIMEDEANISM

The most significant and most central theme of Dworkin's work is his rejection of all attempts to address questions in moral, legal, or political philosophy from a standpoint outside of our ordinary ways of thinking about them. He thus refuses to engage in what is sometimes taken to be the defining project of philosophy, that is, the project of finding an "Archimedean point" outside of our ordinary ways of thinking about things, a point that will give us some special purchase on the questions that we find most difficult to address. Expounding the principle of levers, Archimedes is reported to have said "give me something to stand on and I can move the world."

Archimedes's metaphor has appealed to philosophers ever since. From Plato to Habermas, philosophers have sought to find some standpoint outside of the human practices that puzzled them from which to evaluate those practices. Dworkin explains that Archimedean theories "purport to stand outside a whole body of belief, and to judge it as a whole from premises or attitudes that owe nothing to it."[10]

This image of standing outside the ordinary can be understood in two fundamentally different respects: it can be understood in terms of our particular beliefs about particular topics, such as judicial review or assisted suicide, or, alternatively, it can be understood in terms of our ordinary ways of reasoning and debating such topics. The first way of understanding what counts as ordinary moral thought is inherently conservative and, more significantly, ultimately incoherent, because nobody seriously entertains the possibility that particular views are correct simply because they are widely held. Ordinary moral thought itself includes the idea that people can relate their particular views to their other views, offer general grounds for them, and so on. The second way of understanding ordinary moral thought, by contrast, takes account of this and indeed elevates it to the central command of moral thought. On this view, which Dworkin implicitly endorses in all of his writings and has explicitly developed in a few more recent pieces, the only kind of arguments about practical life that is of any significance is the kind of familiar, first-order arguments that we all know how to recognize.

In the twentieth century, Archimedean approaches to philosophy have been subject to criticism from a wide variety of quarters, ranging from Wittgenstein's attack on certainty, through W.V.O. Quine's holism[11] and Wilfrid Sellars's attack on the idea that knowledge has a foundation[12] of a presuppositionless mode of discourse, to Donald Davidson's claim that only a belief can justify another belief.[13] Whatever the force or merits of these criticisms, they have all focused primarily on the problems with the Archimedean metaphor in theoretical philosophy. The task of the anti-Archimedean is comparatively easier here, because the first-order claims that philosophers seek to understand are (at least usually) not themselves controversial. Philosophers may wonder about what entitles us to talk about physical objects, say, but, except for the skeptic manufactured to serve as the interlocutor in such a debate, nobody seriously doubts the conclusion that we are entitled to do so. Even skeptics are happy to follow Hume's advice and "speak with the vulgar" about such things. If an Archimedean point can be found, the skeptic about knowledge or physical objects can be answered. The failure of attempts to find such an Archimedean point may lead people to wonder if something has gone wrong, and in the twentieth century many philosophers suggested that something had, indeed, gone wrong, and that at bottom the skeptic is not entitled to an answer. Anti-Archimedeans in theoretical philosophy typically deny that ordinary thought and argument have either realist or anti-realist implications.[14]

But Archimedeanism owes its prominence not just to philosophical concerns about skepticism. Indeed, it has always owed much of its appeal – Plato and Habermas provide very different illustrations – to its promise to provide a secure point that will enable us to stand above the fray of *normative* argument and resolve the disputes that animate it. Much legal and constitutional thought of the twentieth century was drawn to Archimedean positions. Oliver Wendell Holmes noted that law "abounds" in moral language, and he went on to dismiss it as a façade covering what were, ultimately, nothing more than questions of social policy. In the 1930s, the "Legal Realist" movement in the American legal academy had carried the Holmesian idea further. In what became the manifesto for that movement, "Transcendental Nonsense and the Functional Approach,"[15] Felix Cohen argued that legal concepts were mere obfuscations, and that the only things that withstood serious scrutiny were assessments about the likely effects of competing resolutions of legal debates. Although realism itself collapsed by the 1950s, its spirit lives on. Many American academic lawyers will say that "we are all realists now." More significantly, the Archimedean picture that motivated it survived in the form of an emphasis on questions of policy and the desire to treat any other forms of moral argument as meaningless.

All of Dworkin's contributions to philosophy reflect his resolute rejection of Archimedeanism. He has written directly on the topics of truth and objectivity in practical discourse, but his most significant contribution does not come so much from those arguments, which are broadly continuous with prominent positions elsewhere in philosophy and are, in his own view, "pointless, unprofitable, wearying interruptions."[16] The most important response to Archimedeanism comes from Dworkin's engagements with the fundamental questions of legal and political philosophy from a resolutely anti-Archimedean perspective. Dworkin has not rested content with making the abstract point that only first-order normative argument can resolve normative disagreements. Instead, he has offered a model of the alternative.

FROM REFLECTIVE EQUILIBRIUM TO INTERPRETATION

In an early article, and again, at more length in *A Theory of Justice*, John Rawls introduced the idea of what he called "reflective equilibrium" as an account of the nature of moral justification. Rawls remarks that "justification is argument addressed to those who disagree with us, or to ourselves when we are of two minds. It presumes a clash of views between persons or within one person, and seeks to convince others, or ourselves, of the reasonableness of the principles upon which our claims and judgments are founded. Being designed to reconcile by reason, justification proceeds from what all parties to the discussion hold in common."[17] Rawls suggests that the best way to achieve justification in this sense is to seek an equilibrium between the general principles that seem most compelling and the considered judgments that we make about particulars.

The Rawlsian account of moral justification has attracted wide support in moral philosophy, though it has also attracted criticism from those who are unwilling to regard considered convictions about particular cases as anything more than evidence of socialization or useful heuristics.[18] Rawls's approach precludes the possibility that any particular set of normative claims, such as the utilitarian or Legal Realist emphasis on consequences, has an "epistemic or logical head start."[19] Instead, both general principles and considered judgments are potentially subject to revision.

Dworkin's approach to justification is continuous with the Rawlsian account, but it is more ambitious in two ways. First, on Rawls's own deployment of it, reflective equilibrium began as a general account of the decision procedure for ethics, but in his later work, Rawls argued that a narrower reflective equilibrium, confined to questions about the legitimate use of coercion, was the appropriate object of justification in political philosophy. Dworkin argues that a careful interpretation of ordinary practices of moral argument reveals a much greater continuity between personal and public morality. That continuity does not require that every person organize his or her life around impartiality or the achievement of justice, but it does require that public arguments resound with the convictions of ordinary citizens about what is valuable in their lives. As a result, "public reason" cannot be sequestered from comprehensive views about value, even if the best public arguments turn out to demand that the state remain neutral in many particular disputes. Second, Dworkin broadens the idea of reflective equilibrium to a more general account of *interpretation*, which is concerned with explaining how our judgments about various domains of value can be correct. To understand the meaning of a work of art is to engage in an interpretive exercise that seeks to account for the work's artistic features in terms of a view of its value. To interpret a statute is to explain the meaning of its clauses in terms of an account of the values underlying the legal system in general. Moral justification is yet another special case of this interpretive exercise.

For Dworkin, the interpretive approach has fundamental implications for the ways in which we think about questions of legal and political philosophy. If he is correct in his contention that law is an interpretive concept, then no purely conceptual Archimedean theory of law can be correct, because conceptual arguments are put forward as noninterpretive. Similarly, no conceptual argument about the relation between liberty and equality can engage with the normative concerns that make those concepts command our attention. At a more general level, no Archimedean argument can dislodge our confidence in the ordinary moral arguments that are the stuff of moral and political debate.

OBJECTIVITY AND TRUTH

If Dworkin's claim that moral, legal, and political concepts are all ultimately interpretive can be made out, there is no room for certain kinds of skeptical arguments that periodically present themselves in moral and political philosophy. Dworkin characterizes these as forms of "external" skepticism, which seek to undermine either particular moral claims or, more generally, the very possibility of moral claims by showing that they lack certain types of plausible epistemological credentials. Dworkin confronts different forms of such Archimedean skepticism in different places, arguing that it afflicts a wide variety of positions, ranging from the those of Legal Realists of the early part of the twentieth century, through the Critical Legal Studies Movement of the late part of that century, as well as economic theorists of law, certain self-described Pragmatists, and technical Analytic philosophers of language. These positions differ in important ways that Dworkin acknowledges, but his general strategy in engaging with them is the same.

Skeptical challenges to moral arguments can be understood in one of two ways. If their skepticism is external and Archimedean, then it is an objection to the entire enterprise of moral or legal argument, but one that nobody who has ever taken a substantive position in any such argument has any reason to acknowledge.[20] The external skeptic supposes that there is some place to stand outside of ordinary ways of reasoning about such questions that, nonetheless, has direct bearing on them. Often skeptics point to the fact of disagreement to explain why people should lack confidence in their moral convictions, but Dworkin suggests that this has to be wrong:

Whether [diversity of opinion in some intellectual domain] has skeptical implications depends on a further philosophical question: it has such implications only if the best account of the content of that domain explains why it should. The best account of scientific thought does explain when and why disagreement in scientific judgments is suspicious...we do not conclude from the diversity of philosophical views (which is more pronounced than moral disagreement) that no positive philosophical thesis is sound.[21]

Alternatively, such skepticism can be read as internal, as offering moral reasons to change our moral views. Dworkin is happy to engage with the internal skeptic because, on his analysis, the internal skeptic is engaged in the same interpretive exercise as the rest of us. Indeed, Dworkin sometimes suggests that the external skeptic is really just an internal skeptic in the grip of a series of unhelpful metaphors. Internal skepticism is the worry that one's own substantive moral views are wrong. It haunts morally serious people from time to time, and its only remedy is moral argument and reflection. The internal skeptic's worry is rooted in a commitment to the objectivity of moral judgments: we worry we may be wrong only because we suppose there is something to be wrong about. If that is right, then there are "no arguments for the objectivity of moral judgments except moral arguments, no arguments for the objectivity of interpretive judgments except interpretive arguments, and so forth."[22]

Dworkin attributes something like this form of internal skepticism to Hand's views about constitutional interpretation. Hand did not think that the decision in *Brown* could be justified and thought that attempts to focus on "neutral" principles of constitutional adjudication simply avoided the difficult question "whether, in the end, the interpretations of the legislatures or those of the judges will prevail, and though lawyers who dislike either answer call for something in between, there is, as Hand pointed out, no logical space for anything in between."[23] On Dworkin's analysis, this type of skepticism about judicial review is a form of internal skepticism, motivated by a political view of the superiority of elected representatives over unelected judges as arbiters of moral questions. The only way to engage with Hand's form of skepticism is to provide a moral argument for empowering judges.

INTERPRETATION

The concept of interpretation is central to Dworkin's work. His account of it needs to be understood in the light of his more general opposition to Archimedean philosophy: his account of interpretation is itself interpretive. It is supposed to provide an account of interpretive reasoning and argument, as well as of interpretive success. In so doing, it provides an account both of itself and of his claim that legal and political philosophy are always interpretive and so can never get beyond ordinary first-order argument. The only way to clarify the concept of law, or equality, or democracy is to engage with it through ordinary moral and political argument.

Discussing the work of H. L. A. Hart and Isaiah Berlin, Dworkin characterizes Berlin as an Archimedean political philosopher committed to the view that "the project of analyzing what liberty really means . . . must be pursued by some form of conceptual analysis that does not involve normative judgment, assumptions, or reasoning." He continues:

> Other political philosophers have treated other political values in a parallel way. It is a very popular idea, for example, that democracy means majority rule. That definition is set to leave open, for substantive decision and argument, such questions as whether democracy is good or bad, and whether it should be compromised by constraints on majority rule that might include, for example, a constitutional system of individual rights against the majority enforced by judicial review. These latter questions, according to the Archimedean view, are substantive and normative, but the threshold question, of what democracy is, is conceptual and descriptive. These various accounts of liberty and democracy are Archimedean because though they are theories about a normative social practice – the ordinary political practice of arguing about liberty and democracy – they claim not themselves to be normative theories. They claim rather to be philosophical or conceptual theories that are only descriptive of social practice and neutral among the controversies that make up that practice.[24]

Dworkin mounts parallel arguments against positivist views about the concept of law and, in political philosophy, about the concept of responsibility, as well as the concepts of liberty and equality. This sort of debate can be made to look like it is just about words: why object to the plausible stipulation that "democracy" means majority rule? Dworkin does not need to deny that it makes sense to ask whether, and when, majority rule is or is not a good thing, working with a fairly sharply defined (or stipulated) sense of what majority rule amounts to. Dworkin's contention is not just that this is not what we do when we use the word "democracy," but, more generally, that any sort of stipulative definition carries no significant weight in moral argument, and such stipulations do not stand outside of ordinary argument. The concept of law, for example, could be equated with some people saying things that cause other people to do things, but such an account would purchase its simplicity and neutrality at the cost of irrelevance. As Hart himself made clear, the concept of law is not to be equated with the concept of a "gunman situation writ large" through which orders are issued and obeyed.[25] An overly simplistic account of what law is, such as the issuing and following of orders, is so thin that it completely fails to engage with the questions about the rule of law that gave it its interest, whether those are moral questions about what attitude to take toward some existing legal system, or even the much more technical questions that arise within every legal system. Those questions, Dworkin contends, are always interpretive.

Interpretation merges justification and criticism with description. In an early essay about Lord Devlin's now-notorious claim that society is entitled to protect its moral character against anything ordinary people view with "intolerance, indignation, and disgust," Dworkin remarks that terms like "moral position" and "moral conviction" function in our conventional morality

> as terms of justification and criticism, as well as of description. It is true that we sometimes speak of a group's "morals," or "morality," or "moral beliefs," or "moral positions" or "moral convictions," in what might be called an anthropological sense, meaning to refer to whatever attitudes the group displays about the propriety of human conduct, or goals. We say, in this sense, that the morality of Nazi Germany was based on prejudice, or was irrational. But we also use some of these terms, particularly "moral position" and "moral conviction," in a discriminatory sense, to contrast the positions they describe with prejudices, rationalizations, matters of personal aversion or taste, arbitrary stands, and the like.[26]

It may be possible to give a descriptive characterization of some group's morality, even if you are a member of that group, but participants in moral debates do not ordinarily focus on morality in this descriptive sense. If they did, it would never be of any help to them in deciding what to do or resolving their disagreements. Those disagreements, instead, are interpretive, and as such they presuppose other substantive moral claims. Devlin goes wrong in supposing that moral responses are purely visceral and in ignoring the place of reason-giving in ordinary ways of thinking about morality. As a result, he imagines that he can take a detour around questions about what there is reason to do and focus only on the supposedly more neutral question of how people react. There are no detours, however, because moral concepts are interpretive, and like other interpretive concepts, they "function in ordinary thought and speech as interpretive concepts of *value*: their descriptive sense is contested, and the contest turns on which assignment of a descriptive sense best captures or realizes that value."[27]

The idea of a social practice is central to this focus on interpretation. For Dworkin, a social practice cannot be analyzed as a convention, made up of rules that all of the parties to the convention somehow grasp, whether implicitly or explicitly. Nor is a practice made up of some set of the settled rules and a further set of open-ended applications of them. Instead, a practice contains all of the disputed claims about the topic, including the debates that sometimes arise about what is, or is not, included within the topic under discussion. Dworkin's opposition to Archimedean accounts precludes him from individuating distinct practices, such as law, politics, or art, except in terms of particular interpretations of them. The boundaries of practices are subject to disputes, some of which share features with some of the disputes that take place within those practices. The fact that the identity conditions of a particular practice are not available preinterpretively may look like it generates a problem: how can you participate in a practice if you do not know which practice it is? From Dworkin's perspective, however, the problem must be seen as nothing more than a holdover from the same Archimedean ideas that he resists. Practices need definitive preinterpretive contours only if someone wants to police a practice while remaining outside of it. Real debate, whether about art, law, or justice, takes place when people are already participating in the practice, and they do not need any guidance from outside of that to show them the way in. At most, they need guidance from inside, but that is just more interpretation on Dworkin's account.

To understand Dworkin's specific arguments and interventions in specific debates, then, it is essential to be clear about the *status* of those arguments. Dworkin's engagements with legal positivism refuse to accept the positivist understanding of the issue that separates them. He denies that there can be a purely descriptive concept of law and so denies that he and the positivist disagree about the role of morality in this descriptive concept. His conclusions, however, are supposed to be genuinely inconsistent with the positivist's rather than simply being answers to different questions.[28] Again, his account of democracy, or responsibility, has substantive political implications, but at the same time they are meant to compete with putatively descriptive or conceptual accounts of these concepts. How can they compete if they are answering different questions? The short answer is that none of these purely descriptive accounts really is what it purports to be. Instead, for Dworkin, accounts that seek to be Archimedean and descriptive are finally incoherent and need to be interpreted as themselves interpretations, though ones that are pessimistic about various aspects of moral or legal argument. To contend that the meaning of a literary or constitutional text is to be identified with the intentions of the author or framers, for example, is to put forward a substantive claim about why that text should command our aesthetic or moral attention rather than to offer a neutral analysis of the concept of meaning. Thus, Dworkin suggests that Hart's defense of the separation between law and morality must be read as an interpretive theory rather than as a neutral conceptual analysis.

AN INTERPRETIVE THEORY OF INTERPRETATION

At its highest level of abstraction, Dworkin's account of interpretation is itself interpretive. He rejects Archimedean theories of interpretation, according to which a successful interpretation captures what is going through an author's mind or, in the more prominent versions, the proper interpretation of the Constitution depends on what was going through the minds of the Framers, or what they would have said or thought in response to particular issues. The idea of Framers' intent remains prominent in American legal thought, so that questions about whether, for example, the death penalty is an example of "cruel and unusual punishment" is sometimes said to depend on what the Framers would have thought about that question. If they would not have characterized it as cruel or unusual, then, on this account, it passes constitutional scrutiny. For Dworkin, such an approach goes wrong at a number of different levels, only one of which is relevant here. Although an interpreter must always accord some authority to the person or persons who created the text that is being interpreted, the question of what sort of authority and at what level of abstraction is itself an interpretive question. As such, the relevance of what the Framers of the American Constitution thought about a particular matter can be addressed only through an interpretive engagement with the questions of value that are at stake in every interpretation.

I will illustrate this point with two examples from Dworkin's writing, neither of which is central to the specific topics discussed elsewhere in this book, but each of which is illustrative of the broad structure of his approach to all philosophical questions.

In a series of articles beginning in the late 1970s, Dworkin pointed to parallels between literary and legal interpretation. In both cases, a reader is confronted with a meaningful text and hopes to understand its significance. Dworkin argues that the way to determine the meaning of such a text is through what he calls "the aesthetic hypothesis" that the work is a valuable instance of its genre.[29] To pursue this hypothesis, the reader must have views about the genre into which the text fits, which can be formed only by reading the text itself. At the same time, reading the text to classify its generic markers is not enough, because generic markers themselves are subject to interpretation. Instead, the reader must try to understand the text as the best text that it can be, that is, as having the features that make it most valuable. In so doing, the reader will construct an interpretation that will answer many questions about the text that did not have clear answers prior to the interpretation. Not every question will have an answer, but many will.

In the case of literature, the interpretive strategy requires reading the text as a unified whole that succeeds at some set of aesthetic ambitions. In the case of law, it requires reading the law as a whole. The law is considerably harder to interpret as a whole than either a poem or novel, but Dworkin suggests that the interpretive strategy must be exactly the same. To make the law the "best it can be," the reader must first try to understand the parameters of the relevant law and so come up with competing interpretive hypotheses based on the relatively uncontroversial aspects of the law, but he or she must also consider the different directions in which the law might extend in the light of competing interpretations. The reader (or lawyer, or judge) must then consider which interpretation makes the law the best it can be, that is, determine which competing interpretation shows the law in its morally best light. Dworkin illustrates this point by comparing the law to a chain novel, written by a series of authors, each of whom must write a chapter based on the chapters already written. He argues that, as the novel gets longer, the successive chain novelists find themselves more and more constrained by what has gone before, until they reach the point at which there may be only one plausible way of continuing the novel.

As Dworkin acknowledges, the chain novel analogy applies to some aspects of legal interpretation but not others. In particular, the point of legal interpretation is given by political morality rather than artistic merit. It is, as he puts it in *Law's Empire*, to make the law "the best that it can be" in terms of its justice and integrity. Interpreters always start from somewhere, based on some understanding of the task before them.

Scott Shapiro's chapter on the Hart/Dworkin debate will take up the relevance of this argument to the debates in legal philosophy that it joins, and Sanford Levinson's chapter will take up the difficult issue of its relation to interpreting morally odious laws. My purpose here is to use it as an illustration both of Dworkin's broader methodological commitments as well as of the misunderstandings that those commitments have sometimes generated. "It's all interpretation" has come and gone as a fashionable slogan in the humanities. The interpretive nature of understanding is often taken to be a threat to objectivity and truth because, it is suggested, different interpretations can be equally good, and any interpretation must presuppose things that others might dispute. For example, Stanley Fish has made this type of argument, both at a general level and against Dworkin in particular. Fish contends that interpretation depends on what he calls an "interpretive community," which he understands as an entirely contingent social and historical matter. Which connections people see, and which ones they find obvious, interesting, or compelling are simply features of their socialization, and might have been other than what they are. As a result, the text that is subject to interpretation provides no real constraint apart from the community, and it makes no sense to talk about what a text means except from the standpoint of a particular interpretive community.

Fish hopes to deploy this general line of argument against Dworkin by pointing to the sociological differences between interpretive communities for law and other interpretive exercises, such as literature. Literary interpretation tends to lead to a proliferation of competing interpretations, while legal interpretation generates much more agreement. Those differences reflect differences between legal education and graduate programs in literature, rather than any features of the underlying texts. For Fish, only social factors determine which interpretation will seem to be best. In law, the relevant factors tend toward convergence, including both common professional training and the career advantages that attach to conformity. The desires of judges to have their decisions withstand appellate scrutiny or to earn the esteem of colleagues will make it more likely that they will see the law narrowly. Fish gives this point rhetorical flourish by suggesting that *Law's Empire* be read as a rhetorical manual for lawyers and judges who want to maximize their chances of convincing others in the particular professional context in which they find themselves.[30] In literary studies, by contrast, professional advantage attaches to novelty, and thus there will be much less convergence in interpretations. These contingent features, rather than either facts about texts or views about morality, determine interpretive outcomes.

Fish gets little attention from philosophers, and I mention his objections here not because he deserves more, but because they are symptomatic of what Dworkin regards as the wrong way to think about interpretation. The details of Dworkin's response to Fish are less significant for present purposes than its general strategy. Fish seeks to undermine the idea that the text constrains interpretation by pointing to the fact that different sociological communities might give different interpretations of a single text. Fish's objection is to a specific thesis about interpretation, according to which interpretation is fully controlled by the text. As such, it fails to engage with Dworkin's distinctive view about interpretation, because the position that Fish criticizes is a noninterpretive thesis about interpretation, a sort of causal hypothesis about which interpretation will, in fact, win. Dworkin defends something very different, an interpretive account of successful interpretation, according to which the point of the entire enterprise of interpretation is internal to it, that is, of making the text under consideration the best that it can be. Dworkin does not need to deny that particular interpretations will be subject to sociological pressures like the one that Fish emphasizes precisely because his claim is about how interpretation should go, and his only mode of argument in support of his interpretation of interpretation is the way in which it fits with ordinary understandings of the aspirations of interpretation. As Dworkin observes in the context of a discussion of the value of such character traits as sensibility or personal integrity, "Some enterprising social Darwinian might one day show that these traits and ambitions had survival value in ancestral savannahs. But that is not how they appear to us . . . We rather consider these values as aspects or components of, not instrumental means toward, an attractive, fully successful life."[31] In the same way, an account of the values that properly inform legal or other interpretation is consistent with various hypotheses about the sociohistorical mechanism by which they came to seem important and plausible, as well as with sociological hypotheses about why particular views prevail. For Dworkin, then, Fish's account needs to be understood as, finally, an Archimedean theory about interpretation, a theory that stands outside of our ordinary practices of making and defending interpretive claims. Unlike other Archimedeans, Fish does not aim to provide a guide to interpretation, because he denies that any such guide is possible. But from Dworkin's standpoint, Fish turns out to be just a disappointed Archimedean, for he imagines that an adequate theory of interpretation would need to provide a method for interpreting texts that was somehow supposed to guarantee the correct interpretation. Dworkin, by contrast, contends that the correctness of an interpretation is internal to interpretive practice.

WALZER

Focusing on "our practices" invites a second interpretation, which Dworkin also rejects. Other philosophers and theorists have tried to avoid

Archimedean commitments by focusing on practices in a different sense. In his book *Spheres of Justice*, Michael Walzer defends a view that he calls "complex equality" through examining particular goods that can be distributed according to different criteria of equality. Walzer relies heavily on historical examples and explains his reason for doing so in terms of a rejection of Archimedean approaches to philosophy, which he identifies with Plato. In the *Republic*, Plato famously introduces the parable of the cave to show that the role of philosophy is to get beyond our ordinary ways of thinking about things and to find the tools to govern our lives according to the way that things really are. Walzer urges a different conception of political philosophy that, as he puts it, "begins in the cave." In a review of Walzer's book, Dworkin illustrates his own position at two levels. First, he questions Walzer's claim to identify the social meanings and conventions making up our practices through examples and historical analysis. The difficulty, Dworkin points out, is that political philosophy, whether in Walzer's approach or his own, gets some of its interest and importance from the fact that we *disagree* about those practices. For example, the social meaning of health in the United States continues to be debated, and the status quo at any time is not an argument for or against any position in that debate. As he puts it, "Our political arguments almost never begin in some shared understanding of the pertinent principles of distribution."[32] When there are no shared understandings, "no solution can possibly be just" on Walzer's account. Second, Dworkin goes on to suggest that the root of the difficulty is the assumption that the relevant conventions and the borders between spheres are fixed in advance and thus that political debate requires only careful investigation of shared practices. That view is just the Archimedean premise again, the idea that ordinary ways of doing things come clearly demarcated in advance.

THE ORGANIZATION OF THIS VOLUME

In a widely discussed essay, "The Hedgehog and the Fox,"[33] the late Isaiah Berlin contrasted two styles of philosophical thinking. Berlin expressed suspicions about those thinkers he characterized as hedgehogs, on the grounds that they try to assimilate everything to one big idea. The fox, who attends to the particular details of the human situation, is more realistic in both his assessment of it and his prescriptions for improving it. Although Dworkin was a friend and admirer of Berlin, he is a self-described hedgehog. He is currently at work on a book, *Justice for Hedgehogs*, that will bring together the various themes from all of his work. His aim, as he describes it in a recent draft, is to articulate an account of justice that combines "a defense against hedgehogs gone mad and the need for a different liberalism of hope against lazy and selfish foxes."

The present book is organized around Dworkin's aspiration to remain a hedgehog without falling into monistic or totalizing thought, while at the same time resisting the quietism and resignation that comes from an excessive focus on the particular. The chapters engage with Dworkin's particular interventions in and elaborations of debates in legal and political philosophy. The only way to understand the aspirations or assess the success of a hedgehog is to look at his engagements with particular issues in the light of his single organizing set of ideas. The first chapter, by Scott Shapiro, looks at Dworkin's debate with H. L. A. Hart and other legal positivists and thus illuminates the central theme in all of Dworkin's writings – the distinctively moral nature of law. The second chapter, by David Dyzenhaus, discusses Dworkin's views about democracy and the rule of law. The third, which I have written, examines his account of distributive justice and its relation to freedom. The fourth, by Benjamin Zipursky and James Fleming, assesses his interventions in debates about life and death. The final chapter, by Sanford Levinson, looks at his particular approach to the American Constitution.

Every hedgehog has a central organizing idea, and someone familiar with Dworkin's views in one debate will not be surprised by the general direction of his views in other debates. His antidote to the "madness" that hedgehogs sometimes court, however, is to engage with particular debates, interpreting them so that the opposed positions within a debate share a common and morally significant subject matter.

The quote opening this introduction recounts a conversation Dworkin had with his successor in the Chair of Jurisprudence at Oxford, John Gardner. Dworkin reports "I said I thought that legal philosophy should be interesting. He jumped on me. 'Don't you see?' he replied. 'That's your trouble.' I am guilty of his charge."[34] Dworkin misreports his own position here, inviting Gardner's "jump." On the best interpretation of Dworkin's interpretive view, it is not that legal or political philosophy can be done either in an interesting, interpretive way or in a boring, analytic or conceptual way and that Dworkin simply prefers the interesting one, but that he thinks others have a reason, external to the doing of political philosophy, to choose the interesting one. Instead, his view is not that legal philosophy should be interesting, but that it is.

Notes

1. For discussion of his international impact, see the essays in the *International Journal of Constitutional Law* 1(2003): 4.
2. Ronald Dworkin, "Law's Ambitions for Itself," *Virginia Law Review* 71, no. 2 (March 1985): 187.
3. Adam Liptak, "The Transcendent Lawyer," *The Law School* 15 (Autumn 2005): 15 (available online at http://www.law.nyu.edu/pubs/magazine/autumn2005/documents/p12_23.pdf).
4. Those interested in some of these details can consult Liptak, "The Transcendent Lawyer."
5. Nicola Lacey, *A Life of H. L. A. Hart: The Nightmare and the Noble Dream* (New York: Oxford University Press, 2004), 186.
6. Lacey reports that Hart later wrote in his diary of the possibility that Dworkin might produce "*Philosophical Investigations to my Tractatus.*" Nicola Lacey, *A Life of H. L. A. Hart: The Nightmare and the Noble Dream*, 291–3.
7. Liptak, "The Transcendent Lawyer," 16.
8. Ronald Dworkin, "Learned Hand," in *Freedom's Law: The Moral Reading of the American Constitution* (New York: Oxford University Press, 1996), 339–40.
9. Ronald Dworkin, "Rawls and the Law," in *Justice in Robes* (Cambridge, MA: The Belknap Press of Harvard University Press, 2006), 261.
10. Ronald Dworkin, "Objectivity and Truth: You'd Better Believe It," *Philosophy and Public Affairs* 25, no. 2 (Spring 1996): 88.
11. W.V.O. Quine, *Word and Object* (Cambridge, MA: MIT Press, 1961).
12. Wilfrid Sellars, *Empiricism and the Philosophy of Mind* (1956; reprinted Harvard University Press, 1997).
13. Donald Davidson, *Inquiries into Truth and Interpretation* (Oxford: Oxford University Press, 1980).
14. See, for example, John McDowell, *Mind and World* (Cambridge, MA: Harvard University Press, 1995) and Arthur Fine, "And Not Anti-Realism Either," *Noûs* 18, no. 1 (March 1984): 51–65.
15. Felix Cohen, "Transcendental Nonsense and the Functional Approach," *Columbia Law Review* 35, no. 6 (June 1935): 809–49.
16. Dworkin, "Objectivity and Truth," 139.
17. John Rawls, *A Theory of Justice* (Cambridge, MA: Belknap Press of Harvard University Press, 1971), 580.
18. It is no surprise that these critics come, almost entirely, from the utilitarian tradition, because considered judgments about particular cases are often brought forward as counterexamples to utilitarianism. The standard utilitarian strategy, at least since Sidgwick in *The Methods of Ethics*, is to treat judgments about particular cases as nothing more than applications of rules that work most of the time but have no independent normative standing. The Rawlsian response to this approach is straightforward: the most general principles, however self-evident they may seem to someone adopting such an approach to justification,

are subject to the same objection that they, too, may be overgeneralizations of something particular, or the result of socialization. The moral that most philosophers have drawn from this conflict is the one that Dworkin draws: the only way to engage with or defeat any first-order moral argument is with other first-order moral arguments.

19. Dworkin, "Objectivity and Truth," 135.

20. As Dworkin notes in different places, almost all of the skeptical challenges do seek to vindicate some moral position – usually a consequentialist one – and so, on their own terms, fail to move even those who put them forward.

21. Dworkin, "Objectivity and Truth," 113–14.

22. Ronald Dworkin, "On Interpretation and Objectivity," in *A Matter of Principle* (Cambridge, MA: Harvard University Press, 1985), 171.

23. Dworkin, "Learned Hand," 343.

24. Ronald Dworkin, "Hart's Postscript and the Point of Political Philosophy," in *Justice in Robes*, 146–7.

25. H. L. A. Hart, "Positivism and the Separation of Law and Morals," in *Essays in Jurisprudence and Philosophy* (New York: Clarendon Press of Oxford University Press, 1983), 59.

26. Ronald Dworkin, "Liberty and Moralism," in *Taking Rights Seriously* (Cambridge, MA: Harvard University Press, 1977), 248.

27. Dworkin, "Hart's Postscript," 150.

28. Joseph Raz claims that Dworkin offers an account simply of the American legal system rather than of the concept of law. Even this cannot be quite right, because Dworkin's claim is not that law is an interpretive concept in certain legal systems at certain times but rather that it always and everywhere is.

29. Ronald Dworkin, "How Law Is Like Literature," in *A Matter of Principle*, 146–66; Ronald Dworkin, *Law's Empire* (Cambridge, MA: The Belknap Press of Harvard University Press, 1986), 228–38.

30. Stanley Fish, "Dennis Martinez and the Uses of Theory," in *Doing What Comes Naturally: Change, Rhetoric, and the Practice of Theory in Literary and Legal Studies* (Durham, NC: Duke University Press, 1989), 392.

31. Dworkin, "Hart's Postscript," 158.

32. Ronald Dworkin, "What Justice Isn't," in *A Matter of Principle*, 216.

33. Isaiah Berlin, *The Hedgehog and the Fox: An Essay on Tolstoy's View of History* (New York: Simon and Schuster, 1953). Berlin begins his essay with a quote from a fragment from the Greek poet Archilochus: "The fox knows many things, but the hedgehog knows one big thing."

34. Ronald Dworkin, "Hart's Postscript and the Point of Political Philosophy," in *Justice in Robes*, 185.

1 | The "Hart–Dworkin" Debate: A Short Guide for the Perplexed

SCOTT J. SHAPIRO

For the past four decades, Anglo-American legal philosophy has been pre-occupied – some might say obsessed – with something called the "Hart–Dworkin" debate. Since the appearance in 1967 of "The Model of Rules I," Ronald Dworkin's seminal critique of H. L. A. Hart's theory of legal positivism, countless books and articles have been written either defending Hart against Dworkin's objections or defending Dworkin against Hart's defenders.[1] Recently, in fact, there has been a significant uptick in enthusiasm for the debate from its already lofty levels, an escalation no doubt attributable to the publication of the second edition of *The Concept of Law*, which contained Hart's much anticipated, but alas posthumous, answer to Dworkin in a postscript. Predictably, the postscript generated a vigorous metadebate about its cogency, with some arguing that Hart was wrong to reply to Dworkin in the way that he did[2] and others countering that such criticisms of Hart are unfounded.[3]

In this essay, I will not take sides in this controversy over Hart's reply to Dworkin. I will be interested, rather, in a more preliminary matter, namely, in attempting to set out the basic subject matter of the debate. My chief concern, therefore, will be to identify the core issue around which the Hart–Dworkin debate is organized. Is the debate, for example, about whether the law contains principles *as well as* rules? Or does it concern whether judges have discretion in hard cases? Is it about the proper way to interpret legal texts in the American legal system? Or is it about the very possibility of conceptual jurisprudence?

To pinpoint the core of the debate, I will examine at some length the main argumentative strategies employed by each side to advance their cause. Thus, I will begin by exploring Dworkin's characterization and critique of Hart's positivism and will then follow up by presenting the rebuttals offered by Hart and his followers. My hope is that by laying bear the basic structure of the debate, we will be able not only to explain why the jurisprudential community has been fixated on this controversy, but also to determine the most profitable direction for the debate to proceed in the future.

Capturing the essence of a philosophical debate, however, can be a tricky business for several different reasons. First, as in any debate, participants may not agree on what they are arguing about. One side may firmly believe that the issue is whether X is true, whereas the other supposes that it is whether Y is true. Notoriously, the Hart–Dworkin debate began on just such a note. In "The Model of Rules I," Dworkin claimed that the dispute between him and Hart concerned whether the law is a model of rules. This formulation of the debate, though, is misleading – and has misled several generations of law students – because, as it is now generally recognized, Hart never claimed that the law is simply a model of rules (in Dworkin's sense of "rule"), nor is he committed to such a position.[4]

Second, philosophical debates are hard to characterize because, unlike formal debates, they are not usually about just one issue. In philosophy, everything is ultimately connected to everything else, and hence philosophical controversies tend to range over many different, though in-the-end related, questions. Thus, the Hart–Dworkin debate concerns such disparate issues as the existence of judicial discretion,[5] the role of policy in adjudication,[6] the ontological foundations of rules,[7] the possibility of descriptive jurisprudence,[8] the function of law,[9] the objectivity of value,[10] the vagueness of concepts,[11] and the nature of legal inference.[12]

Third and last, philosophical debates are difficult to represent because they are typically moving targets. Philosophers are remarkably agile advocates and tend to shift their positions to accommodate the objections of their opponents. The critique of legal positivism that Dworkin offered in 1967, for example, differs dramatically from the one that he presented in 1986. Any description must, therefore, attempt to capture this fluidity by treating the debate as an evolving entity that over time adapts to rational pressures coming from without and within.

Despite these complications, I think that there is an important unity to the Hart–Dworkin debate that can be described in a relatively straightforward manner. I will suggest in what follows that the debate is organized around one of the most profound issues in the philosophy of law, namely, the relation between legality and morality. Dworkin's basic strategy throughout the course of the debate has been to argue that, in one form or another, legality is ultimately determined not by social facts alone, but by moral facts as well. In other words, the existence and content of positive law is, in the final analysis, governed by the existence and content of the moral law. This contention, therefore, directly challenges and threatens to undermine the positivist picture about the nature of law, in which legality is never determined by morality but rather by social practice. For if judges must consider what morality requires in order to decide what the law requires, social facts alone cannot determine the content of the law. As one might expect, the response by Hart and his followers has been to argue that this dependence of legality on morality is either merely apparent or does not, in fact, undermine the social foundations of law and legal systems.

Because the Hart–Dworkin debate is, as mentioned earlier, a dynamic entity, I will try also to show how Dworkin modified his critique to circumvent the responses of Hart's followers. As we will see, however, virtually no attention has been paid to this latter challenge, which is especially surprising given that none of the previous positivistic defenses are helpful against it. I will then sketch out a possible response positivists might offer to this extremely powerful objection. My aim in this last part of the paper will be not merely to defend positivism, but also to show why it is important that it be defended. As I will argue, the primacy that positivism affords to social facts reflects a fundamental truth about law, namely, that the law guides conduct through the authoritative settlement of moral and political issues. Moral facts cannot ultimately determine the law, as I will show, because they would unsettle the very questions that the law aims to resolve.

1. THE OPENING BLAST

Whatever else the Hart–Dworkin debate is about, it is at least about the validity of Hart's version of legal positivism. To understand the debate, therefore, we must first examine how Dworkin characterized its core commitments. Once this has been set out in Section A, we will turn to Dworkin's first critique of that position in Section B.

A. Three Theses

In "The Model of Rules I," Dworkin sets out three theses to which he believes Hart and most legal positivists are committed.

> (1) "The law of a community ... can be identified and distinguished by specific criteria, by tests having to do not with their content but with their *pedigree* or the manner in which they were adopted or developed."

> (2) "The set of these valid legal rules is exhaustive of 'the law,' so that if someone's case is not clearly covered by such a rule (because there is none that seem appropriate, or those that seem appropriate are vague, or for some other reason) then that case cannot be decided by 'applying the law.' It must be decided by some official, like a judge, 'exercising his discretion.'"

(3) "To say that someone has a 'legal obligation' is to say that his case falls under a valid legal rule that requires him to do or to forbear from doing something."[13]

Because this description of Hart's theory is somewhat idiosyncratic, we should dwell on it for a moment.

The first thing to notice about the first proposition, which we can call the Pedigree Thesis, is that although Dworkin portrays it as a singular commitment, it is in fact a composite claim. The initial part asserts that in any community that has a legal system, there exists a master rule for distinguishing law from non-law. The latter part places an important restriction on this rule: the criteria of legality set out by the master rule may refer only to social facts – in particular, to whether the rule has the appropriate social "pedigree" or source. Such a rule may, for example, require that the norms related to certain subject matter be enacted solely by the legislature by majority vote, or it may recognize the actions of other bodies, such as courts or administrative agencies, in these regards. The master rule of any legal system, however, may not set out criteria of legality that either refer to a norm's moral properties or require for their implementation the exercise of moral reasoning. No master rule, therefore, may condition legality on morality.

Dworkin clearly intends the Pedigree Thesis to capture Hart's doctrine of the rule of recognition.[14] One might question, however, whether it does so. For example, Hart nowhere imposes a pedigree requirement on the rule of recognition; indeed, in certain places, he specifically allows that the criteria of legality may explicitly refer to moral considerations.[15] In addition to being too strong, the Pedigree Thesis is too weak. For Hart specifically claims that the rule of recognition is a "social" rule, that is, a convention among judges to treat certain rules as authoritative. The Pedigree Thesis, however, places no social requirement on the master rule. Thus, a test for legality may satisfy the Pedigree Thesis and still not be a rule of recognition in Hart's sense.

The second positivistic thesis holds that the law consists solely in legal rules. Accordingly, if a case is not clearly covered by an existing legal rule, either because there seems to be no applicable legal rule or because the rule contains vague or ambiguous terms, the deciding judge cannot apply the law but must exercise his or her discretion to resolve the case. Call this the Discretion Thesis. Finally, the third thesis is the counterpart of the Discretion Thesis for "legal obligation": it claims that legal obligations can be generated only by legal rules. Call this the Obligation Thesis.

Whereas the Pedigree Thesis is at least recognizable as a colorable commitment of Hart's theory, the Discretion and Obligation Theses do not seem to state peculiarly positivistic positions. After all, what else does the law consist in if not *rules*? And where else would legal obligations arise if not from them? To understand the distinctive nature of the Discretion and Obligation Theses, we must first understand what Dworkin means by a "rule" and how rules differ from other norms that he calls "principles."

In Dworkin's terminology, rules are "all or nothing" standards.[16] When a valid rule applies in a given case, it is conclusive or, as a lawyer would say, "dispositive." Because valid rules are conclusive reasons for action, they cannot conflict. If two rules conflict, then one of them cannot be a valid rule.

By contrast, principles do not dispose of the cases to which they apply.[17] They lend justificatory support to various courses of actions, but they are not necessarily conclusive. Valid principles, therefore, may conflict and typically do. Moreover, in contrast to rules, principles have "weight." When valid principles conflict, the proper method for resolving the conflict is to select the position that is supported by the principles that have the greatest aggregate weight.

Given the logical distinction between these two types of norms, we can see that the Discretion and Obligation Theses are far from trivial. The Discretion Thesis holds that the law consists solely of legal rules; no principles, in other words, are legal principles. Likewise, the Obligation Thesis states that legal obligations can be generated only by legal rules. Where legal rules are inapplicable, legal obligations do not exist, and judges by necessity must look beyond the law to decide the case.

B. Against Judicial Discretion

In "The Model of Rules I," Dworkin argues that legal positivism, so characterized, cannot account for the manifest existence of legal principles. Hart's theory, or any such positivistic account, is a "model of and for a system of rules"[18] and, as such, must be rejected.

Dworkin begins his critique by arguing that the Discretion Thesis is implausible insofar as it ignores the many cases where judges regard themselves as bound by law even though no rules are clearly applicable. In *Henningsen v. Bloomfield Motors*, for example, the court was asked to hold an automobile maker liable for injuries sustained as the result of defective manufacturing despite the fact that the injured plaintiff signed a waiver of liability.[19] The court could find no explicit rule that would authorize it to ignore such a waiver but nevertheless held for the plaintiff. In support of its decision it cited a number of legal principles, including "freedom of contract is not such an immutable doctrine as to admit of no qualification in the area in which we are concerned"[20] and "in a society such as ours the automobile manufacturer is under a special obligation in connection with the construction, promotion, and sale of his cars."[21] These principles, the court reasoned, were of such great importance that they outweighed contrary principles, such as those supporting the freedom to contract, which militated in favor of enforcing the waiver.

According to Dworkin, *Henningsen* was not an aberration. "Once we identify legal principles as separate sorts of standards, different from legal rules, we are suddenly aware of them all around us. Law teachers teach them, law books cite them, legal historians celebrate them."[22] In fact, legal principles are most conspicuously at play in hard cases, where they guide and constrain judicial decision making in the absence of legal rules. Legal positivism ignores the existence of these norms precisely because it holds, via the Discretion Thesis, that cases such as *Henningsen* are not governed by law. Legal positivism, in other words, is a model of rules only.

Dworkin is careful to point out that there are several "weak" senses in which judges must exercise discretion even in hard cases.[23] Judges must exercise discretion in the sense that they are required to use their judgment in reasoning from legal principles to legal conclusions. At least sometimes as well, they have discretion in the sense that they have the final say in a particular case. Dworkin denies, however, that judges must exercise what he calls "strong" discretion, namely, the idea that they must look beyond the law and apply extralegal standards to resolve the case at hand. Once one recognizes the existence of legal principles, Dworkin claims, it becomes clear that judges are bound by legal standards even in hard cases.

C. Content, Not Pedigree

According to Dworkin, the pervasiveness of legal principles not only falsifies the Discretion Thesis, it also discredits the Pedigree Thesis. This is so because the legality of principles depends, at least sometimes, simply on their content.

> The origin of [the *Henningsen* principles] as legal principles lies not in a particular decision of some legislature or court, but in a sense of appropriateness

developed in the profession and the public over time. Their continued power depends upon this sense of appropriateness being sustained. If it no longer seemed unfair to allow people to profit by their wrongs, or fair to place special burdens upon oligopolies that manufacture potentially dangerous machines, these principles would no longer play much of a role in new cases, even if they had never been overruled or repealed.[24]

Insofar as positivism requires legality to be purely a function of pedigree, it cannot account for the existence of principles such as those operative in *Henningsen*, whose legal recognition is conditioned on the moral perception that, for example, it is "fair to place special burdens upon oligopolies that manufacture potentially dangerous machines."[25]

Dworkin does not, of course, claim that pedigree is legally irrelevant. He concedes that legal principles usually have institutional support and that having such support is normally crucial to their legality. "True, if we were challenged to back up our claim that some principle is a principle of law, we would mention any prior cases in which that principle was cited, or figured in the argument. . . . Unless we could find some such institutional support, we would probably fail to make out our case."[26] Dworkin does, however, deny that a positivistic master rule could be constructed that would test a principle based on its institutional support.

> We argue for a particular principle by grappling with a whole set of shift-ing, developing and interacting standards (themselves principles rather than rules) about institutional responsibility, statutory interpretation, the persua-sive force of various sorts of precedent, the relation of all these to contem-porary moral practices, and hosts of the other standards. We could not bolt all of these together into a single 'rule', even a complex one, and if we could the result would bear little to Hart's picture of a rule of recognition, which is the picture of a fairly stable master rule specifying 'some feature or features, possession of which by a suggested rule is taken as a conclusive affirmative indication that it is a rule.'[27]

Dworkin's argument appears to be this: the legal impact of a principle's institutional support on its legality and weight is itself determined by prin-ciples, namely, those relating to institutions and their authority. For exam-ple, whether a judge should recognize the principles in *Henningsen* and, if so, how much weight to attribute to them depends on a whole constel-lation of principles relating to the institutional authority of common law courts, their relations to legislatures, and to ordinary moral practices. These institutional principles, in turn, are supported by very broad principles of political morality.[28] Dworkin believes that no rule could be fashioned that accurately reflects the verdicts of all these political principles, presumably because the possibilities that would have to be considered and codified are infinite in number. Moreover, these principles and their weights fluctuate over time, based on their own degree of institutional support, and hence any resulting master rule would fail to be stable.

According to Dworkin, therefore, the Pedigree Thesis must be rejected for two reasons. First, legal principles are sometimes binding on judges simply because of their intrinsic moral properties and not because of their pedigree. Second, even when these principles are binding in virtue of their pedigree, it is not possible to formulate a stable rule that picks out a principle based on its degree of institutional support. Having previously disposed of the Discretion Thesis, Dworkin concludes that legal positivism must be rejected as an adequate theory of law.

2. THE ISSUE

Dworkin is often criticized for having ascribed to Hart a highly implausible view, namely, that the law consists solely of rules, never of principles. When Hart spoke of legal rules, it is usually pointed out, he did not mean to single out only "all or nothing" standards that cannot conflict and lack the dimension of weight.[29] He simply intended to refer to standards that are binding in a particular legal system and have as their function the guidance and evaluation of conduct.

These criticisms are not entirely fair, however. Understood charitably, Dworkin's attribution to Hart was an exercise in charitable interpretation. On this reading, Dworkin was not reporting anything that Hart actually said; rather, he was attempting to explain Hart's doctrine of strong discretion by attributing to him a view that he never expressed but nonetheless held. Why, Dworkin asked, did Hart believe that judges are not bound by law in hard cases, despite the fact that they appeal to principles to resolve such cases? It must be, he answered, that Hart did not believe that these principles are part of the law. If the law contains only rules, then when the rules "run out," so must the law.

Although Dworkin's interpretation of Hart is fair, I don't think it is the best explanation for Hart's theory of judicial discretion. Its major defect stems from the fact that Hart explicitly offered a very different, and more plausible, explanation for his doctrine of strong discretion. According to Hart, judicial discretion is a necessary byproduct of the inherent indeterminacy of social guidance. It is impossible, Hart argued, to transmit to others standards of conduct that settle every contingency in advance. Guidance by precedent is imperfect because, although the exemplar is identified, the relevant standard of similarity is not. While common sense will eliminate certain similarity standards as inappropriate, there will always be a healthy number of conflicting standards that seem more or less reasonable. Whereas guidance by legislation might settle some of these doubts, Hart maintained that the use of general terms in statutes cannot eliminate them all. This is so because of the "open texture" of language. "In all fields of experience, not only that of rules, there is a limit, inherent in the nature of language, to the guidance which general language can provide. There will be plain cases constantly recurring in similar contexts to which general expressions are clearly applicable . . . but there will also be cases where it is not clear whether they apply or not."[30]

Thus, Hart's doctrine about judicial discretion is not predicated on a model of rules. It rests, rather, on a picture of law that privileges social acts of authoritative guidance. For Hart, a legal rule is a standard that has been identified and selected as binding by some social act, be it an individual directive, a legislative enactment, a judicial decision, an administrative ruling, or a social custom. Judicial discretion is inevitable, according to Hart, because it is impossible for social acts to pick out standards that resolve every conceivable question.

As we can see, the debate between Hart and Dworkin does not concern whether the law contains principles as well as rules. This cannot be *the* issue of the debate because it was never *an* issue of the debate.[31] Contrary to Dworkin's interpretation, Hart never embraced the model of rules, either explicitly or implicitly.

Nor would it be accurate to claim that the core issue of the debate revolves around the question of judicial discretion. To be sure, Hart and Dworkin did disagree about whether judges have strong discretion in hard cases. Yet this dispute is a derivative one: both sides take their positions on judicial discretion because of their very different theories about the nature of law.

As we have just seen, Hart held that judges must sometimes exercise strong discretion because he takes the law to consist in those standards socially designated as authoritative. Dworkin, on the other hand, believes that judges do not have strong discretion precisely because he denies the centrality of social guidance to determining the existence or content of legal rules. Recall that the point of Dworkin's critique in "The Model of Rules I" is to show that the law contains norms that are binding even though they have not been the subject of past social guidance. They are binding, rather, because of their moral content. Moreover, even with respect to those norms that have been the subject of past social guidance, the bindingness of those norms, according to Dworkin, does not depend on the fact that they have been socially designated as binding. They are binding because the principles of political morality make them binding. Thus, even when social guidance runs out, the law does not, for moral guidance does not.

The "real" debate between Hart and Dworkin, therefore, concerns the clash of two very different models of law. Should law be understood to consist in those standards socially designated as authoritative? Or is it constituted by those standards morally designated as authoritative? Are the ultimate determinants of law social facts alone or moral facts as well? Dworkin's challenge purports to demonstrate that we must choose the latter. As we will see, the positivist response has been to argue that Dworkin has shown no such thing.

3. THE RESPONSES

The traditional moniker "the Hart–Dworkin debate" is slightly deceiving, for it tends to create the impression that Hart and Dworkin have been the sole participants in the debate. In point of fact, however, Hart never directly responded in writing to Dworkin's critique during his lifetime.[32] He apparently left to others the task of defending his theory.

In this section, I will survey the two main responses offered by Hart's followers to Dworkin's challenge. As we will see, some positivists accepted Dworkin's characterization of legal positivism but rejected his proposed explanation for why legal principles are part of the law. For them, legal norms are never valid because of their moral content – the principles that Dworkin cites either have social pedigrees or they are not law. Others accepted Dworkin's explanation for the legality of principles as conceptually possible, and even empirically plausible, but rejected his characterization of legal positivism. For these theorists, legal principles can be valid in virtue of their moral content without rejecting the core commitments of legal positivism.

A. Exclusive Legal Positivism

Although Hart himself seemed to reject the Pedigree Thesis, some legal positivists agreed with Dworkin about its centrality to positivism and, hence, enthusiastically embraced it. For them, tests of legality must always distinguish law from non-law based exclusively on their social source and must be implementable without resort to moral reasoning. Traditionally, these positivists have been known as "hard" or "exclusive" legal positivists.[33]

How, then, do exclusive legal positivists respond to Dworkin's claim that judges are often bound by principles that have no pedigree? One reply has been to point out that these norms do have pedigrees, appearances notwithstanding.[34] For these principles typically have been used by courts over a period of time as the basis for their decisions. This usage amounts to the existence of a "judicial custom," thereby constituting an adequate social pedigree from the perspective of the Pedigree Thesis.

The weakness of this response, however, is that judges often take themselves to be obligated to apply principles that seem entirely novel. As Dworkin pointed out, no court before *Henningsen* applied the principle that automobile manufacturers are subject to a greater standard of care. Yet that court nevertheless felt compelled to apply that norm.

Accordingly, exclusive legal positivists have offered a second, more nuanced response. They concede that judges are sometimes legally obligated to apply principles that lack any institutional pedigree. But this fact, they contend, does not impugn the Pedigree Thesis. For in such cases, judges are simply under a legal obligation to apply *extralegal* standards.

According to this second response, first made prominent by Joseph Raz, Dworkin's critique assumes that the law of a system consists of all those standards that judges of that system are required to apply.[35] From this it follows, of course, that if judges are required to apply moral principles that lack pedigrees, these principles must be *legal* principles. However, Raz argues, this assumption is mistaken. In choice of laws cases, for example, judges are often required to apply the law of a foreign jurisdiction. Yet the obligation to apply foreign rules does not transmute them into local rules. The distinction between normative systems is preserved even when one system borrows from another. Analogously, Raz claims, the judicial obligation to look to morality does not ipso facto incorporate morality into the law.[36]

According to Raz, therefore, when pedigreed standards run out, judges are under a legal obligation to look to moral principles to resolve the case at hand. Furthermore, in such cases, judges are exercising strong discretion insofar as they are obligated to look beyond the law and apply these extralegal principles to the case at hand. Strong discretion does not, therefore, entail the existence of "extra-legal principles [a judge] is *free* to apply if he *wishes*."[37] Rather, judges are legally constrained to apply certain extralegal principles, namely, the morally best ones.[38]

B. Inclusive Legal Positivism

Most legal positivists, however, have not taken the exclusivist route. Instead, they have sought to deflect Dworkin's critique by rejecting his characterization of positivism. Legal positivism, they have argued, does not prohibit moral tests of legality.[39] Hence, even if Dworkin is right and judges are sometimes obligated to apply principles that lack pedigrees in mature systems such as our own, positivism would remain unscathed. Positivists who embrace this position are usually known as "soft" or "inclusive" legal positivists.

This response to Dworkin begins by setting out a more traditional version of legal positivism, one that sees it as defined by two commitments. The first thesis, sometimes called the "Separability Thesis," denies any necessary connection between legality and morality. For the positivist, there is some possible legal system where the legality of a norm does not depend on any of its moral properties: in that system, an unjust law is still a law. The second thesis, sometimes known as the "Social Fact Thesis," holds that the existence and content of the law are ultimately determined by certain facts about social groups. Legal facts are grounded, in the final analysis, on social, not moral, facts.

Clearly, the Separability Thesis does not rule out master tests that incorporate moral criteria of legality. It states simply that tests of legality need not be moralized, not that they *could* not. Would the existence of such tests, however, offend the Social Fact Thesis? Not necessarily, according to the inclusive legal positivist. The Social Fact Thesis would be satisfied, on this view, just in case such tests of legality themselves have social pedigrees. For as long as the criteria of legality are set out in a rule whose existence is underwritten by a social fact, the law would have the appropriate social foundations.

In fact, the inclusive legal positivist points out that Hart's master rule, the rule of recognition, has the requisite pedigree. As mentioned earlier, the rule of recognition is necessarily a *social* rule – it is a convention among judges to recognize certain norms that bear certain characteristics as binding. The Social Fact Thesis is compatible with rules of recognition that set out nonpedigree, moral criteria of legality, for, contrary to the exclusive positivist, it does not require every legal rule to have a social source – it merely requires that the rule of recognition have one. Thus, as long as legal positivism's commitment to social facts can be satisfied by the existence of a social rule of recognition, there is no bar to treating morality as a condition of legality.[40]

The simplicity of this response, however, is offset by a hidden weakness. It would seem that the inclusive legal positivist cannot claim that the rule of recognition requires judges to resolve hard cases by resorting to moral principles and still maintain that the rule of recognition is a social rule. The difficulty stems from the fact, as Dworkin pointed out in "The Model of Rules II,"[41] that the contents of social rules are determined by agreement. A social rule imposes an obligation to p if and only if members of the group agree that p is required. Controversy about the requirements of a social rule, thus, seems impossible: social rules rest on agreement, whereas controversy entails disagreement.

Yet, the objection continues, in hard cases, judges disagree with one another about which principles they are required to apply. If the rule of recognition required judges to apply moral principles, hard cases would, therefore, involve controversy about the content of the rule of recognition. However, as mentioned above, controversy about a social rule is impossible. Hence, if inclusive legal positivists maintain that the rule of recognition requires hard cases to be resolved by reference to moral principles, then the rule of recognition cannot be a social rule.

In "Negative and Positive Positivism," Jules Coleman showed how to overcome this objection.[42] Coleman distinguished between two types of disagreements. The first type involves disputes over the content of the rule of recognition. Call these "content disputes." By contrast, certain disagreements presuppose consensus about the content of a rule but involve disputes about its implementation. Call these "application disputes."

Coleman suggested that we see hard cases as involving disputes about the applicability of the rule of recognition. They are application disputes, not content disputes. In controversial cases, there exists an accepted convention among judges to look toward the principles of morality to resolve legal disputes. When judges disagree about which principles to apply, they are disagreeing over the correct application of the rule of recognition, not about its content. All judges agree, in other words, that the rule of recognition requires them to look toward moral principles in adjudication, thereby making those moral principles valid law. They simply disagree about which principles are moral principles (and hence legal principles).

It should be noted that Hart eventually endorsed Coleman's strategy in the Postscript to *The Concept of Law*. First, Hart rejected Dworkin's contention that exclusive legal positivism was the only true positivism. "In addition to such pedigree matters the rule of recognition may supply tests relating not to the factual content of laws but to their conformity with substantive moral values or principles."[43] Moreover, he dismissed Dworkin's inference that controversy entails the absence of a convention. "Judges may be agreed on the relevance of such tests as something settled by established judicial practice even though they disagree as to what the tests require in particular cases."[44]

4. ACT TWO

A detailed examination and comparison of these two versions of legal positivism, and their respective responses to Dworkin, are clearly beyond the scope of this essay. I will, however, simply assert without argument that Hart's followers have succeeded in blunting the force of Dworkin's critique in "The Model of Rules I." The fact that judges are sometimes obligated to apply moral principles in hard cases does not show, by itself, that legal positivism is false. This is not to say, of course, that such a critique could not be made out but only that Dworkin has yet to make it.

Perhaps Dworkin sensed the impasse as well, for his critique changed dramatically after "The Model of Rules I." As we will see, the new objection, first broached in "The Model of Rules II" but fully developed only in *Law's Empire*, attempts to show that legal positivists are unable to account for a certain type of disagreements that legal participants frequently have, namely, those that concern the proper method for interpreting the law. The only plausible explanation for how such disagreements are possible, Dworkin claimed, is that they are moral disputes. Contrary to legal positivists, therefore, Dworkin argued that the law does not rest on social facts alone but is ultimately grounded in considerations of political morality.

As we will see, this critique of positivism is extremely powerful. Moreover, none of the responses to the first critique mentioned earlier are effective against it. Whether positivists have any defense against it is a matter to which I will return at the end of the essay.

A. Theoretical Legal Disagreements

At the beginning of *Law's Empire*, Dworkin argues that the law is a social phenomenon that has a special structure. Legal practice, he claims, is "argumentative,"[45] by which he means that the practice consists largely in participants advancing various claims about what the law demands and defending such claims by offering reasons for them. "Every actor in the practice understands that what it permits or requires depends on the truth of certain propositions that are given sense only by and within the practice; the practice consists in large part in deploying and arguing about these propositions."[46]

To understand the law as a social phenomenon, then, one must appreciate that, for the most part, it is a practice of argumentation. Legal philosophers must, therefore, study the different modes of argumentation that legal participants actually use when engaging in legal reasoning. However, as Dworkin argues, modern jurisprudence fails utterly in this regard. Following the dominant approaches in legal philosophy, he claims, many of the disagreements that legal participants engage in either do not exist or are complete nonsense.

To formulate this charge, Dworkin begins by introducing two related sets of distinctions. He first distinguishes between "propositions of law" and "grounds of law."[47] A proposition of law is a statement about the content of the law in a particular legal system, such as "the law forbids states to deny anyone equal protection within the meaning of the Fourteenth Amendment" and "the law requires Acme Corporation to compensate John Smith for the injury he suffered in its employ last February." Propositions of law may be true or false. The proposition "motorists are not legally permitted to drive in California over 65 miles per hour" is true, whereas "motorists are not legally permitted to drive in California after sunset" is false.

Propositions of law are true in virtue of the "grounds of law." In California, for example, propositions of law are true (roughly speaking) if a majority of state legislators vote for bills that contain texts to those effects and the governor then signs it. These acts of legislation make propositions of California law true and hence are grounds of law in the California legal system.

Given the distinction between propositions and grounds of law, Dworkin argues that two different types of legal disagreements are possible.[48] The first type involves disagreements about whether the grounds of law have in fact obtained. Parties could dispute, for example, whether Congress passed a certain law by the requisite majorities or whether the president vetoed the bill. Dworkin calls these "empirical disagreements."

The second type of disagreement does not relate to whether the grounds of law have obtained; rather, it involves conflicting claims about what the grounds of law are. For example, one party to a dispute might argue that a statute is valid because Congress has the authority to enact a certain kind of legislation and has so acted. The second party might concede that the formal conditions for enactment have been met but nevertheless claim that Congress lacks the authority to so legislate. These parties are not embroiled in an empirical disagreement inasmuch as they agree about the historical record. According to Dworkin, they are engaged in a "theoretical" disagreement about the law. They are disagreeing about the identity of the grounds of law, that is, about what must take place in their legal system before a proposition of law can be said to be true or false.

With these distinctions in tow, Dworkin declares: "Incredibly, our jurisprudence has no plausible theory of theoretical disagreement in law."[49] This is so because "our jurisprudence" is committed to a "plain-fact" view of law.

The plain-fact view, according to Dworkin, consists of two basic tenets. First, it maintains that the grounds of law in any community are fixed by consensus among legal officials. If officials agree that facts of type f are grounds of law in their system, then facts of type f are grounds of law in their system. Second, it holds that the only types of facts that may be grounds of law are those of *plain historical* fact.

> The law is only a matter of what legal institutions, like legislatures and city councils and courts, have decided in the past. If some body of that sort has decided that workmen can recover compensation for injuries by fellow workmen, then that is the law. If it has decided the other way, then that is the law. So questions of law can always be answered by looking in the books where the records of institutional decisions are kept.[50]

As Dworkin convincingly argues, the plain-fact view cannot countenance the possibility of theoretical legal disagreements. For if, according to its first tenet, legal participants must always agree on the grounds of law, then it follows that they cannot disagree about the grounds of law. Any genuine disagreement about the law must involve conflicting claims about the existence or nonexistence of plain historical facts. They must, in other words, be purely empirical disagreements.

B. The Prevalence of Theoretical Disagreements

Dworkin proceeds to argue that, *pace* the plain-fact view, theoretical disagreements do exist in the law. He makes his case by presenting numerous examples where it is plausible to suppose that legal participants all agree about the historical record but dispute their legal significance. For example, in *Tennessee Valley Authority v. Hill*, several conservation groups sued the Tennessee Valley Authority (TVA) to prevent them from completing a $100 million dam project.[51] They claimed that the dam would threaten the existence of the snail darter – a three-inch fish of no particular scientific, aesthetic, or economic interest – and hence would violate the Endangered Species Act of 1973. The TVA, however, argued that the Endangered Species Act did not apply to a project authorized, funded, and substantially constructed before it was passed and, hence, should not be construed to prohibit the dam's completion.

The Supreme Court sided with the conservationists. Although Chief Justice Burger, writing for the majority, admitted that halting the project would involve an enormous waste of public funds and, from a policy perspective, could not be justified, he noted that the text clearly requires the government to terminate projects posing risks to species designated as "endangered." Furthermore, he could find no indication that Congress intended otherwise. Burger thus concluded that the Court had no choice but to issue the injunction, even at so late a date.

The dissent, led by Justice Powell, argued that courts should not construe texts to lead to absurd results, except where it can be demonstrated that such results were intended by the legislature. Because it would be ludicrous to shut down a nearly completed $100 million construction project simply to save an unimportant, albeit endangered, fish and because Congress did not clearly endorse this result, the Court is obligated to give an interpretation that "accords with some modicum of common sense and the public weal."[52]

Dworkin argues that the disagreement between Burger and Powell is ultimately theoretical in nature.[53] Both sides agreed that the Endangered Species Act of 1973 is valid law, that halting the construction of the dam is terribly wasteful even in the light of the benefits to the snail darter, and that Congress never considered this type of case when drafting or voting on the legislation. Their disagreement concerned the legal relevance of these plain facts. According to Burger, the plain meaning of the text should control even when absurdities follow unless compelling evidence can be found to show that Congress did not intend the absurd result. Powell, on the other hand, argued that plain meaning should not control when absurdities follow unless compelling evidence can be found that Congress *did* intend the absurd result.

Those who subscribe to the plain-fact view are, of course, aware that legal participants often seem as though they are engaged in theoretical disagreements. But, they claim, appearances are deceiving. In these types of cases, when participants seem to be disagreeing about what the law is, they are actually disagreeing about what the law ought to be. According to the plain-fact view, therefore, the debate between Burger and Powell concerned the law's repair. Burger should be understood as seeking to *extend* the reach of the Endangered Species Act to construction projects that were substantially completed by the time the act was passed. Powell, on the other hand, should be taken as arguing that the Act, in the light of the wasteful consequences of such an expansion, should not be so expanded.

If judges are not actually engaging in theoretical disagreements, why do judges act as though they are? The standard answer supplied by the plain-fact view is that judges are trying to conceal the true "legislative" nature of their actions. In systems of separated powers, where legislatures alone are authorized to make law and judges are required to apply it, it is dangerous for judges to admit that they are exercising discretion and attempting to repair the law. Courts preserve their legitimacy when they act as though there really is law "out there" to discover rather than admitting that the law is sometimes indeterminate and that they are filling in the gaps.

Dworkin finds this response implausible for two reasons. First, he cannot see why, if the plain-fact explanation is true, the general public has yet to uncover the ruse. "If lawyers all agree there is no decisive law in cases like our sample cases, then why has this view not become part of our popular political culture long ago?"[54] Second, Dworkin points out that if judges were seeking to repair, not report, the law, it would be difficult in many cases to explain why they end up deciding as they do. In *TVA*, for example, Burger claimed that halting the dam's construction was disfavored from a policy perspective. If he wanted to repair the law, why did he come to such a decision? By Burger's own admission, the Court's ruling would result in an enormous waste of public funds for no apparent benefit.[55]

Dworkin infers from *TVA v. Hill* and cases like it that theoretical disagreements not only take place but abound. Because the plain-fact view cannot account for the possibility of these disputes, Dworkin concludes that it does not capture the argumentative structure of legal practice and as a result must be rejected.

C. The Possibility of Theoretical Disagreements

How, then, are theoretical disagreements possible? Dworkin's explanation centers on the claim that legal interpretation is, at bottom, "constructive" interpretation. Constructive interpretation is the process of "imposing purpose on an object or practice in order to make it the best possible example of the form or genre to which it is taken to belong."[56] A purpose makes an object the best that it can be when it both "fits" *and* "justifies" the object better than any rival purpose. A purpose "fits" the object to the extent that it recommends that the object exists or that it has the properties it has. A purpose is "justified" to the extent that it is a purpose worth pursuing.

To determine which facts are grounds of law in a particular legal system, Dworkin believes that the interpreter must engage in constructive interpretation. She must first impute a point to the particular practice that presents it in its best light, namely, one that best fits and morally justifies it. Then, she must use this point to ascertain the grounds of law for the particular system.

By treating the determination of legal grounds as a process of constructive interpretation, Dworkin is able to account neatly for the possibility of theoretical interpretations in law. Disagreements about the grounds of law are predicated on disagreements about the moral value of law and/or law's relation to practice. Thus, unlike the plain-fact view, this account need not treat theoretical disagreements as incoherent or insincere: insofar as the content of the law is dependent on which principles portray legal practice in its morally best light, genuine *moral* disagreements will induce genuine *legal* disagreements.

5. THE TWO CRITIQUES COMPARED

Dworkin's critique of legal positivism in *Law's Empire* has many similarities to the one he put forth in "The Model of Rules I." Both characterize positivism as committed to a Pedigree Thesis. Both claim that positivism cannot explain judicial behavior in hard cases. And both maintain that the proper explanation for such behavior involves understanding judges looking to morality to resolve the legal matters at hand. Despite these commonalities, however, Dworkin's latter critique is a vastly different and, as we will soon see, more effective one.

The distinction between critiques becomes plain when the first is recast using the terminology of the second. To translate between critiques, we start by noting that a "criterion of legality" (in the language of the first critique) tests whether certain "grounds of law" (in the language of the second critique) obtain in a particular case. For example, the criterion "All rules passed by both houses of Congress that regulate interstate commerce are laws of the United States" takes the facts of bicameral passage and regulation of interstate commerce as grounds of law in the U.S. legal system. Thus, instead of speaking of kinds of criteria of legality, we can speak simply in terms of the kinds of grounds of law that these criteria set out.

On this translation, the first critique can be understood as purporting to show that in hard cases judges take morally relevant facts to be grounds of law. It does this by examining cases such as *Henningsen* where judges regard themselves as bound by principles whose legal authority derives from their moral content. But positivism is committed to the plain-fact view, which precludes moral grounds of law. Hence, the first critique concludes that legal positivism cannot explain judicial behavior in hard cases.

Whereas the first critique seeks to exploit the alleged fact that judges often take the grounds of law to be moral in nature, the second critique tries to capitalize on the alleged fact that judges often disagree with one another about what the grounds of law are. The dispute in *TVA*, for example, was grounded in a dispute about whether to privilege the statutory text even in the face of absurd results. Positivism cannot explain such disagreements, the second critique concludes, because it is committed to the plain-fact view, according to which the grounds of law are fixed by agreement.

Thus, though both *Henningsen* and *TVA* are hard cases, they are hard for different reasons. *Henningsen* is hard because, although the court agreed on the grounds of law, figuring out whether those grounds obtain in the particular case is a demanding question that reasonable people may disagree about. *TVA* is hard because to determine the correct outcome of the case, the court had to first resolve what the grounds of law are, and reasonable people can disagree about that question as well.

As we saw earlier, hard cases like *Henningsen* are not hard for the positivist to accommodate. For example, the positivist may take the exclusivist route and claim that, in such cases, judges are legally obligated to apply extralegal norms. Or she can take the inclusive route and simply admit that the grounds of law can be moral in nature, provided that there is a convention among judges to regard those facts as grounds of law. But cases like *TVA* cannot be explained away in either manner. For it is common ground between exclusive and inclusive legal positivists that the grounds of law are determined by convention. How can they account for disagreements about the legal bindingness of certain facts whose bindingness, by hypothesis, requires the existence of agreement on their bindingness?[57]

Curiously, positivists have had little to say about this problem. Indeed, it is one of the great ironies of modern jurisprudence that in spite of the huge amount of ink spilled on the Hart–Dworkin debate, so little attention has been paid to this second, more powerful objection. To be sure, legal positivists have relentlessly attacked Dworkin's positive theory of constructive interpretation. Yet they have made almost no effort to defend their own theory against Dworkin's negative arguments in *Law's Empire*. They have made no attempt to show how theoretical legal disagreements are possible.

One explanation for this neglect may be that positivists have not recognized that these later objections differ in kind from the earlier ones. They may have thought that their responses to the "Model of Rules I" critique are equally applicable to the *Law's Empire* critique. This, we have just seen, is a mistake. Dworkin's later critique seeks to show that the grounds of law cannot be determined by convention, whereas the positivistic responses to the earlier critique presuppose that the grounds of law are indeed fixed conventionally. There is another possibility, however. Positivists may have recognized the differing nature of the second critique and may simply be unmoved. For they might still cling to the repair argument: they might maintain that theoretical disagreements about the law are impossible, that when judges appear to be occupied by such disputes they are, for various political reasons, really engaged in covert arguments about repairing the law, and that nothing Dworkin has said has given them any reason to think otherwise.

To be fair to the positivist, it must be said that Dworkin's specific responses to the positivist argument about repair are not particularly compelling. Recall that Dworkin objected to the repair argument by wondering why, if the positivist is correct, the public has yet to pick up on the judicial ruse. But the explanation for such a fact – if it is indeed a fact – is simple: the law is a professional practice and lay persons are either ignorant of its ground rules or too intimidated by legal officials to challenge them. Dworkin also argued that the repair argument makes it difficult to explain why judges make the rulings they make. If Burger were interested in repairing the law, Dworkin reasoned, he would not have shut down the construction project to save the snail darter. But this objection overlooks the possibility that Burger had bigger fish to fry. Burger might have wanted to repair not the specific statute itself but rather the norms of statutory interpretation. His concern, in other words, might have been with denying judges the discretion to deviate from the statutory text when they happen to disagree with its result. Understood in this way, Burger's ruling in favor of the snail darter was a rational choice for legal repair.

Although Dworkin's objections to the repair argument are not, to my mind, convincing, I think that it would be a mistake to dismiss his entire critique so quickly. For it is relatively simple to refashion his objections in such a way that the repair argument no longer looks particularly attractive. One need notice only that judges are not the only ones who engage in theoretical disagreements – legal scholars do so as well. The law reviews, after all, are filled with articles arguing for the legal propriety of one interpretive methodology over another. Indeed, the great disputations of legal theory – those between originalism and dynamism, textualism and purposivism, documentarianism and doctrinalism – have been precisely about theoretical disagreements in the law. Judges may have a great political interest in hiding the true nature of their activities, but scholars generally do not. No doubt, some theorists tailor their interpretive theories to fit their politics. But if theoretical disagreements were incoherent, trying to convince one's peers in this manner would be folly, for surely they would see right through it.

Positivists, therefore, appear to be in an awkward position. If they wish to deny the existence of theoretical legal disagreements, they are forced to say that legal scholars are so confused about the practice they study that they routinely engage in incoherent argumentation. This result is unattractive but perhaps not fatal. For it cannot be demanded that legal theories fit every lawyerly preconception. Lawyers can certainly be wrong about the practice in which they participate. What the positivist must show, however, is that there are compelling theoretical reasons to either dismiss or reinterpret the self-understanding of these experts. Whether this can be shown is a question that positivists have yet to face.[58]

6. ACCOUNTING FOR THEORETICAL DISAGREEMENTS

There is one more option available to the positivist. Instead of trying to explain away theoretical disagreements, she might nevertheless attempt to account for them within a positivistic framework. She might, in other words, show how proper interpretive methodology might be anchored in social facts. It is to this possibility that we now turn.

A. Looking for Social Facts

The first step in accounting for theoretical disagreements in a positivistic framework, I believe, is to concede that the plain-fact view, or any other account that privileges interpretive conventions as the sole source of proper methodology, ought to be rejected. Because theoretical disagreements abound in the law, interpretive methodology may be fixed in ways other than specific social agreement about which methodologies are proper.[59] The positivist should also agree with Dworkin that when theoretical disagreements are plenty ascertaining proper interpretive methodology involves attributing a purpose to legal practice. One cannot understand disagreements over interpretive methodology unless one sees them as disputes about the point of engaging in the practice of law. Finally, the positivist should also maintain with Dworkin that in such cases proper interpretive methodology for a particular legal system is primarily a function of which methodology best harmonizes with the objectives of that system.

Here, however, the agreement must end. Although ascertaining interpretive methodology involves attributing a purpose to legal practice, the positivist cannot, of course, treat this attributive process in a Dworkinian manner, namely, as an exercise in moral and political philosophy. The positivist, rather, must seek *social facts*. The fact that some set of goals and values represents the purposes of a certain legal system must be a fact about certain social groups that is ascertainable by empirical, rather than moral, reasoning. Proper interpretive methodology would then be established by determining which methodology best harmonized with these goals and values. In this way, the positivist will have blunted Dworkin's critique: by claiming that interpretive methodology is a function of empirically derivable objectives, the positivist will have grounded the law in social fact. Moreover, the positivist will have established the social foundations of law in a manner that does not rely on specific conventions about proper interpretive methodology, thereby accounting for the possibility of theoretical disagreements. Theoretical disagreements would simply be a product of disputes over which purposes are in fact the objectives of the system or about which methodology best harmonizes with those objectives.

This proposed response, of course, is purely schematic, for it does not specify how the political objectives are to be ascertained. The proposal does not tell us, for example, whose objectives are relevant to determining the purposes of a legal system, nor how these objectives must be related to the actual behavior of legal participants. No doubt, these are questions that any adequate positivistic theory of legal interpretation must address. The above proposal, however, merely sets out a strategy: it claims that for the positivists to account for the possibility of theoretical disagreements, they should drop their conventionality requirement, concede that proper methodology is a function of systemic purpose, and yet maintain nevertheless that systemic purpose is a matter of social fact.

B. Settling on an Ideology

To be sure, it is not enough for positivists to advance a theory of legal interpretation that grounds interpretive methodology in social facts. Their account must be plausible as well. What, then, would a plausible positivist theory of legal interpretation look like? Although space limitations prohibit a detailed exposition of such an account, I will attempt in the remainder of this section to sketch the outlines of one such theory.[60]

The proper task of the legal interpreter, I would like to suggest, is to impute to legal practice the political objectives that the current designers of the legal system sought to achieve.[61] The purposes that are legally relevant, in other words, are those that *explain*, rather than justify, the current practice. These objectives might be laudable ones, such as promoting democratic self-rule and protecting individual liberty, or they may be more morally suspect, such as seeking to implement the will of God or hastening the proletariat revolution. The proper methodology for a particular legal system would be the one that best harmonizes with the ideological objectives of those who designed the current system, regardless of the moral palatability of their ideology.

According to this proposal, proper interpretive methodology is grounded in social fact because the specific purposes of a legal system are matters of social fact. Whether a legal system ought to be understood as advancing some political goal G or realizing some value V depends on whether those who destroyed the system designed it to advance G or realize V. To uncover the political objectives of a legal system, the interpreter must analyze its institutional structure and determine which goals and values best explain why the legal system has its current shape. Thus, one might conclude that a system that made provisions for voting, representation, elections, and some protection for public deliberation is a system in which democratic self-rule is prized. By contrast, an institutional structure that empowered clerics to decide matters of principle and policy and minimized the degree to which secular forces can affect the direction of the law would be a system in which religious values are designed to be promoted.

It should be emphasized that the reason to privilege the objectives of legal designers in legal interpretation is not simply motivated by the desire to answer Dworkin's objections. More importantly, deference to the ideology of designers is necessary if designers are to do their job, *which is to settle questions about which specific objectives the group should pursue.*[62]

To see why this is so, let us start with the idea that the fundamental function of all legal systems is to achieve certain very general political and moral objectives. These objectives include the maintenance of order, the prevention of undesirable and wrongful behavior, the promotion of distributive justice, the protection of rights, the provision of facilities for private ordering, and the fair settling of disputes. How legal systems should go about attaining these objectives, of course, is likely to be a complex and contentious matter. What rights do individuals have and which deserve legal protection? Which distribution of goods is the just distribution? Against which moral metric is behavior to be assessed? These questions are apt to provoke serious doubts and disagreements. It is reasonable to suppose that without some mechanism for settling on which specific goals and values the legal system ought to pursue, there is a significant risk that the massive amount of coordinated behavior necessary for the law to achieve its moral mission will not take place.[63]

It is one of the primary functions of legal designers to resolve these very issues. They settle questions about specific political objectives through the process of institutional design, that is, by distributing rights and responsibilities in such a way that the exercise of the allocated powers and the observance of the assigned duties achieve the goals and realize the values they wish to promote. In this way, the behavior of members of the community will be channeled in the direction of the selected objectives. This is not to say that the law's fundamental functions will be achieved simply through deference to the institutional structure. Indeed, if the designers are untrustworthy and design the system poorly, the broad moral objectives mentioned earlier are guaranteed not to be met. The point, rather, is that if the designers are basically trustworthy, which is what the law always supposes, deferring to their judgments about how to attain the fundamental aims of the system is a highly effective strategy for actually attaining those ends.[64]

Once it is recognized that legal designers play this "settling" function, one can see why their resolutions concerning particular ends and values must be privileged when ascertaining interpretive methodology. For if members of the group are permitted to engage in moral and political philosophy to determine the proper justification for legal practice, they would effectively unsettle these matters. We might say that accounts of legal interpretation, such as Dworkin's, defeat the purpose of having legal authorities – they allow subjects to reopen the questions that authorities resolved by designing a legal system. After all, the judgments of designers are just more fodder for constructive interpretation. Their judgments will receive only the amount of deference that the Dworkinian interpreter deems to be morally appropriate in the light of current practice. To make that judgment, the interpreter will be forced to engage in abstract philosophical reflection and confront questions that have baffled humanity for the past few millennia.

Once we see the necessity of deferring to authoritative settlements about *which* particular objectives to pursue, the same argument counsels respect for decisions about *how* specifically they ought to be pursued. For authorities don't will just the *ends*, they will the *means* as well. It is also their task, in other words, to determine how to allocate rights and responsibilities based on their assessments of the competence and character of various members of the group. If, after having designed a particular institutional arrangement, those members were then to ask themselves afresh "Which assignment of power to me would best justify the practice?" they would be undoing precisely what the designers intended to do.

To preserve the ability of legal designers to design (and redesign) a legal system, the interpreter must defer not merely to the designers' decisions about specific political objectives, but also to those decisions concerning roles and trust. Thus, the interpreter must figure out how those with authority to design the system divided labor and which roles they entrusted to various participants. She must also determine which judgments or claims of trust and distrust underwrite such a division of labor. Thus, for example, broad grants of power to certain participants, with comparatively few attendant duties, might evidence high degrees of confidence in the competence and character of those individuals, whereas highly diffused distribution of power, with few opportunities for the exercise of discretion, might suggest low degrees of trust instead.

How should an interpreter process this information about ends and means? The interpreter might begin by drawing up a list of possible interpretive methodologies and attempting to ascertain their basic properties. She should try to discover, for example, whether certain methodologies require a great deal of expertise to implement or comparatively little, and whether they are easy to abuse or hard to manipulate. Having ascertained the basic properties of the candidate methodologies, the interpreter should then attempt to extract certain information from the institutional structure of the legal system in question. She ought to ascertain the attitudes of those who designed the system regarding the competence and character of certain participants, as well as the objectives that they are entrusted to promote. Finally, the interpreter should apply the information culled from the first two tasks to determine proper interpretive methodology. She must try to figure out which interpretive methodologies best further the extracted goals in the light of the extracted attitudes of trust. The relationship between interpretive method and systemic ideology can often be quite complex, but it can also be rather simple. Here is an example of a straightforward connection: an interpretive methodology that requires for its effective implementation a high degree of competence or moral character will be inappropriate for systems where high degrees of trust are inappropriate; instead, hermeneutic procedures that are easier to apply and less subject to abuse – perhaps ones that defer to plain meaning, instead of purpose – would be more fitting.

As mentioned previously, a virtue of this type of proposal is that, insofar as interpretive methodology is not determined by a specific convention about proper interpretive methodology, it is able to account for the possibility of theoretical disagreements. Participants in a practice can disagree over proper interpretive methodology because they disagree about any of the steps mentioned above. They might disagree about the demands imposed by particular methodologies, the ideological purposes of the system, its distribution of trust and distrust, or which methodology best harmonizes with such purposes and judgments of competence and character.

Notice further that this theory is strongly positivistic. Because it takes a regime's animating ideology as its touchstone, this account may end up recommending an interpretive methodology based on a morally questionable set of beliefs and values. The legal system in question, for example, may exist to promote racial inequality or religious intolerance; it may embody ridiculous views about human nature and the limits of cognition. Nevertheless, the positivist interpreter takes this ideology as given and seeks to determine which interpretive methodology best harmonizes with it.

This account of legal interpretation is positivistic in the most important sense, namely, it roots interpretive methodology in *social facts*. That a legal system has a certain ideology is a fact about the behavior and attitudes of social groups. The account privileges social facts, as mentioned earlier, not out of fanatical desire to save positivism at all cost, but because the alternative would render legal systems incoherent. Imputing to legal systems purposes, division of roles, and judgments of trustworthiness that are morally justified undercuts the basic division of labor between those who settle such matters and those who implement such settlements.

It is possible, then, for the positivist to maintain that the grounds of law are determined by social facts *and* to account for theoretical disagreements about those very grounds, Dworkin's contention in *Law's Empire* notwithstanding. The commitment to the social foundations of law, I have tried to show, can be satisfied in the absence of a specific convention about proper interpretive methodology just in case a consensus exists about the factors that ultimately determine interpretive methodology. The law will be grounded in social facts, that is, if the current designers agree about the basic objectives of the system, the competence and character of participants, and the proper distribution of roles.[65] The fact that interpretive methodology is determined by these factors not only renders theoretical disagreements possible, it explains why they are so prevalent. For it is highly likely that participants will disagree with one another about what these shared understandings are and which methodologies are best supported by them.

To be sure, it is a consequence of this approach that, in the absence of these shared understandings, disagreements about proper interpretive methodology will be irresolvable. And even if shared understandings do exist, they may be quite thin and thus will provide neither side much leverage in interpretive debates. I am not sure, however, that these implications undermine the solution I am offering. First, although thin shared understandings may not determine a unique methodology, they might nevertheless rule out certain interpretive stances. There may be no right answer to these disputes, but there are usually wrong ones. Second, and more important, a theory of law should account for the *intelligibility* of theoretical disagreements, not necessarily provide a resolution of them. An adequate theory, in other words, ought to show that it makes sense for participants to disagree with each other about the grounds of law. Whether a unique solution to these disputes actually exists is an entirely different, and contingent, matter, and a jurisprudential theory should not, indeed must not, demand one just because participants think that there is one.

7. THE FUTURE OF THE HART-DWORKIN DEBATE

In a recent article, "Beyond the Hart/Dworkin Debate," Brian Leiter makes the following provocative claim:

> The moment now seems opportune to step back and ask whether the Hart/Dworkin debate deserves to play the same organizing role in the jurisprudential curriculum of the twenty-first century that it played at the close of the twentieth. I am inclined to answer that question in the negative, though not, to be sure, because I can envision a jurisprudential future without Hart's masterful work at its center. Rather, it seems to me – and, I venture, many others by now – that on the particulars of the Hart/Dworkin debate, there has been a clear victor, so much so that even the heuristic value of the Dworkinian criticisms of Hart may now be in doubt.[66]

Needless to say, Leiter thinks that Hart has been the clear winner and that, given this resounding victory, the Hart-Dworkin debate no longer deserves the scholarly and pedagogical pride of place that it has been accorded for the past four decades.

To some extent, I agree with Leiter. If we identify the Hart-Dworkin debate solely by Dworkin's criticisms in "The Model of Rules I" and the discussion generated by them, which is how Leiter and many others understand it, then I think that the positivists clearly have "won," at least in the sense that they have successfully parried Dworkin's challenge. Narrowly construed, the Hart-Dworkin debate is indeed past its intellectual sell-by date. For whether positivism can account for the fact that judges are often required to apply nonpedigreed principles in hard cases is a question that, as lawyers say, has been asked and answered.

Yet, as I have tried to show, Dworkin's critique of Hart and legal positivism did not end with "The Model of Rules I." His challenge evolved over time and, in the process, became resistant to the existing positivistic defenses. Thus, I part company with Leiter when he writes that "The point is not, I hasten to add, that there remain no challenges to legal positivism, but rather that the significant issues that face legal positivists are now different, often in kind, from the ones Dworkin made famous." I have argued, however, that positivism is particularly vulnerable to Dworkin's critique in *Law's Empire*. To overlook this challenge, which most positivists have done, is to ignore the most serious threat facing legal positivism at the beginning of the twenty-first century.

Reports of the demise of the Hart-Dworkin debate, therefore, would be greatly exaggerated. The particulars have changed, but the basic issue, and its fundamental importance, remains the same today as it did forty years ago. Is the law ultimately grounded in social facts alone, or do moral facts also determine the existence and content of the law? Only the future will tell who has the right to claim victory in this debate.

ACKNOWLEDGMENTS

I thank Michael Bratman, Les Green, Brian Leiter, Joseph Raz, and Arthur Ripstein for extremely helpful comments that enabled me to improve the present draft substantially. Thanks are also due to Mark Greenberg for many helpful discussions related to the matters discussed in the paper. This essay was written while a Fellow at the Center for Advanced Study in the Behavioral Sciences. I am grateful for financial support provided by the Andrew W. Mellon Foundation.

Notes

1. Ronald Dworkin, "The Model of Rules I," reprinted in *Taking Rights Seriously* (Cambridge, MA: Harvard University Press, 1977).
2. See Scott J. Shapiro, "On Hart's Way Out," in *Hart's Postscript: Essays on the Postscript to "The Concept of Law,"* ed. J. Coleman (Oxford: Oxford University Press, 2001); "Law, Morality and the Guidance of Conduct," *Legal Theory* 6 (2000): 127–70; Jules L. Coleman, "Incorporationism, Conventionality and the Practical Difference Thesis," in *Hart's Postscript*.

3. See Kenneth Einar Himma, "H. L. A. Hart and the Practical Difference Thesis," *Legal Theory* 6 (2000): 1–43; W. J. Waluchow, "Authority and the Practical Difference Thesis: A Defense of Inclusive Legal Positivism," *Legal Theory* 6 (2000): 45–81; Matthew Kramer, "How Morality Can Enter Into the Law," *Legal Theory* 6 (2000): 83–108; Matthew Kramer, "Throwing Light on the Role of Moral Principles in the Law: Further Reflections," *Legal Theory* 8 (2002): 115–43.

4. In the Postscript, Hart accepts some responsibility for the confusion: "Much credit is due to Dworkin for having shown and illustrated [the] importance [of legal principles] and their role in legal reasoning, and certainly it was a serious mistake on my part not to have stressed their non-conclusive force." H. L. A. Hart, *The Concept of Law*, eds. Penelope Bulloch and Joseph Raz (Oxford: Clarendon Press, 1994), 263. Yet he goes on to disavow Dworkin's interpretation of his views: "But I certainly did not in my use of the word 'rule' claim that legal systems comprise only 'all or nothing' standards or near conclusive rules."

5. Compare Ronald Dworkin, "Judicial Discretion," *Journal of Philosophy* 60 (1963): 624–638 and "Model of Rules I" with Hart's *Concept of Law*, Ch. 7.

6. Compare Dworkin's "Hard Cases" in *Taking Rights Seriously* with Hart's *Concept of Law*, 128–36; Kent Greenawalt, "Discretion and Judicial Decision: The Elusive Quest for the Fetters that Bind Judges," *Columbia Law Review* 75 (1975): 359, 391.

7. Compare Dworkin's "The Model of Rules II," reprinted in *Taking Rights Seriously*, with Hart's *The Concept of Law*, 55–7 and 254–9.

8. Compare Ronald Dworkin's *Law's Empire* (Cambridge, MA: Harvard University Press, 1986), Chs. 1–2; Stephen Perry's "Interpretation and Methodology in Legal Theory," in *Law and Interpretation*, ed. A. Marmor (Oxford: Clarendon Press, 1995); and Jeremy Waldron's "Normative (or Ethical) Positivism," in *Hart's Postscript* with Hart's *Concept of Law*, vi, 248–50 and Jules Coleman's *The Practice of Principle* (Oxford: Oxford University Press, 2001), Ch. 12.

9. Compare Dworkin's *Law's Empire*, 93 with Hart's *Concept of Law*, 249.

10. Compare Dworkin's "On Interpretation and Objectivity," in *A Matter of Interpretation*, *Law's Empire*, 76–86. and "Objectivity and Truth: You'd Better Believe It," *Philosophy & Public Affairs* 25 (1996): 87–139 with Hart's "American Jurisprudence through English Eyes: The Nightmare and the Noble Dream," in *Essays in Jurisprudence and Philosophy* (Oxford: Clarendon Press, 1983), 139–40, and "Legal Duty and Obligation," in *Essays on Bentham* (Oxford: Clarendon Press, 1982), 149, 159.

11. Compare Dworkin's "Is There Really No Right Answer in Hard Cases?" reprinted in *A Matter of Principle* (Cambridge, MA: Harvard University Press, 1985), and "On Gaps in the Law," in *Controversies about Law's Ontology*, eds. Neil MacCormick and Paul Amselek (Edinburgh: Edinburgh University Press, 1991) with Hart's *Concept of Law*, 123–36, Joseph Raz's "Legal Reasons, Sources, and Gaps," in *The Authority of Law* (Oxford: Clarendon Press, 1979), and Timothy Endicott's *Vagueness in Law* (Oxford: Clarendon Press, 2000), esp. Chs. 4 and 8.

12. Compare Dworkin's "Model of Rules I," 41 and "Model of Rules II" with Hart's *Concept of Law*, Chs. 5 and 6.

13. Ronald Dworkin, "The Model of Rules I," 17.

14. Ibid., 39.

15. See, for example, Hart's *Concept of Law*, 204.

16. Ronald Dworkin, "The Model of Rules I," 24.

17. Ibid., 25–7.

18. Ibid., 22.

19. 32 N.J. 358, 161 A.2d 69 (1960), discussed in Dworkin, *Taking Rights Seriously*, 25–6.

20. 32 N.J. 388, 161 A.2d 86.

21. 32 N.J. 387, 161 A.2d 85.

22. Dworkin, "Model of Rules I," 28.

23. Ibid., 31–4.

24. Ibid., 40.

25. Ibid.

26. Ibid.

27. Ibid., citing Hart's *The Concept of Law*, 94.

28. See Dworkin, "Model of Rules I," 41: "We might argue, for example, that the use we make of earlier cases and statutes is supported by a particular analysis of the point of the practice of legislation or the doctrine of precedent, or by the principles of democratic theory, or by a particular position on the proper division of authority between national and local institutions, or some thing else of that sort."

29. See, for example, Raz, "Legal Principles and the Limits of Law," *Yale Law Journal* 81 (1972): 823, 845; Shapiro, "On Hart's Way Out," 163; Leiter, "Beyond the Hart-Dworkin Debate," *American Journal of Jurisprudence* 48 (2003): 17, 20; and Lyons, "Principles, Positivism and Legal Theory," *Yale Law Journal* 87 (1977): 415, 422. See also Hart's comments in the Postscript to his *Concept of Law*, as I quoted in footnote 5.

30. Hart, *Concept of Law*, 126.

31. Although no one disputes that the law contains principles as well as rules, some have objected to the way Dworkin distinguishes between these two classes of norms. In particular, they have argued that rules do not always operate in an "all or nothing" fashion. See, for example, Raz, "Legal Principles and the Limits of Law" and George Christie, "The Model of Principles," *Duke Law Journal* 17 (1968): 649. For Dworkin's response, see Dworkin, "Models of Rules II," 71–80.

32. Hart did criticize Dworkin's positive proposals on several occasions. See Hart, "Legal Duty and Obligation," 147–53; "American Jurisprudence through English Eyes: The Nightmare and the Noble Dream," 137–41; "Law in the Perspective of Philosophy," in *Essays in Jurisprudence and Philosophy*, 153–8; and "Comment on Dworkin, 'Legal Theory and the Problem of Sense'," in *Issues in Contemporary Legal Philosophy: The Influence of H. L. A. Hart*, ed. Ruth Gavison (Oxford: Clarendon Press, 1987).

33. Joseph Raz, exclusive legal positivism's leading advocate, refers to his view as the commitment to the Sources Thesis. The Sources Thesis was first set out in "Legal Positivism and the Sources of Law," in Raz, *The Authority of Law* and received its most vigorous defense in his "Authority, Law and Morality," reprinted in Raz, *Ethics in the Public Domain* (Oxford: Clarendon Press, 1994). Raz further develops his position in Joseph Raz, *The Concept of a Legal System*, 2nd ed. (Oxford: Clarendon Press, 1980), 211–12; "The Problem about the Nature of Law," "The Inner Logic of the Law," and "On the Autonomy of Legal Reasoning," all appearing in *Ethics in the Public Domain*; and "Postema on Law's Autonomy and Public Practical Reasons: A Critical Comment," *Legal Theory* 4 (1998): 1.

34. See, for example, Genaro Carrio, *Legal Principles and Legal Positivism*, (Buenos Aires: Abeledo-Perrot, 1971), 25.

35. See Joseph Raz, "Postscript to 'Legal Principles and the Limits of Law'," in *Ronald Dworkin and Contemporary Jurisprudence*, ed. Marshall Cohen (Totowa, NJ: Rowman & Allanheld, 1983), 84–5.

36. Raz, *The Authority of Law*, 46.

37. Dworkin, "Model of Rules I," 29 (emphasis added).

38. See, for example, Joseph Raz, "Legal Principles and the Limits of Law," 847–8. Timothy Endicott has recently argued that when judges are legally required to apply moral principles to plug a gap in the law, and those principles dictate a unique solution, judges lack strong discretion. This represents somewhat of a compromise view: with Dworkin, Endicott believes that judges do not always have strong discretion in hard cases; with Raz, he believes that in these situations, judges are making, not finding, law. See Timothy Endicott, "Raz on Gaps – The Surprising Part," in *Rights, Culture and The Law*, eds. L. H. Meyer, S. L. Paulson, and T. W. Pogge (Oxford: Oxford University Press, 2003).

39. For this type of response see Philip Soper, "Legal Theory and the Obligation of a Judge: The Hart–Dworkin Dispute," *Michigan Law Review* 75 (1977): 473; David Lyons, "Principles, Positivism and Legal Theory," *Yale Law Journal* 87 (1977): 415; Jules Coleman, "Negative and Positive Positivism," in *Markets, Morals and the Law* (Cambridge: Cambridge University Press, 1988); Wilfred Waluchow, *Inclusive Legal Positivism* (Oxford: Clarendon Press, 1994).

40. Some positivists took a slightly different tack: they claimed that as long as a norm is morally derivable from a legal norm that has a pedigree, the morally derivable norm need not have a pedigree to be law. Suppose, for example, that a norm imposing a duty of reasonable care on everyone has a legally appropriate pedigree and that reasonable care requires homeowners to clear snow from the sidewalk in front of their house. These positivists – sometimes called "incorporationists" – hold that the snow-clearing norm is a legal norm despite its lack of a pedigree because it is morally entailed by a pedigreed norm. For such a response, see Rolf Sartorious, "Social Policy and Judicial Legislation," *American Philosophical Quarterly* 8 (1971):151.

41. Ronald Dworkin, "Model of Rules II."

42. Coleman, "Negative and Positive Positivism," 20.

43. Hart, *Concept of Law*, 258.
44. Ibid., 258–9.
45. Dworkin, *Law's Empire*, 13.
46. Ibid.
47. Ibid., 4.
48. Ibid., 4–6.
49. Ibid., 6.
50. Ibid., 7.
51. Tennessee Valley Authority v. Hill, 437 US 153 (1978).
52. Ibid., 196.
53. Dworkin, *Law's Empire*, 23.
54. Ibid., 37.
55. Likewise, in *Riggs v. Palmer*, Judge Gray argued in dissent that beneficiaries who murder testators should be permitted to collect their bequests, even though this interpretation of the Statute of Wills results in absurdity. If judges are supposed to be acting in these cases as legislators, as the plain-fact view urges, then their actions are inexplicable – they routinely choose the less socially beneficial course of action.
56. Dworkin, *Law's Empire*, 52.
57. It is important not to conflate the objection from theoretical disagreements with the argument Dworkin calls the "semantic sting." In *Law's Empire*, Dworkin introduces the semantic sting argument *after* he makes the objection from theoretical disagreements. See ibid., 43–4. The semantic sting is used to explain why positivists require the grounds of law to be determined by consensus. Dworkin hypothesizes that positivists insist on consensus because they tacitly subscribe to a criterial semantics, according to which concepts may be shared only if the criteria for the proper application of the concepts are shared. Thus, a criterial semantics for the concept of law would require that community members can share the same concept of law – and hence have meaningful dialogue about their law – only if they share the same criteria for the application of the concept. Since the criteria for the application of the concept of, say, U.S. law are just the grounds of U.S. law, a criterial semantics demands that communities share the same grounds of law in order to share the same concept of law. Dworkin argues that criterial semantics is defective precisely because criterial semantics is unable to account for theoretical legal disagreements. This is the semantic sting argument. Notice that the semantic sting argument is no objection to positivism if positivism is not committed to criterial semantics. See, for example, Joseph Raz, "Two Views of the Nature of the Theory Law: A Partial Comparison," in *Hart's Postscript*; Jules Coleman and Ori Simchen, "'Law'" *Legal Theory* 9 (2003): 1.
58. There is a third possible reason why positivists have misjudged the force of Dworkin's critique: they may have conflated the objection from theoretical disagreements with the semantic sting argument, as discussed in the previous note. The thought goes as follows: since positivism is not committed to criterial

semantics and since the semantic sting argument is an objection to criterial semantics, the semantic sting argument poses no threat to positivism. This is true, of course, but given that the semantic sting argument is not the same as the objection from theoretical disagreements, the failure of the former is irrelevant to the success of the latter.

59. It should be noted that sometimes courts settle theoretical disagreements. See, for example, *Edwards v. Canada* (Attorney General) [1930] A.C. 124, where the Privy Council rejected originalism as an appropriate method of constitutional interpretation. I thank Les Green for making this point to me.

60. I explore these issues in much greater detail in *Interpretation and the Economy of Trust* (forthcoming).

61. Because legal systems always contain mechanisms for revision, the designers of a system will change as the structure of the system is intentionally revised. The designers of the present American system include not only the framers and ratifiers of the Constitution of 1787, but the numerous agents over the past two hundred years who have changed the complexion of the system. The framers and ratifiers of the 14th Amendment are as much the designers of the current regime as the framers and ratifiers of the original constitution. How the objectives of a system change as the institutional structure is revised is a complex question that I cannot explore here.

62. Not every legal system has designers or has been designed. In some cases, the structure of a legal system, or some part thereof, is the result of custom. In these situations, there may be no ideology that underlies the system's institutional structure and thus no way to resolve theoretical disagreements (indeed, in these cases theoretical disagreements are not even possible). I say that there *may* be no ideology because legal officials may theorize previously untheorized customary aspects of a certain system and develop the system in the direction of this new ideology. These officials will then be considered designers, and theoretical disagreements can be resolved by reference to their ideology.

63. Even in those rare instances where there is a very broad consensus in the community on which specific political objectives to pursue, how conflicts between them should be adjudicated, and how they ought to be implemented institutionally, there will still be a pressing need to have mechanisms that can quell dissent, should it arise. Given that in politics not everyone wins, there is always the threat that the loser will challenge the results, and without some way of settling these sorts of disputes, the ability of the legal system to achieve its fundamental ends will be significantly imperiled.

64. It should be clear that this argument does not entail that members of the community are always morally obligated to defer to the system designers. For when the designers are not trustworthy, or otherwise not entitled to deference, there may be no reason to defer to their judgments about fundamental aims.

65. Similarly, there must exist a shared understanding among participants in the system about who the designers are and which institutional structures they have created.

66. Leiter, "Beyond the Hart-Dworkin Debate," 18.

2 The Rule of Law as the Rule of Liberal Principle

DAVID DYZENHAUS

[T]he "rights" conception [of the rule of law] assumes that citizens have moral rights and duties with respect to one another, and political rights against the state as a whole. It insists that these moral and political rights be recognized in positive law, so that they may be enforced *upon the demand of individual citizens* through courts or other judicial institutions of the familiar type, so far as this is practicable. The rule of law on this conception is the ideal of rule by an accurate public conception of individual rights. It does not distinguish, as the rule-book conception does, between the rule of law and substantive justice; on the contrary it requires, as part of the ideal of law, that the rules in the rule book capture and enforce moral rights.[1]

– Ronald Dworkin

INTRODUCTION

In popular opinion, the rule of law is essential to legitimate government. Philosophers of law do not dispute popular opinion but divide over an ambiguity in it. They agree that a legitimate government is one that, among other things, operates under the constraints of the rule of law. They disagree about whether the constraints suffice to make government to some extent legitimate. As we will soon see, this disagreement turns in part on political considerations about the role of judges in democracy. But it also turns on the debate between positivists and antipositivists about the nature of law. If, as antipositivists argue, there is some necessary connection between law and morality, the rule of law is to some extent the rule of good law. If, as positivists argue, the rule of law is simply the rule of the rules certified as valid in a particular legal order, it is the rule of those rules with the content they happen to have.

Positivists concede that the rule of law makes a difference to government. Rules are applied in accordance with the requirements of strict legality so that official coercion is authorized only if there is a clear legal warrant for it, like cases are treated alike, and so on. Under a regime of legitimate government, it is important that strict legality is by and large observed, and thus legitimate government requires the rule of law. But, positivists maintain, an oppressive regime can also operate under the constraints of the rule of law. Since its rules will be rigorously enforced, its rule might be morally worse for its subjects than that of an equally evil but disorganized regime.

Ronald Dworkin's account of the rule of law as the rule of liberal principles is the most recent in a long line of distinguished attempts to loosen positivism's grip on legal theory. Its power is evidenced by the fact that positivists have found themselves forced to concede that the rule of law is not just the rule of rules, since it is also the rule of principles. As Dworkin argues, such principles play a central role in judicial decision of "hard cases," cases where there is reasonable disagreement about what the law requires.

Positivists do not, however, suppose that that concession damages the fundamental tenet of legal positivism – the "separation thesis," which asserts that there is no necessary connection between law and morality. They think that Dworkin fails to show that the rule of principles is necessarily the rule of liberal principles, thus illustrating their contention that any attempt to show that the rule of law is the rule of good law must fail.

In the next section, I identify the main problems that an antipositivist account of the rule of law faces. With one exception, they come in a package of positivist objections to the tradition of judicial antipositivism to which Dworkin belongs. Then, in a long expository section, I show that Dworkin's account of the rule of law cannot surmount these problems, and thus I close by arguing that his account should be modified.

But before I embark on my account of a complex debate, I want to note a curious feature of it. Most of the principal figures in philosophy of law in the twentieth century paid little attention to the issue of the rule of law because for them that issue was approached by first determining what the *law* is that rules, after which there is little left to say about the *rule* of law. We will see that in Dworkin's case there seems little left to say, which is why the essay from which my epigraph is taken is a rare example of focus on the rule of law.[2] It is more true of his position than of any other that his account of the rule of law is an account of the particular theory of liberal justice that he argues is embedded within the law. I will narrow the scope of discussion by focusing on three central objections to Dworkin's theory of the rule of law.

THREE OBJECTIONS TO DWORKIN

The first positivist objection to an antipositivist account of the rule of law is that it is politically dangerous. To suggest that the rule of law is the rule of good law is to support oppressive regimes in their claim to legitimacy merely because they observe the rule of law. But this is not the only political danger positivists detect in antipositivism, at least in the judicial antipositivism of the common law tradition to which Dworkin belongs, a tradition that maintains that the common law is the repository of the morality of the law and that judges are the guardians of its principles.

Jeremy Bentham regarded this view as the main weapon in the armory of the self-aggrandizing, usurpatory legitimacy claims made by judges. His positivism was clearly put in the service of debunking the claims of judges minded to uphold a private order that privileged property-owning elites in the face of democratic legislative reforms. This political association of positivism with democracy, and a preference for statutes as the primary form of law against liberal antipositivists who may seem to give an exalted role to judges and the common law, is a constant theme in debates about the rule of law. It informs the critique of judges in what we might think of as populist conceptions of democracy, which require law to be nothing more than the expression of what the people in fact want, unconstrained insofar as this is possible by formal legal requirements and completely unconstrained by judicially interpreted principles.

The main stream of contemporary positivism, however, follows H. L. A. Hart in detaching legal positivism from democratic theory, indeed from any particular political commitments. Although contemporary positivism stresses the political dangers of antipositivism, it ultimately relies on a conceptual reason for adopting positivism – the need for a general theory of law.[3] A theory of law must be general not only in that it can account for the fact that law can be used as an instrument of oppression. It must also be able to account for the fact that legal orders have very different institutional features, for example, the institution of constitutional review of the United States of America and the Westminster model of parliamentary supremacy, which requires judicial deference to clearly expressed legislative intention.

So a second objection to antipositivist accounts of the rule of law is not so much political as theoretical. It is that such accounts are parochial, unable to offer a general account of the law. They rely on features of legal systems that are entirely contingent – for example, a written constitution giving judges the authority to test legislation against a bill of liberal rights and freedoms.

The structure of the positivist claim for superiority over antipositivism makes life difficult for judicial antipositivism. Positivists distinguish between a general theory of law and theories of adjudication that tell judges how to decide hard cases. They also claim that in hard cases the positive law does not supply an answer. Since the positive law supplies no answer, and since law is positive law, the question is settled by the discretion of the official with final authority. In other words, the official, who may be a judge, has to legislate an answer. An account of the proper exercise of such discretion is a theory of adjudication whose details will depend both on the institutional makeup of the particular legal order and on political arguments about the considerations on which judges may legitimately rely. The particularity of such a theory of adjudication tells us that it cannot provide a theory of law given that a theory of law must aspire to be general. In sum, judicial antipositivism is more than theoretically inadequate and politically suspect; it does not even live in the same space as a general theory of law.[4]

The last problem for judicial antipositivism is not so much an objection put by positivists as one to which their theory of law is not vulnerable. However, it is damaging to judicial antipositivism.

The central issue of the rule of law in the twentieth century stemmed from changes in the form of law – the growth of the regulatory state, brought about by legislative creation of administrative agencies that are often hybrid in nature since they combine legislative and adjudicative functions. These agencies can be given the task of developing the legislation – the policy mandate – that they are charged with implementing as well as the task of adjudicating conflicts that arise about the interpretation of that legislation. Usually, the officials who staff these agencies will get their authority from a statute, and then the question is what are the limits set by the statute or by other sources of law, for example, the constitution or the common law.

In hard cases about the scope of official authority, the statutory grant of authority to the official is usually couched in discretionary terms. The official, or panel of adjudicators when an administrative tribunal has to decide, will get its authority either explicitly or by clear implication from the legislature. So for positivists it follows that in this situation – the ordinary situation that faces common law judges in judicial review within administrative law – judicial discretion as to what the law requires is piled on top of administrative discretion on the same issue.

All that positivist legal theory can say about this situation is that it is shot through with discretion. However, this is not a concern for positivism since it does not assume a division of power between the legislature, which makes the law; the judiciary, which interprets it; and the administration, which implements it.[5] Since positivists maintain that judges make as well as apply the law, the change in the form of law seems to positivists to be no change at all but merely the addition of another hybrid body to many legal orders.

Dworkin, in contrast, does generally assume a strict division of powers between legislature, judiciary, and administration, whereby the legislature has a monopoly on making law, the judiciary on interpreting the law, and the administration merely implements the law. Hence, the change in the form of law provides the basis for a third objection to his theory of the rule of law.

THE RULE OF LIBERAL PRINCIPLES

A. An Attack on Two Fronts

In his "Introduction" to *Taking Rights Seriously*, Dworkin undertook to supply a "general theory of law" that would unseat "the ruling theory of law" of legal positivism.[6] By general theory he meant something different from the positivist thought that a general theory of law does not depend on contingent institutional features or political ideologies. For him, a general theory unites a normative – or politically prescriptive – part with a conceptual part. Bentham, Dworkin said, was the "last philosopher in the Anglo-American stream to offer" such a general theory of law, one that united positivism with the normative theory of utilitarianism. Dworkin saw his task as an argument against the two streams that flow on seemingly separate[7] courses from Bentham's general theory: the conceptual legal positivist stream, which holds that one's legal rights are simply those the positive law explicitly states; and the economic/utilitarian stream, which holds that the only ground for protesting a legislative decision is that it does not in fact serve the general welfare.

In the "Introduction," Dworkin outlined the distinction for which *Taking Rights Seriously* is best known, namely, the distinction between policy and principle, according to which the role of judges is to be the guardians of the moral "principles" immanent in the law, whereas legislatures make decisions about policy or collective welfare – decisions that are legitimate unless they violate the principles. But he also said that another distinction was more fundamental – one between "two forms of political rights":

> background rights, which are rights that hold in an abstract way against decisions taken by the community or the society as a whole, and more specific

institutional rights that hold against a decision made by a specific institution. Legal rights may then be identified as a distinct species of a political right, that is, an institutional right to the decision of a court in its adjudicative function.[8]

To appreciate the importance of this distinction, recall the positivist claim that the rule of law does not guarantee legitimate rule. That claim is strongly supported if any attempt at refutation cannot stop short of equating the rule of law with the rule of good law, meaning rule by a full theory of liberal justice.

To succeed, then, an antipositivist theory has to show more than that the rule of law is the rule of principles. It has to show – without making the fatal equation – that the principles of the rule of law are sound moral principles. Hence it is the distinction between background and institutional rights, rather than the one between principle and policy, that "provides a bridge between the conceptual and normative parts"[9] of Dworkin's own theory.

It is clear from the way Dworkin drew the distinction that judges are at center stage in determining institutional rights. Since he wanted to highlight a principled basis for the decisions of courts "in their adjudicative function," the rule of law is the rule of institutional rights based on the principles exposed in adjudication. It is rule by judges based on their interpretation of the principled basis of their law. This rights model of the rule of law – the rule of liberal principles over which judges have an interpretative monopoly – must seem like judicial antipositivism written as large as it can be. And so Dworkin hastened to assure the reader that the bridge his "normative theory of adjudication" provides is one that also shows that "judicial decisions based on arguments of principle are compatible with democratic principles."[10]

B. The Conceptual Challenge

Dworkin's conceptual challenge to legal positivism demonstrates the pervasive role of principles in adjudication. Since this challenge is the topic of other essays in this volume, and since positivists responded by acknowledging that principles play a pervasive role, I want simply to note the main form of the positivist response – that the operation of principles is the subject matter for a theory of adjudication, not a theory of law. The question of what principles are available will depend on contingent features of a particular legal order, and their role in adjudication will depend on a political theory about how judges should exercise their discretion.

This response is problematic since it accounts for principles by opening up an ever-widening gap of discretion for judges and thus may seem even more suspect from the point of view of a populist democratic political theory than Dworkin's attempt to build a theory of law out of a theory of adjudication.[11] But Dworkin cannot provide sufficient grounds for rejecting the response, unless he can show that the right to a particular decision in a hard case, and thus the judge's duty to give that decision, is both a moral and a legal right. And this is so even if the contemporary normative developments of Bentham's utilitarianism are wrong, for Dworkin's theory shows that in a democracy individuals have rights that "trump" collective judgments about welfare.[12] Such a theory shows only that rights should be recognized in law, not that they are already recognized. Yet it is the latter result that Dworkin needs if he is to show that the role of principles goes beyond a conceptual challenge to positivism, because only that result establishes the link between law and morality that positivism denies.

C. A Bridge Too Far?

Dworkin's foundation for his bridge is the distinction between background and institutional rights. It is supposed to show the difference between the questions "What are moral rights, whatever the law says?" and "What are the moral rights under the law of this particular legal order?"

Dworkin sets out the bridge in "Hard Cases." Again his foil is legal positivism, described as making two main claims. First, positivism puts judges "in the shadow of legislation" – they should "apply the law that other institutions have made; they should not make new law." Second, when judges have to make law because of the inherent vagueness of legal rules, they should act "not only as deputy to the legislature, but as a deputy legislature" and make "law in response to evidence and arguments of the same character as would move the superior institution if it were acting on its own." This, says Dworkin, "is a deeper level of subordination because it makes any understanding of what judges do in hard cases parasitic on a prior understanding of what legislators do all the time. This deeper subordination is thus conceptual as well as political."[13]

If, however, judges should decide on the basis of principle rather than policy, they move – Dworkin supposes – legitimately out of the shadow of the legislature. The legal order is one in which there is no subordination of judges to the legislature, but there is a division of labor between the legislature, whose province is policy, and the judiciary, whose province is principle.

Legislatures may rely on arguments of principle, but they may also rely on policy considerations alone.

According to Dworkin, a democratic objection to an enhanced judicial role has most force if we suppose that judges' decisions are based on policy. Judges arc not in as good an institutional position as legislatures to adjudicate competing claims of interest, and they should not determine people's rights retrospectively on the basis, say, of an assessment of wise economic policy. But if judges decide on the basis of principle, it makes sense to insulate them from "the demands of the political majority." Judicial decisions enforce "existing political rights" because the principles on which they are based are to be found in "institutional history." But institutional history cannot by itself supply the answer – the judge has to make a "fresh judgment" about what those rights are, one which engages his or her sense of justice at the same time as his or her understanding of history.[14]

This claim about engagement is important because it opposes the idea that judges have discretion. "Judges," says Dworkin, "do not decide hard cases in two stages, first checking to see where the institutional constraints end, and then setting the books aside to stride off on their own." Rather, there is a "pervasive interaction" of "personal and institutional morality."[15]

Judges, like "all political officials," are subject to a doctrine of political responsibility that requires them to make "only such political decisions as they can justify within a political theory that also justifies the other decisions they propose to make." This requirement is one of "articulate consistency," demanding of judges arguments of principle, which show that the principle cited is "consistent with earlier decisions not recanted, and with decisions that the institution is prepared to make in hypothetical circumstances."[16]

Dworkin summarizes his claims in the "rights thesis," the thesis that a party has a right in a hard case to the decision supported by principle. This is not a right to the decision that would be given by "background rights," the "rights that provide a justification for political decisions by society in the abstract," but a right to the decision in terms of "institutional rights, that provide a justification for a decision by some particular and specified political institution." And within both categories of right, he distinguishes between "abstract" and "concrete" rights, where the former are general political aims, whereas the latter are more precisely defined to "express more definitely the weight they have against other political aims on particular occasions."[17] The rights thesis provides, then, that judges decide hard cases by "confirming or denying concrete rights," which are institutional rights rather than background rights, and legal rights "rather than some other form of institutional rights."[18]

But though they are institutional rights, they are, Dworkin asserts, genuine rights despite the fact that institutional autonomy will insulate an "official's institutional duty from the greater part of background political morality."[19] The judge who accepts the "settled practices of his legal system...must, according to the doctrine of political responsibility, accept some general theory that justifies these practices."[20]

In "Hard Cases," Dworkin examines three kinds of legal material – written constitutions, statutes, and the common law. Here I confine myself to his discussion of statutes and the common law since an antipositivist conception of the rule of law cannot rely on the contingent presence of a written constitution.

Even if Dworkin need not rely on the existence of a written constitution, he does rely on the claim that a judge in any legal order requires a "constitutional theory." The judge's approach to statutes and to precedent – his or her doctrine of political responsibility – will be informed by a constitutional theory, in the sense of an overarching theory of what justifies his or her approach to both statute and precedent as authoritative sources of law.[21] This bare understanding of constitutionalism moves one out of the terrain of conceptual challenge and into the terrain of normative political theory. Dworkin's foil here is not Hart's conceptual positivism but Bentham's general theory. And that theory is a foil to Dworkin's judicial antipositivism since it is a theory of legislative positivism, one that seeks to subordinate judges as far as possible to the will of the majority, expressed as clearly as possible in the only form of law that Bentham thought politically responsible – statutes.

What then is the constitutional theory that informs judicial antipositivism? According to Dworkin, a judge interpreting a statute has to ask which interpretation of the statute best "ties the language the legislature used to its constitutional responsibilities."[22] The policy of the statute is determined by a combination of interpretation of the language used by the statute with a sense of the legal rights of the individuals affected by plausible interpretations. The judge must select the interpretation that best lives up to his or her sense of the legislature's constitutional responsibilities. Dworkin emphasizes that this is not a theory of what the legislature would have done or should have done had it contemplated the particular situation, but of what it did do, with the limits of what it could plausibly be said to have done set by the words of the statute.[23]

The common law in contrast does not operate by setting limits through language to judicial interpretation. Here Dworkin introduces a distinction between "enactment force" and "gravitational force," where enactment force is about the limits on the political decisions that may be ascribed to an authority and are set by language, whereas gravitational force is a kind of authority that "escapes...language." It is explained by the principle of fairness, which requires that like cases be treated alike. But likeness here is likeness with respect to principle. The gravitational force of earlier decisions is limited "to the extension of the arguments of principle necessary to justify those decisions."[24]

Dworkin does not, however, suppose that statutes have only enactment force, whereas judicial decisions always have gravitational force. On his account, a judge deciding a hard case must seek to show that his or her interpretation of the law is best on two dimensions – fit and soundness.[25] The judge must show that the interpretation is among those consistent with – that fit – relevant institutional history and that of these interpretations it is soundest in that it shows that history in its best moral light. The set of principles that shows all the law of a particular jurisdiction in its best light is what Dworkin terms a theory of law.

Total consistency or fit is not achievable, and so the judge will have to develop a theory of "institutional mistakes." Dworkin emphasizes that a theory of mistakes cannot be "impudent" – a judge cannot declare as mistaken any piece of institutional history merely because it is incompatible with his or her own theory of law, otherwise the requirement of consistency would be "no genuine requirement at all." A judge will often lack authority to overrule either statutes or past judicial decisions, and so, even if his or her theory deems these to be mistakes, they are "embedded" mistakes. Here the judge should deal with the mistake by limiting its legal force to its enactment force – to what its explicit language requires.[26]

But even the decision so to limit the force of a past decision must be constrained by the principle of fairness, since that principle will say that a decision declaring a past decision a mistake is "prima facie weaker than one that does not." This gives rise to two maxims a judge must observe:

> If he can show, by arguments of history or by appeal to some sense of the legal community, that a particular principle, though it once had sufficient appeal to persuade a legislature or court to a legal decision, has now so little force that it is unlikely to generate any further such decisions, then the argument from fairness that supports that principle is undercut. If he can

show by arguments of political morality that such a principle, apart from its popularity, is unjust, then the argument from fairness that supports that principle is overridden.[27]

Now the second maxim clearly allows the judge's own convictions about justice to decide the issue.[28] Thus it immediately attracts the charge that it permits the judge to decide on the basis of his or her own convictions, which, Dworkin acknowledges, many will regard as "unfair, contrary to democracy, and offensive to the rule of law."[29]

Dworkin points out that even if a judge decides in hard cases to defer to the community's sense of justice, such deference relies on a conviction about justice – that this is what the judge's institutional duty requires. So it might seem that one can characterize the issue as one between the populist democrat judge who regards his or her duty in such cases as requiring deference to community morality, understood as conventional morality, and a judge who relies on his or her own convictions about morality.

Dworkin argues that this is a mischaracterization. His judge, whom he calls Hercules because of his "superhuman skill, learning, patience, and acumen,"[30] does not "enforce his convictions against the community's." Rather, the judge takes the "record" of the community's "moral traditions" to be that "captured in the whole institutional record that it is his office to interpret." This record establishes a "constitutional morality," one that may be at odds not only with conventional morality – the opinion of the day – but also with other discrete bits of the record. "There is," he says, "no question as to how such a conflict must be resolved":

> Individuals have a right to the consistent enforcement of the principles on which their institutions rely. It is this institutional right, as defined by the community's constitutional morality, that Hercules must defend against any inconsistent opinion, however unpopular.[31]

We can now see why the distinction between background and institutional rights is so important. In hard cases, judges are deciding what legal rights individuals have, and those rights depend on moral principles. But the principles are not the moral principles that the judge would enact into the law, had he or she the power to do so. Rather, they are the principles already established by the legal record. Since that record is a legal one – established by the political decisions of a particular community over time – the community cannot complain that the judge relies illegitimately on his or her own convictions about justice in interpreting that record, even if that interpretation is both unpopular and declares some part of the record to be mistaken. For the judge is interpreting that community's record, the moral principles it regarded as so important that it gave them public expression in its law. In short, there is no objection from democracy, since the morality on which the judge relies is a community's own constitutional morality. Nor is there an objection from the rule of law, since a judge in deciding such cases has to rely on his or her substantive convictions about justice at some point.

Dworkin acknowledges that occasionally a judge will find that his or her sense of justice will be in conflict with concepts in institutional morality. Generally, this will not be the case because "he is likely to value most of the concepts that figure in the justification of the institutions of his own community," and so he "will be able to put to himself, rather than to some hypothetical self, questions about the deep morality that gives the concept value." But if such conflict arises, the judge will find that his or her inquiry will be more "sociological" in nature; the judge will ask what are the convictions about morality held by those who enacted that part of the record rather than what his or her own convictions are.[32]

Positivists think this acknowledgment is fatal. A distinction is useful here, one that falls within Dworkin's category of principles, between substantive and procedural principles. The distinction is notoriously slippery, since procedural principles are often valued for substantive reasons. But it usefully captures the difference between, on the one hand, principles about the rights and liberties of the individual and, on the other, the principles that like cases should be treated alike and that, in a legal regime of legislative supremacy, judges should defer to the will of the legislature.

Now imagine a legal order where these two procedural principles hold and the legislature is the captive of a minority racial group, which uses its power both to enact racist principles into the law and to ensure that most judges are either supporters of its policies or at least are likely to adopt the view that in hard cases their duty lies in deferring to the group's views. Moreover, legislative and judicial reaction to the decisions of the few liberal judges who make it to the bench shows that the legal community regards as legitimate this conventionalist mode of interpretation. In this legal order, the substantive principles of the law are racist, whereas the procedural principles require their faithful enforcement. Even in cases where some room for interpretation is available, it seems clear how judges are supposed to use that room.

This profoundly undemocratic legal order is not fanciful – it is pretty much the legal order of apartheid South Africa, which was frequently cited as a counterexample to Dworkin's theory of law. For the apartheid legal order seemed to show that a liberal judge who emulates Hercules will be driven by his adherence to the distinction between institutional and background morality to an ever more sociological inquiry. And such an inquiry will detect racist substantive principles as the animating principles behind both statute and common law.[33]

At first, Dworkin appeared to concede this point. He said that the liberal judge would either have to resign or to make "the difficult moral decision" to lie about what the law is.[34] As Hart pointed out, that concession raises insuperable difficulties for Dworkin's claim that a judge always has a moral reason to apply the soundest theory of the law.[35] It concedes that the substantive principles of the law can be morally odious. Hence, it concedes the positivist case against equating the rule of law with the rule of good law.

Dworkin thus offered two further responses. First, he said that it is a mistake to take wicked legal systems as a crucial test for the connection he claims exists between moral and legal rights, since that assumes that we know what people's legal rights are in such systems, and we can know that only if we have a theory of legal rights. "Wicked legal systems should be treated, that is, like hard cases that turn on which conception of law is best rather than like easy cases whose proper resolution we already know and can therefore use to test any particular conception for adequacy."[36] In this regard, he suggested that his conception of law would prove adequate in a "wicked legal system" as long as one distinguishes between explanation and justification so as to see that an explanation does not "provide a justification of a series of political decisions if it presents, as justificatory principles, propositions that offend our ideas of what even a bad moral principle must be like." And he asserted that he had more faith than he had expressed in earlier work in the "screening power of the concept of a moral principle" – the power of the justificatory dimension of his test for hard cases to rule out blatantly discriminatory principles.[37]

Second, he said it is a mistake to suppose that the source of the moral weight of the judge's duty to apply the soundest theory of the law is found in the principles that figure in the soundest theory itself. Rather, the source of the moral weight is a "general political situation . . . that the central power of the community has been administered through an articulate constitutional structure the citizens have been encouraged to obey and treat as a source of rights and duties, and that the citizens as a whole have in fact done so." In short, the moral reason – or "moral kind of reason," as he qualifies it – is whether the public accepts the legitimacy of the law.[38]

The first response is problematic since it seems to collapse explanation or fit into justification. The more the liberal judge's convictions about background morality are put under stress, the less the test of fit counts in his or her approach to hard cases until the point where all that counts is his or her convictions. The distinction between institutional rights and background rights disintegrates when the judge finds the moral content of the law obnoxious. And Dworkin's suggestion that he might say of such a situation that there are no legal rights because the law seems so devoid of morality does not help since it raises the same problem of equating law with good law.

The second response is problematic because it collapses justification into explanation. It appears to concede that the principled basis of the law will not of itself legitimate the legal order because the substantive principles might be morally obnoxious. It therefore resorts to an external source of legitimacy – large scale public endorsement of the law. But it is unclear why such endorsement will provide judges with a reason to enforce the law, unless it is the case that one might expect that where there is such endorsement, it occurs in part because principles attractive to the majority are already incorporated into the law. It will follow, of course, that most judges will also find the principles of the law morally attractive, and so they will think there is a moral reason to apply them. But this provides a sociological explanation of why judges are likely to think there is a moral reason to apply the law of the land, not a normative argument about why there is such a reason.

In sum, the wicked legal system seems an effective counterexample to a liberal model of the rule of law. Dworkin's first response to the wicked legal system pushes the bridge the model builds from law to morality too far because it equates law and morality. His second response has the bridge stop short of reaching the moral shore, at the same time as it seeks to tint that situation with morality. It is perhaps awareness of this dilemma that led Dworkin to remark that wicked legal systems "are not very important hard cases, from the practical point of view, because the judgments we make about foreign wicked legal systems are rarely hinged to decisions we have to take."[39] But this remark, made in the midst of articulating his first response, tied his argument to the fatal concession of his second response – that his theory of the rule of law is contingent on judges' finding themselves in a legal order in which the substantive principles are not badly out of line with liberal morality. And, as we will now see, an analogous dilemma bedevils his rights model of the rule of law, even in democratic legal orders where it should be most at home.

D. Is Administrative Law a Mistake?

We saw that Dworkin has a theory of "institutional mistakes," which explains when a judge is entitled either to expunge some bit of the public record of law or to limit its force. There is another sense of institutional

mistake in the history of legal theory, one that pertains not to the substance
of particular bits of the record but to whole institutions. Bentham, for example, thought that to give judges the kind of authority over the interpretation
of the law that licenses judicial antipositivism is to make a grave political
mistake. In his view, the institution of the common law is a mistake that
must be confined or, even better, eradicated. Therefore, a constitutionalism
that explicitly gives judges the authority to strike down statutes is that same
mistake writ large.

Conversely, A. V. Dicey's model of the rule of law is designed to find
that the law made by administrative agencies is a mistake because it is in
tension with the common law. This is in part for the reason that his model
of the rule of law cannot accommodate administrative agencies with hybrid
functions of making and interpreting the law, since the model requires that
legislatures have a monopoly on making the law and judges have a monopoly
on interpreting the law.[40] But it is also – and more fundamentally – because
Dicey is opposed to the political program of regulation and redistribution
of economic and social resources, which prompted the development of the
administrative state.

For Dicey, what was fundamentally wrong with the administrative state
was that it flouted the principles of a morality of liberty and protection of
private property, a kind of constitutional morality in Dworkin's sense, which
had been embedded in the common law. Since these principles formed
the backdrop for judicial interpretation of statutes, statutes that delegated
both legislative and adjudicative power to agencies removed them from the
control of a constitutional morality whose guardian is the judiciary. And
this same theme is to be found in Lord Hewart's *The New Despotism*[41] and
in F. A. Hayek's *The Road to Serfdom*.[42]

Dworkin's account of the substance of the liberal principles that judges
should protect is different from Dicey's, Hewart's, or Hayek's, all of whom
are libertarians concerned to maximize the space of negative liberty for
individuals by limiting state intervention to the greatest possible extent. As
an egalitarian liberal, Dworkin has argued that equality, not negative liberty,
is the foundational value of liberalism. And he gives the state a large role in
redistribution, as long as redistributive decisions do not violate a principle
of state neutrality expressed in what he takes to be the fundamental liberal
principle of equal concern and respect.

But though there is this political difference between Dworkin and libertarians about the content of what is protected by the rule of law, there is
little or no difference from the perspective of legal theory. The libertarians
and Dworkin agree that the rule of law exists when judges protect some core

of liberal principles from majoritarian decision making. And this stance of "judicial supremacism" is made up of two components that together create enormous difficulties for judicial review of administrative action, whatever the details of the liberal ideology behind it.

The first component is institutional – the place of judges in "Law's Empire." No less than Dicey, Dworkin understands legislatures as having a monopoly on making law and judges a monopoly on its interpretation. There is no room in his account for administrative agencies that have an authority to make or interpret the law in the sense that such administrative decisions are ones to which courts have reason to defer. At most, Dworkin can concede to administrative agencies the authority to make decisions about the policy implications of their constitutive statutes – utilitarian calculations about what decision will best advance the policy – or decisions about what the effects of different arrangements of natural justice might be. But they have no authority over legal principles – the exclusive province of the judiciary.[43]

The second component is substantive – the assumption that the essence of law is some particular substance, a coherent conception of the common good. It does not matter so much what the precise content of that vision is – more or less libertarian, more or less egalitarian – as that there is such an assumption. For it is such an assumption that requires that judges have the institutional place just sketched.[44]

Together these two components create difficulties familiar to administrative lawyers in common law legal orders. On the one hand, Dworkin's understanding of the imperialism of principles over which judges preside invites the extension of principles derived from one area of law into another, and thus, for example, invites judges to attempt to govern the public law regimes of administrative law in the light of their understandings of private law.[45]

On the other hand, the distinction between principle and policy in Dworkin's account of adjudication suggests that when one is on the policy side of the divide, no crucial issues of legal principle arise.[46] The administration either gets squeezed into a procrustean common law bed or left to its own devices because it is somehow not for the most part involved in law, properly so called.

In the last section Dworkin's dilemma was between an implausible equation of the principled content of the law with liberal morality and a concession that the principled content of the law is only contingently sound. Here the dilemma is between a judicial supremacism hostile to the administrative state and a concession that judges do not have an interpretative monopoly. But the root cause of both dilemmas is the same – an equation of the principled basis of the law with a particular set of principles of liberal morality. And that equation makes Dworkin's position vulnerable to the various objections listed earlier: of ascribing legitimacy to unjust regimes merely because they govern through law, of supporting usurpatory legitimacy claims made by judges, and of a parochial dependence on a particular kind of legal order.

CULTURES OF LAW

I remarked that few philosophers of law focus on the issue of the *rule* of law, because most regard that issue as resolved by first determining what the *law* is that rules. The main exception is Lon L. Fuller, for whom the rule of law involves principles of legality that, taken together, amount to an "inner morality" of law.

Fuller argued that eight principles of legality inhere in the idea of the rule of law: generality, promulgation, nonretroactivity, clarity, noncontradiction, possibility of compliance, constancy through time, and, the one he took to be the most complex, congruence between official action and declared rule.[47] These principles are more procedural in nature than substantive in that they are supposed to pinpoint what is involved in the production of valid law.

A system that fails completely to meet one principle, or fails substantially to meet several, would not, in Fuller's view, be a legal system. It would not qualify as government under law – as government subject to the rule of law. Further, a tyrant who wanted to govern through the medium of law would have to comply with the eight principles, and this would preclude rule by arbitrary decree and secret terror, which, Fuller said, is the most effective medium for tyranny.[48]

Positivists argued that Fuller's principles of legality merely enhance the ability of law to guide behavior,[49] and Dworkin joined vigorously in this positivist critique.[50] He suggested that Fuller had missed his positivist target altogether, since Fuller's arguments were about a purported inner morality of law, whereas the separation thesis is about a connection between law and substantive moral standards external to law.[51]

Dworkin also said that if tyrants preferred not to rule through law, this would be because they feared publicity and not because there was any constraining inner morality of law.[52] Thus, he challenged Fuller's claim that laws enacted to achieve evil ends are necessarily vague and lacking in the quality of legality, saying that a "perfectly evil statute can be drafted with exquisite precision." The only substance in Fuller's position, Dworkin thought, was that if we have to interpret a law whose fundamental purpose is obnoxious to our sense of morality, we might have difficulty in understanding the law because we would "gain no help from our sense of fairness in making discriminations under it."[53]

Finally, Dworkin claimed that the project of establishing an inner morality of law is fundamentally mistaken because it fails to see an important difference between law and morals – that a "moral principle . . . cannot be established by deliberate act, as some sorts of law can."[54] His point here is that whereas there might be criterial standards of morality analogous to Fuller's criteria for legality – for example, the rule against self-contradiction – such moral criterial standards do not tell us whether an act is moral or immoral. Only the standards of substantive morality can tell us that; hence, the criterial standards of morality do not identify the standards of morality in the way that the criterial standards of law might.

In making this point, Dworkin relied explicitly and with wholehearted approval on Hart's account in *The Concept of Law* of the relationship between moral and legal obligation, specifically on the section where Hart maintained that certain important differences between law and morality arise from the fact that morality, unlike law, is immune from deliberate change. Hart said that "the idea of a moral legislature with competence to make and change morals is repugnant to the whole notion of morality."[55]

But this idea is not obviously repugnant. Something like the idea of a "moral legislature" with "competence to make and change morals" animates the democratic tradition, including Bentham's utilitarianism. By supposing otherwise, Hart and Dworkin affirm a crude dichotomy between liberalism and democracy.

On the one hand, we have liberals determined to preserve the substantive standards of morality from statutory encroachments by democratic legislatures. They thus hold up the judiciary as the legal guardian of the political constitution. The ideal system for many liberals, especially in the United States of America, entrenches liberal political morality in a written constitution – one that gives to judges the authority to strike down statutes as invalid when these cannot be interpreted in a fashion consistent with that morality. On the other hand, we have the populist democrats referred to earlier, who require law to be nothing more than the expression of what the people in fact want, unconstrained insofar as this is possible by formal legal requirements and completely unconstrained by judicially interpreted principles.

Curiously, what these liberals and democrats share is an instrumental, basically positivist, account of law. Law is just the instrument of substantive values established by political morality, and disagreement is about only whether it is liberal political philosophy or "the people" who should decide on the content of morality. And if it seems odd to suggest that Dworkin turns out to be a positivist in this very limited sense, one should recall that a constant criticism of his theory has been that it boils down to a version of American constitutionalism – to a political theory with a claim to have established itself in a particular legal order.

It is also worth recalling that Fuller too argued against the positivist account of adjudication and, especially in the 1960s, advanced a theory of adjudication that was in many respects quite similar to Dworkin's.[56] However, he never tied his theory of adjudication to a particular version of liberal political morality, nor did he rest his challenge to the separation thesis on such a theory. He stuck to his idea that a sincere commitment to government within the constraints of legality involves moral constraints on government and that it is in attending to the values that such constraints serve that judges, like other legal officials, will express their fidelity to law. In other words, Fuller's theory of adjudication is a subtheory within his main theory, which is a theory of law as legal order or legality. And it is the moral order put into place by the legal order to which judges must be faithful rather than to any particular political ideology.

Fuller's antipositivism thus agrees with one of positivism's principal objections to Dworkin's position – that Dworkin goes wrong in trying to build a theory of law out of a theory of adjudication. The error seems demonstrable in Dworkin's case because he ties his account of adjudication to a particular version of liberalism and so commits himself either to the odd claim that every legal order must instantiate that particular political ideology or to the counterintuitive claim that judges are morally as well as legally bound to apply morally unsound law.

Further, Dworkin – with the positivists – failed to appreciate the complexity of Fuller's principle of publicity. Publicity for Fuller is not only about stating one's aims in public. Rather, publicity involves a commitment to a process of reasoned justification by legal authority to those subject to it. A public law is one that is the result of such a process.[57] And in general all of Fuller's principles are best understood as instantiations of the two main democratic principles – participation and accountability – principles that can be realized in very different ways within legal institutions with no thought that judges have a monopoly on their guardianship.

In my view, the embryonic forms of democratic accountability are found merely in an insistence on positive law as the form that political policy must adopt. Not only is positive law highly visible, but it also establishes a standard to which those with power can be called to account. In other words, the existence of positive law is linked to its justification – visibility plus accountability.[58] As the idea of what ensures accountability changes, so will ideas of what legal institutions are required and thus of what the fundamental forms of law are. But such ideas will always be linked to the moral principles that legal forms are meant to serve.

I have argued elsewhere that how they are linked can best be understood by distinguishing between three different conceptions of legal culture: a Dworkinian liberal culture of neutrality, which requires judges to uphold liberal standards on judicial review; a positivistic culture of reflection, in which law merely mirrors or reflects judgments made in the political arena and judges are required to defer submissively to the clearly expressed will of the legislature; and the Fullerian culture of justification, in which law is justified when it is adequately supported by reasons, and thus the judicial duty is to promote a culture of reason giving.[59] It is that idea that provides the principled basis of an accommodation of the change in the form of law brought about by the regulatory state, one that neither consigns administrative decision making to the positivist black hole of discretion, nor sets up judges as supreme arbiters of the law.

CONCLUSION

It is a mark of Dworkin's great influence that most positivists became almost entirely focused on adjudication – on putting together a conceptual response to Dworkin's demonstration of the role of principles in adjudication. Recently, however, some positivists, against the trend of conceptualism, have returned to the task of trying to build what we saw Dworkin call a general theory of law.[60] They sense that the place of the democratic legislature in legal order has almost completely disappeared from legal theory. And they seek to marry a positivistic account of legal institutions with a political account of legitimacy, thus beginning a response to the challenge Dworkin articulated more than twenty years ago in *Taking Rights Seriously*.[61]

The return of positivism to its substantive political roots will, I suspect, highlight even more starkly the problems faced by Dworkin's account of the rule of law. His most significant contribution to our understanding of the rule of law could then come to be seen as his prompting of a revival of legal positivism. But that result would not be ironical if one understood Dworkin's project in line with his "Introduction" to *Taking Rights Seriously*. That is, Dworkin's primary aim was not so much to provoke acceptance of his theory of adjudication as to show that the issues raised by that theory compelled legal positivists and others to resituate the great debates of legal theory within political philosophy.

It would, or so I have suggested, be a mistake to leave Fuller out of the story. A revival of the Fuller-Dworkin debate might well hold the clues to a stronger, antipositivist theory of the rule of law. In particular, one would want to dwell on those moments in Dworkin's theory of law that I have neglected in this chapter because, when push comes to shove, Dworkin himself has chosen another path. Here I refer to the idea that judicial fidelity to law is not primarily about the judicial role in promoting articulate consistency or integrity with principles of some substantive vision of political morality. Rather, judges, together with the other institutions of legal order, namely, the legislature and government, have a role in promoting integrity with the principles of legality – the more procedural morality of the rule of law.[62]

ACKNOWLEDGMENTS

I thank Alan Brudner, Sujit Choudhry, Evan Fox-Decent, Arthur Ripstein, and Hamish Stewart for comments on drafts of this chapter. My greatest debt in regard to its themes goes back to discussions between 1984 and 1988 with a highly imaginative and conscientious thesis supervisor, Ronald Dworkin. With time I have come to understand better the luck involved in working with a supervisor whose only concern was to help his students make their arguments into the best they could be.

Notes

1. Ronald Dworkin, "Political Judges and the Rule of Law," in *A Matter of Principle* (Cambridge, MA: Harvard University Press, 1985), 11–12 (his emphasis).
2. And, as one commentator has pointed out, there is hardly any mention of the phrase "the rule of law" within Dworkin's major work on legal theory, *Law's Empire* (London: Fontana Press, 1986). See Paul Craig, "Formal and Substantive Conceptions of the Rule of Law: An Analytical Analysis," *Public Law* (Autumn 1997): 467–87. In part, this is a product of the highly parochial nature of American public law discourse, which assumes that debate about the rule of law is a debate about U.S. style constitutionalism. (For an exception, see Richard H. Fallon, Jr.,

"'The Rule of Law' as a Concept in Constitutional Discourse," *Columbia Law Review* 97, no. 1 [January 1997]: 1–56.) It is thus unsurprising that Dworkin's only sustained treatment of the rule of law occurs on the occasion of a lecture to the British Academy and that the best work on his legal theory and the rule of law is by a British administrative lawyer, Trevor Allan; see, for example, Allan's "The Rule of Law as the Rule of Reason: Consent and Constitutionalism," *Law Quarterly Review* 115 (1999): 221–44, and, more recently, *Constitutional Justice: A Liberal Theory of the Rule of Law* (Oxford: Oxford University Press, 2001). More recently, Dworkin has taken up the topic of the rule of law in response to Jeremy Waldron, "The Rule of Law as a Theatre of Debate," in *Dworkin and His Critics*, ed. Justine Burley (Oxford: Blackwell, 2004), 387–8. In other work Dworkin has suggested that the way forward in legal philosophy is to see that the concept of law is answerable to an ideal of legality. See Dworkin, "Hart's Postscript and the Character of Political Philosophy," *Oxford Journal of Legal Studies* 24, no. 1 (Spring 2004): 23–5. Note that there is renewed interest in the topic of the rule of law after 9/11. Here Dworkin has played an important public intellectual role in defending civil liberties in the pages of the *New York Review of Books*. I discuss the implications of 9/11 for debate about the rule of law in *The Constitution of Law: Legality in a Time of Emergency* (Cambridge, UK: Cambridge University Press, 2006).

3. See especially the posthumously published "Postscript" to H. L. A. Hart's *The Concept of Law*, 2nd ed. (Oxford: Clarendon Press, 1994), 239–44.

4. I ignore in this essay the "incorporationist" or "soft" versions of legal positivism. They not only share many of the problems of Dworkin's account of the rule of law, but they also seem to subvert the positivist project, as I try to explain in "Positivism's Stagnant Research Programme," *Oxford Journal of Legal Studies* 20, no. 4 (2000): 703–22 and in "The Genealogy of Legal Positivism," *Oxford Journal of Legal Studies* 24, no. 1 (Spring 2004): 39–67. Some contemporary positivists deny that positivism subscribes to the separation thesis; see John Gardner, "The Legality of Law," *Ratio Juris* 17, no. 2 (June 2004): 168–81.

5. At least it is not a conceptual concern. It is a political concern, as I mention later, because of issues about political accountability – issues that conceptually driven positivists consign to political theory.

6. See Dworkin, *Taking Rights Seriously* (London: Duckworth, 1978), vii (hereafter *TRS*). My principal focus in what follows is the "Introduction" and Chapters 2, 3, and 4 of *TRS*. In my view, every important element of Dworkin's account of the rule of law is to be found in these chapters, which explains why they had such an immediate and important influence.

7. According to Dworkin, the two streams sometimes converge in the conservative constitutional theory advanced primarily by Robert Bork; see Dworkin, "Law's Ambitions for Itself," *Virginia Law Review* 71, no. 2 (March 1985): 173–87, and Dworkin, *Freedom's Law* (Cambridge, MA: Harvard University Press, 1996), especially the "Introduction" and the essays dealing with Bork in Section III. On pages 33 and 34 of this book, Dworkin suggests that judges may not provide the only official site for the moral elaboration of the requirements of the rule of law.

8. Dworkin, *TRS*, xii.

9. Dworkin, *TRS*, xii.

10. Dworkin, *TRS*, xii.

11. The historic compromise between positivism and the common law was struck
   by John Austin, precisely because he wanted to find a role for judges as a
   bulwark *against* democracy; see Austin, *Lectures on Jurisprudence*, vol. 1, 5th
   ed. (London: John Murray, 1885), 218; and Austin, *Lectures on Jurisprudence*,
   vol. 2, 5th ed. (London: John Murray, 1885), 532–3, 641–7; both may prof-
   itably be read together with his pamphlet, *A Plea for the Constitution* (London,
   1859). The incorporationist or soft positivism referred to in note 4 is perhaps
   best understood as providing the theoretical spin on how to accommodate this
   compromise.

12. Thus Dworkin's argument in "Equality, Democracy, and Constitution: We The
   People in Court," *Alberta Law Review* 28, no. 2 (1990): 324–46, while presenting
   a sophisticated argument for a "nonstatistical" account of democracy, does not
   deal at all with the question of why the law already embodies that account. The
   same judgment holds for the essays on political equality and democracy collected in Ronald Dworkin, *Sovereign Virtue: The Theory and Practice of Equality*
   (Cambridge, MA: Harvard University Press, 2000). It is worth noting in this
   connection Richard Pildes's argument that Dworkin's idea of rights as trumps
   constrains any attempt to understand the fruitful role judges can play in enhanc-
   ing the democratic character of political and legal institutions; see Pildes, "Why
   Rights Are Not Trumps: Social Meanings, Expressive Harms, and Constitutionalism," *Journal of Legal Studies* 27, no. 2 (June 1998): 725–63. Jeremy Waldron
   has suggested that Pildes misunderstands Dworkin's understanding of rights,
   since Dworkin in fact opts for Pildes's preferred understanding of rights as "constraints on the kinds of reasons that government may legitimately act upon"
   rather than as trumps or "simple protections for certain individual interests
   against the demands of the common good." Waldron, "Pildes on Dworkin's
   Theory of Rights," *Journal of Legal Studies* 29, no. 1 (January 2000): 301. But
   this response makes little difference to the substance of Pildes's argument. Even
   if Waldron is right, Dworkin also supposes that the principal constraint on reasons is a requirement that government must treat each individual with equal
   concern and respect.

13. Dworkin, *TRS*, 82.

14. Dworkin, *TRS*, 84–7.

15. Dworkin, *TRS*, 86–7.

16. Dworkin, *TRS*, 87–8.

17. Dworkin, *TRS*, 93.

18. Dworkin, *TRS*, 101.

19. Dworkin, *TRS*, 101.

20. Dworkin, *TRS*, 105.

21. Dworkin, *TRS*, 21.

22. Dworkin, *TRS*, 108.

23. Dworkin, *TRS*, 109–10.

24. Dworkin, *TRS*, 111–13, at 113.
25. The terms "fit" and "soundness" are drawn from later work; see Dworkin, *Law's Empire*.
26. Dworkin, *TRS*, 121.
27. Dworkin, *TRS*, 122–3.
28. Dworkin puts things somewhat more ambiguously in another earlier formulation of this maxim, saying that a decision could be wrong because "unfair, within the community's own conception of fairness" (ibid). For an illuminating discussion of this ambiguity, see Anthony J. Sebok, *Legal Positivism in American Jurisprudence* (Cambridge, UK: Cambridge University Press, 1998): 238ff.
29. Dworkin, *TRS*, 123.
30. Dworkin, *TRS*, 105.
31. Dworkin, *TRS*, 126.
32. Dworkin, *TRS*, 127–8.
33. See Raymond Wacks, "Judges and Injustice," *South African Law Journal* 101, no. 2 (May 1984): 266–85. I deal with these issues in *Hard Cases in Wicked Legal Systems: South African Law in the Perspective of Legal Philosophy* (Oxford: Clarendon Press, 1991) and *Judging the Judges, Judging Ourselves: Truth, Reconciliation and the Apartheid Legal Order* (Oxford: Hart Publishing, 1997).
34. Dworkin, *TRS*, 326–7.
35. See Hart, *Essays in Jurisprudence and Philosophy* (Oxford: Clarendon Press, 1983), 9, and *Essays on Bentham: Jurisprudence and Political Theory* (Oxford: Clarendon Press, 1982), 150–3.
36. Ronald Dworkin, "A Reply," in *Ronald Dworkin & Contemporary Jurisprudence*, ed. Marshall Cohen (London: Duckworth, 1984), 260.
37. Dworkin, "A Reply," 299 4n.
38. Dworkin, "A Reply," 258.
39. Dworkin, "A Reply," 260.
40. For the ideas of legislative and interpretative monopoly in Dicey, see Paul Craig, *Public Law and Democracy in the United Kingdom and the United States of America* (Oxford: Clarendon Press, 1990), 12–55.
41. Lord Hewart, *The New Despotism* (London: Ernest Benn Limited, 1929).
42. F. A., Hayek, *The Road to Serfdom*, 50th Anniversary ed. (Chicago: University of Chicago Press, 1994).
43. See Dworkin, "Principle, Policy, Procedure," in *A Matter of Principle*, 99–101.
44. The problem here is akin to the one Roberto Unger detects when he describes the "two dirty little secrets of contemporary jurisprudence." The first is a "rightwing Hegelian view of social and legal history," one which emphasizes the "cunning of history in developing rational order . . . out of the unpromising stuff of historical conflict and compromise." The second is a "discomfort with democracy" that leads to the marginalization of politics in legal theory, including the work of democratic legislatures, and a focus on what "higher judges" do. The two secrets work together since the "restraints on democracy" that have become the focus of legal theory "open the space in which the self-fulfilling prophecies

of rightwing Hegelianism can come to pass." See Roberto Mangabiera Unger, *What Should Legal Analysis Become?* (London: Verso, 1996), 72–4, and also Jeremy Waldron, *Law and Disagreement* (Oxford: Clarendon Press, 1999), especially Chapter 2. For a sustained and very powerful argument that an understanding of the rule of law requires a Dworkinian account of the common good, see Allan, *Constitutional Justice: A Liberal Theory of the Rule of Law.*

45. The imperial project is subject to the principle of local priority, which allows "departments of law" to deviate somewhat from pure integrity; see Dworkin, *Law's Empire*, 250–4. But all such deviations are a matter of regret, and given the place of judges in the imperial project, it is highly unlikely that a judge should pause to take seriously an administrative agency's sense that the principles of, say, the common law of contract should not govern the interpretation of a collective agreement.

46. See Dworkin's discussion of the distinction between moral harm and bare harm, "Principle, Policy, Procedure," 84ff., and see Genevra Richardson, "The Legal Regulation of Process," in *Administrative Law and Government Action*, eds. Genevra Richardson and Hazel Genn (Oxford: Clarendon Press, 1994), 105. Richardson states, "This is a powerful argument for procedural rights in relation to substantive rights. The corollary is, however, that there are no procedural rights in relation to bare interests. The harm which may result from interference with bare interests is bare harm; there is no moral harm since nothing has been lost to which there is a right, and it is only moral harm that attracts procedural protection. It seems that for Dworkin, once outside the sphere of substantive rights, procedures are essentially matters of policy with any claim to specific procedures being so weak as to be negligible" (ibid., 112–13).

47. These are set out in detail in Lon L. Fuller, *The Morality of Law*, rev. ed. (New Haven: Yale University Press, 1969).

48. Fuller, *The Morality of Law*, especially Chapter 2.

49. See Hart, *Essays in Jurisprudence and Philosophy*, 350–2. For a more recent statement, see Joseph Raz, "The Rule of Law and its Virtue," in his *The Authority of Law: Essays on Law and Morality* (Oxford: Clarendon Press, 1983), 210–29.

50. Dworkin, "Philosophy, Morality, and Law: Observations Prompted by Professor Fuller's Novel Claim," *University of Pennsylvania Law Review* 113, no. 5 (March 1965): 668–90.

51. Dworkin, "Philosophy, Morality, and Law," 671.

52. Dworkin, "Philosophy, Morality, and Law," 672.

53. Dworkin, "Philosophy, Morality, and Law," 672.

54. Dworkin, "Philosophy, Morality, and Law," 684.

55. Dworkin, "Philosophy, Morality, and Law," 694 30n; and see Hart, *The Concept of Law*, 171–3.

56. See especially Fuller, *Anatomy of Law* (New York: Frederick A. Praeger, 1968).

57. Fuller identified his own starting point as a faith in the moral resources of law; in particular, he suggested that when people "are compelled to explain and justify their decisions, the effect will generally be to pull those decisions

towards goodness, by whatever standards of ultimate goodness there are." See Fuller, "Positivism and Fidelity to Law: A Reply to Professor Hart," *Harvard Law Review* 71, no. 4 (February 1958): 632.

58. Such links creep even into the account of law of that allegedly uncompromising advocate of political absolutism, Thomas Hobbes. For further discussion see David Dyzenhaus, "Hobbes and the Legitimacy of Law," *Law and Philosophy* 20, no. 5 (September 2001): 461–98.

59. See David Dyzenhaus, "Form and Substance in the Rule of Law: A Democratic Justification for Judicial Review," in *Judicial Review & the Constitution*, ed. C. Forsyth (Oxford: Hart Publishing, 2000), 141–72. The term "culture of justification" was coined by the late South African administrative lawyer, Etienne Mureinik.

60. See Jeremy Waldron, *Law and Disagreement* as well as *The Dignity of Legislation* (Cambridge, UK: Cambridge University Press, 1999); Jeffrey Goldsworthy, *The Sovereignty of Parliament: History and Philosophy* (Oxford: Clarendon Press, 1999); and Tom D. Campbell, *The Legal Theory of Ethical Positivism* (Aldershot: Dartmouth, 1996).

61. The nature of this challenge is best articulated by Stephen Perry's work on methodology; see Perry, "Hart's Methodological Positivism," *Legal Theory* 4 (1998): 427–67.

62. See, for example, Dworkin's discussion of integrity, his more recent label for articulate consistency, in *Law's Empire*. At 176–7, integrity seems to require judicial fidelity to the law rather than to a substantive conception of justice. But at 190ff. – Dworkin's exploration of the "puzzle of legitimacy" – he seems undecided on this issue. And, if we read this exploration in the light of his discussion of the wicked legal system problem at 101–13, a similar indecision reproduces the problems in this regard, which I outlined earlier. In both cases, Dworkin seems to move on by presuming that ultimately the problems are resolved by political rather than legal theory.

Seen in this light, the claim that Dworkin's theory of adjudication turns out to be parochial need not be considered disrespectful. Although I cannot make this argument here, I suspect that all theories of adjudication are parochial or local, but that their fruitfulness as theories will be judged not only by the way they help us understand what happens at the local level, but also by how they assist debates about more general theories of law. And they will so assist by casting other theories of adjudication and other ways of designing legal order into sharper relief, thus focusing our attention on the most fundamental questions about the nature of law. But for there to be this reciprocal relationship between the local and the more general, there must be some common terms to the debate about the question "What is law?" Those common terms are set by an agreement that the question is to be answered politically, not conceptually.

One might naturally raise here a challenge that, if successful, undermines my conclusion – namely, that the constraints I identify do not amount to a morality. But that challenge assumes a particular conception of morality, for example, a particular liberal list of individual rights and liberties.

3 | Liberty and Equality
ARTHUR RIPSTEIN

More than two decades ago, Ronald Dworkin described equality as "a popular but mysterious political ideal." More recently he described it as the "endangered species" of political ideals. Yet both its claim and its mystery persist. It is mysterious because its demands are not always clear and its relation to other values seldom is. A long tradition in political philosophy supposes that the ideas of liberty and equality conflict irreconcilably. The most we can hope for, on this view, is for some acceptable compromise between them. Dworkin's writings about equality hold out the more appealing prospect that, far from being opposed values, liberty and equality are inseparable.

BACKGROUND

Normative political philosophy had no real place in the English-speaking world in the middle part of the twentieth century. Such political philosophy as there was consisted in the study of great thinkers of the past or conceptual analyses of political concepts. Isaiah Berlin's "Two Concepts of Liberty" sought to clarify the nature of liberty and its relation to other values, arguing that liberty was one among several political values. Equality was another, and they were always potentially in conflict. Berlin cautioned against what he saw as the dreadful costs of overlooking this conflict and pretending that values could be integrated into a seamless web. Citizens and politicians must not try to deny or evade the conflict between those values but must instead face up to the choices between them that must be made.

Normative analysis was largely the province of economists, lawyers, and policy experts, most of whom took it for granted that some form of utilitarianism was correct and that social institutions should be designed so as to bring about the best consequences at the lowest cost. The other normative voice came from critics of liberalism, who regarded its mix of liberty and equality either as misguided or as a mask for the exercise of power.

Beginning with a series of articles in the 1950s and, especially, with the publication of *A Theory of Justice* in 1971, John Rawls gave new life to normative political philosophy. Rawls proposed a simple but compelling thought experiment: if people were asked to choose the basic standards of justice for their society, in circumstances in which they were unaware of their own abilities, bargaining advantage, and conception of the good, but were concerned to advance their ability to set and pursue that conception of the good, what principles would they choose? Rawls argued, against the conventional wisdom of the time, that people in such an "original position" would not choose utilitarianism in any of its forms, because, as he put it, to do so would ignore "the distinction between persons." Instead, he argued, they would choose two distinctive principles of justice. The first was a principle of allowing maximal liberty consistent with a like liberty for others. The second was what Rawls called the "difference principle," according to which inequalities in wealth or power could be justified only by showing that allowing some people to have more than an equal share would raise the absolute share of those having less.

The most prominent initial responses to Rawls's work came from two directions. Some, from the Left, argued that Rawls was insufficiently concerned about equality and too ready to allow differences in income and wealth. The difference principle might be an acceptable compromise with justice in the face of human selfishness, but, these critics argued, it is not itself an expression of justice.

Others, from the Libertarian Right, argued that Rawls was insufficiently concerned about liberty and that the first principle, maximizing liberties, must extend to economic liberties as well, thus precluding the state from any role in redistributing income. The libertarian argument was put most forcefully by Robert Nozick, with a thought experiment of his own. Nozick asked the reader to imagine that his or her ideal of distributive justice had been achieved, whether by Rawls's difference principle or any other standard. He then suggested that if people were allowed to use their distributive shares as they saw fit – for example, each paying twenty-five cents to watch the famous basketball player Wilt Chamberlain play – the ideally just pattern of distributive holdings would be upset. Nozick argued that this problem infected any pattern of distributive justice and showed that the exercise of individual liberty was inconsistent with distributive justice.

Dworkin's account of liberty and equality and the relation between them can be read as a fully developed response to the libertarian and egalitarian challenges to Rawls. Dworkin's own account differs from Rawls's in important ways but, like Rawls, he believes that, far from being opposed values, liberty and equality are intimately related to each other. It can also be read as a response to Berlin's claim to have shown that the concept of liberty necessarily comes into conflict with the concept of equality. For Dworkin, liberty and equality must be interpreted together. When that is done, no conflict remains.

Dworkin's strategy is to realign the terms of this debate in three stages. First, Dworkin advocates a standpoint from which disagreements about the respective importance of liberty and equality can be assessed. He contends that they are not actually disagreements about the weight to be attached to competing and opposed values, with libertarians at one extreme and egalitarians at the opposite one, but rather competing interpretations of equality. Second, he offers his own preferred interpretation of equality. Third, and perhaps most significant, he offers an account of the place of equality in public life. As he observes in the introduction to *Sovereign Virtue*, equality is "the virtue of sovereigns."[1] The demands of equality are not the moral demands of impartiality that are sometimes said to govern all of morality. If they were, and if states were to enforce rigorous demands of impartiality, equality would inevitably be the enemy of freedom because it would always, at least in principle, be prepared to subordinate any individual choice to the broader demands of impartiality. A version of this charge is often leveled against utilitarianism. Utilitarian morality demands that private persons attach no greater weight to their own interests than to those of others. Any defense of freedom is contingent on the fact that each person may be in a better position to advance his or her own interests than those of others. The key idea underlying Dworkin's egalitarianism and his specific account of the relation between liberty and equality is that the state must treat its citizens as equals, not that each person's life must be organized around achieving equality.

THE EGALITARIAN PLATEAU

It seems beyond dispute that competing philosophical positions actually disagree about something. The subject of the disagreement, however, is not always transparent. It is often said that the spectrum running from "Left" to "Right" is outdated, as different people may occupy very different positions – someone may be opposed to state action in the economic sphere but favor state action on social questions; another might be socially liberal but believe that the state has an important place in the economy. More fundamental than the difficulties of the spectrum running in only one direction, however, is the assumption that the different positions along any such spectrum, or series of spectra, represent competing and irreconcilable values that society has no choice but to compromise on in one way or another. Dworkin rejects this second picture and suggests that the "right to equal concern and respect, then, is more abstract than the standard conceptions of equality that distinguish different political theories."[2] And these are all versions of a deeper egalitarian principle that "We cannot reject...outright, because it is absurd that government should show no concern for the lives of its citizens, and immoral that it should show more concern for the lives of some than of others."[3] Understood in this way, competing positions disagree about what it is to treat people as equals. Dworkin points to the intuitive pull of this idea when he remarks that "anyone who thinks that liberty and equality really do conflict on some occasion must think that protecting liberty means acting in some way that does not show equal concern for all citizens."[4] Defenders of liberty would not want to suggest that the protection of liberty is opposed to equal concern, but rather that it is a demand of equal concern. As Will Kymlicka summarizes Dworkin's approach, "This more basic notion of equality is found in Nozick's libertarianism as much as in Marx's communism."[5] The only question that divides these very different views concerns the best interpretation of equality.

Libertarians – whom Dworkin welcomes to the debate under the name "laissez-faire egalitarians"[6] – contend that the only defensible form of equality is the minimal equality before the law that protects each person's claim to have their rights to person and property enforced. On Dworkin's reading of the debate, however, to assert that libertarianism is friendlier to liberty is already to accept that equality is always the supreme value. As a result, the libertarian's argument needs to be understood as an argument of what it is for the state to treat its citizens with equal concern and respect. The libertarian's account of equality may not be a compelling one, but the best way to see what is wrong with it is not to imagine that the libertarian defends liberty and rejects equality, but rather that the libertarian offers what is, finally, an indefensible account of equality.

WHAT IS EQUALITY?

If the conflict between freedom and equality is an artifact of the wrong way of framing the question, a better understanding of equality should defuse the conflict. It should show how the best conception of equality leaves people free to use their distributive shares as they see fit but, at the same time, not use that aspect of equality to undermine the claim of the state to distribute in the name of equality. Equality cannot require that state actions have equal impact in all respects because no set of government policies, and no refusal to make policy on particular matters, will have an equal impact on all citizens in all respects. Instead, the inevitably disparate impact of government policies must be compatible with treating people as equals in the relevant sense.

Equality of Welfare

Dworkin introduces his preferred account of equality – equality of resources – through an investigation of what he sees as its most natural competitor, the idea that welfare should be equalized. He notes that the idea of equal welfare has some plausibility if, for example, a parent is deciding how to care for his or her children. If one of those children has special needs or disabilities, raising that child to the level of the others appears to be more important than improving the situation of the others. Equality of welfare provides, at least initially, a plausible explanation of why this should be so.

Equality of welfare demands that social institutions distribute the resources and opportunities over which they have control so as to ensure that people are equal in their welfare. Because of its conflict with freedom, its defenders often concede that equality of welfare must be balanced against the value of liberty. Because it is sensitive to changes in people's welfare, it is also sometimes thought to be an ideal that can never be fully realized in practice. Although Dworkin does not deny either of these difficulties, his complaint against equality of welfare goes deeper: he argues that it is not a value at all. Far from being a disappointment egalitarians must accept, departures from equality of welfare, considered as such, are without moral importance.

Because of ambiguities in the concept of welfare, equality of welfare is a slipperier concept than might at first be supposed. Should the relevant sense of welfare be limited to the satisfaction of each person's preferences about his or her own well-being, or should it also include, for example, the preferences that one person has about another's happiness, or those that some people might have about the distribution of happiness in a society? Such preferences are familiar and plainly contribute to a person's sense of how his life is going. Parents want their children to be happy, usually more than they want their own happiness; indeed, many parents find that they can be no happier than their least happy child, no matter how well other aspects of their lives may be going. Again, those who believe the societies they live in to be unjust experience disappointment as well as outrage at that injustice, even if they are themselves materially comfortable. Questions about the nature of welfare pose special challenges not because of these puzzling but benign examples, but because of other, equally familiar but less friendly ones. Racists, for example, might think it important that members of groups they despise be less happy. If those hopes are frustrated, must society devote extra resources to satisfying their other preferences? Again, should a person's welfare include the interest he takes in things that have no direct effect on him, such as the desire that outer space be explored? Or should welfare be construed narrowly, so that it includes only a person's success in achieving the ends she sets for herself? This second set of questions poses a different set of challenges since dealing with them in a principled way seems to require that we already have answers to the very distributive question that equality of welfare was supposed to address. If people have preferences about things that do not affect them directly, should they receive compensation if the universe turns out differently than they had hoped? Each of these different conceptions of welfare has partisans who have defended them in a variety of ways. Yet none of them, Dworkin suggests, offers an acceptable vision of equality.

The core intuition underlying equality of welfare can be brought out by considering the situation of people who have low welfare through no fault of their own, owing perhaps to illness or disability. Equality of welfare demands that their welfare deficits be made up. At the root of Dworkin's criticism of equality of welfare is the idea that the reason that people with illness or disabilities merit special attention in the egalitarian society has nothing to do with their welfare, considered as such. He suggests that we can see this by considering the case of people who suffer welfare deficits because they have tastes that are expensive to satisfy. Equality of welfare requires that people with "champagne" tastes receive extra resources to bring *their* welfare up to the level of those with more ordinary ones. This problem arises no matter how we construe welfare. Devoting extra resources to the satisfaction of such preferences is, as Dworkin puts it, "counterintuitive."[7] Subsidizing expensive tastes may require the transfer of resources from people who have less to those who have more, simply because those who already have more have acquired tastes that are expensive to satisfy.

This objection to equality of welfare is a particular expression of a more general line of objection to any moral or political theory that makes welfare its central focus. In other places Dworkin mounts a parallel objection to the economic analysis of law, the proponents of which contend that legal rules should be structured so as to maximize the overall wealth of society, where that wealth is measured in terms of the willingness and ability of people to pay for things.[8] This principle would in some circumstances justify the forced and uncompensated transfer of property from a poor person to a wealthy one, simply because the wealthy person would have been willing to pay more for it. The difficulty is not just that such a result offends our intuitions about justice. Dworkin analyzes it as an expression of a deeper problem: it makes each person's entitlements depend on the choices of others in a way that is inconsistent with the ideas of freedom and independence that are at the heart of liberalism. One person's ability to set and pursue his or her own purposes depends on how badly other people would prefer to use that person's share of resources to pursue different purposes. The objection here is not to the way markets coordinate the choices of people in such a way that the availability of particular options depends on the choices of others. As we shall see, Dworkin does not think *that* is a problem at all. Instead, the difficulty is that each person's claim to his or her share of resources – the means each one has to pursue the life he or she thinks best – is itself hostage to the tastes of others because they must always be surrendered if they can be put to more effective use elsewhere. The example of expensive tastes illustrates the vulnerability of equality of welfare to the same type of objection: each person's distributive share is not his or hers to use in pursuit of a life he or she thinks worthwhile but is instead always hostage to the ways that share can be used to produce welfare for others. This argument parallels Nozick's example because it shows how each person's share must be hostage to the need to maintain an overall pattern. At the same time, it deepens it because the limits on each person's ability to choose how to use his or her share are interlaced with a vulnerability to other people's tastes.

Dworkin argues that the difference between expensive medical needs and expensive tastes underscores two problems for equality of welfare: first, equality of welfare leaves no room for individual responsibility. Equality of welfare requires that people subsidize the choices of others whenever doing so will equalize welfare overall, and it requires people to accommodate the particular tastes of others, regardless of their source or content.

Second, the example of expensive tastes shows that equality of welfare is radically discontinuous with the ways people ordinarily think about their own lives. Expensive tastes are often cultivated. Equality of welfare looks at persons only in terms of their welfare and so must regard any such person as a sort of moral and political aberration. Such a possibility is self-defeating from the perspective of equality of welfare because the person who does so could only expect to lower her own welfare in the process. If the resources available to her remain fixed, then she gets less welfare from drinking champagne than she would if she kept her earlier taste for beer. If they vary because a scheme of equality of welfare has been implemented, they will not increase by enough to bring her back to the level of welfare she enjoyed when she had cheaper tastes, since she is entitled only to the level of welfare that other people in her society enjoy, and their welfare level will decrease if resources that would otherwise have gone to them are transferred to her to enable her to satisfy her expensive tastes.[9] Yet people who knowingly develop expensive tastes are familiar – those who set out to learn more about opera, or painting, or fine wines. They do so not because they expect to derive greater welfare from them but because they believe those things to have value apart from the contribution they make to their welfare.

The problem of expensive tastes thus does double duty in Dworkin's argument. It introduces a problem about unfair subsidies and reveals a tension between conceiving of a life in terms of a series of satisfactions and conceiving of it in terms of its value.

Equality of Resources

In place of the discredited idea of equality of welfare, Dworkin introduces the very different idea of equality of resources. It promises to show how, far from being opposed values, liberty and equality are inseparable. It also promises to reconcile the way a state should think of its citizens with the way those citizens think about their own lives. The basic idea is as powerful as it is simple: if our concern is with equalizing material shares, people must be free to use those shares as they see fit because their relative value, and so whether or not they are equal, cannot be measured except against the competing uses to which other people might wish to put various goods.

> Equality of resources places special emphasis on people's responsibility for the choices they make, not because it supposes, absurdly, that people's choices are causally independent of their culture, history, and circumstance, or that people have chosen the convictions, ambitions, and tastes that influence their choices, but because it aspires to a political morality that makes sense in terms of – and of – each citizen's internal practices of moral and ethical criticism, including self-criticism. These practices suppose – they could make no sense without supposing – that we all have choices to make and cannot avoid moral and ethical responsibility for how we choose.[10]

This integration of equality and responsibility requires a careful specification of what a resource is. In economics, resources are often thought of as vectors to welfare: people want resources so as to improve their welfare, and, conversely, anything that improves welfare is treated as a resource. To make the contrast between equality of welfare and equality of resources, Dworkin must work with a different conception because the economist's conception turns equality of resources merely into a way of implementing equality of welfare. First, it is fundamental to Dworkin's account that not everything that could be used to improve welfare counts as a resource in the requisite sense. Any ability or disposition from which someone could derive a benefit counts as a resource in the economist's sense. If you enjoy singing in the shower, and others could derive welfare if you recorded yourself, then your beautiful voice is a resource in the economist's sense, and someone might think that it should count as one of your resources for purposes of equality of resources. For Dworkin, though, the things that count as resources are external to you. Tiny Tim may have higher welfare than Scrooge because of his cheerful disposition, but that disposition does not count as one of his resources.[11]

Dworkin illustrates the idea that resources are to be equalized with a thought experiment: suppose a group of people shipwrecked on a previously unpopulated island wanted a just way of dividing up the various resources available there. They could find something to use as currency – clamshells, for example – and auction off all of the available resources. The auction would transform their initially equal but worthless allotments of clamshells into bundles of resources that could be used in pursuit of the various particular purposes the Islanders set for themselves. The prices of various resources would depend on the different uses to which different people are willing to put them and the ways different uses of them are interchangeable. These bundles would differ in various ways, reflecting the choices made by the Islanders, but they would be different but still represent equal shares. Each person is the judge of whether his or her bundle is the same size as the bundles of others: if anyone would prefer someone else's bundle to her own, then the bundles are not equal.[12] If the conditions of the auction satisfy the standard assumptions of microeconomics, then carrying it out will guarantee an envy-free allocation.

The auction is only the starting point, however, because the same envy test needs to be applicable across time.[13] In assessing whether I would prefer someone else's bundle to my own, I must look not simply at that person's wealth, but also at the various things that she has foregone to accumulate it. Perhaps I would prefer the income of the successful accountant but would find the work he does uninteresting. If so, then the distribution is still consistent with equality of resources because it is envy free.[14]

Equality of resources is satisfied when each person has the bundle of resources he or she would most like. As Dworkin puts it,

> Equality of resources uses the special metric of opportunity costs: it fixes the value of any transferable resource one person has as the value others forgo by his having it. It deems such resources to be equally divided when the total transferable resources of each person have the same aggregate opportunity costs measured in that way. The imaginary auction is designed to secure exactly that result; if the auction ends, then aggregate opportunity costs, as defined by that auction, are equal.[15]

On this understanding, an equal distribution of different goods cannot even be defined except through some mechanism such as the market, which makes qualitatively different resources equivalent based on the uses to which various people might wish to put them. Each person is entitled to equal opportunities and an equal share of resources, but each person's share reflects his or her choice about which resources to purchase in the light of their availability and price, which in turn reflect the willingness of others to purchase them instead.

If auctions (or markets) are to measure opportunity costs in this way, the goods to be divided must be specified in a way that differentiates them as much as possible. For example, the auction will best enable people to adapt their bids to their priorities if the parcels of land that are available are small enough that they can be used for a wide variety of purposes, including the purpose of combining them with other plots of land. If, instead, only large parcels of land are available, prices will be insensitive to the priorities of those who want smaller parcels than are available. Dworkin describes the process through which the items for sale are determined as a pre-auction auction, which must honor what he calls "the principle of abstraction."[16] Where the principle of abstraction cannot be applied because goods cannot be specified narrowly enough, and so costs of using particular resources cannot be fully internalized, a "principle of correction" steps in to justify legal and regulatory constraints on the rights that come with particular goods.[17] Thus, familiar state activities, ranging from the enforcement of tort law through the articulation of regulations, can be thought of as giving effect to equality of resources.[18]

The metric of opportunity costs requires that people take responsibility for their own choices in a second sense. Dworkin's criticism of equality of welfare focused on the way citizens are responsible for deciding for themselves what matters to them, what tastes to develop, and what ends to pursue. The second sense of taking responsibility for one's own life focuses on the requirement that citizens accommodate their choices to their fair share of resources, where that share, in turn, is determined by the separate choices of others. The two senses of responsibility are plainly related: in deciding what to do, and taking up my own special responsibility in the first sense, I need to do so in a way consistent with the claim of others to do the same. Market transactions enable us to do so, both by measuring our relative consumption of scarce resources and by allowing us to adjust out particular bundles through exchanges.

Neither of the problems associated with expensive tastes arise for equality of resources because those who have or choose to develop such tastes are simply using their own fair share of resources as they see fit. The fact that they end up with fewer other goods or have to work harder to acquire the things they want most is not an objection to equality of resources but an example of it. If a person has expensive tastes, she is not entitled to a greater share of resources. The bundle of goods she will receive in the auction will depend on those tastes, but she cannot complain that her bundle is smaller than someone else's since she remains free to exchange her resources for those of others. Insofar as her bundle appears smaller in material terms – for example, she may have fewer cubic feet of goods in her bundle, fewer calories, fewer dollars, or fewer units of welfare, whatever such units might be – its content reflects her tastes and priorities and so does not show that she has received less than an equal share. The distribution of goods in a society is a function of each person's understanding of what he or she believes to be worth doing.

Rather than entering as an exception to equality, then, responsibility enters equality of resources in a constitutive and systematic way. It is constitutive because the actual exercise of choice – taking responsibility for particular choices – determines the value of particular shares and so enters into their definition. It is systematic, rather than exceptional, because the claim that a person is responsible for her choices is not a hypothesis about how she came to make those choices. People are responsible for their tastes because they have decided to use their share of resources in pursuit of them.[19] The person with "champagne" tastes does not receive a subsidy, even if he can show that he was born with a silver spoon in his mouth and so had "no real choice" about it.

Equality of resources is also supposed to solve the other problem that expensive tastes posed for equality of welfare, that is, the intelligibility of a person's decision to develop a particular taste even though it will be expensive. From the point of view of equality of resources, a person's decision to develop an expensive taste is intelligible and continuous with the way the person him or herself thinks about it. Having noticed that a certain way of living is potentially valuable, a person decides to learn more about it and develop a taste for it, even though he recognizes that doing so may be expensive and require sacrifices in other areas of his life. People do not think of their lives in terms of welfare but in terms of what they believe to be valuable. The person who has expensive tastes (or inexpensive ones, for that matter) typically identifies with those tastes rather than experiencing them as a sort of impulse that overtakes him from without. In addition to taking responsibility in the sense of identification, equality of resources asks that people take responsibility in the sense of bearing the costs that their choices impose on others. Equality of resources allows each person to pursue his or her own conception of what is valuable in life and ensures that people have equal shares with which to pursue it.[20]

CHOICE AND CIRCUMSTANCE: DIFFERENT WAYS OF DRAWING THE LINE

Dworkin articulates this centrality of responsibility in a number of related but distinct ways: equality of resources is "ambition sensitive" but "endowment insensitive." It allows differences based on choices but not on circumstances. It corrects for the effects of "brute luck" but not for those of "option luck." Each of these distinctions is related to the way equality of resources determines what counts as an equal bundle by looking to the opportunity costs that one person's control of that bundle imposes on others. Finally, choices are connected to the tastes with which the agent identifies.

Are these various distinctions equivalent? Individuals might identify with their ethnic heritage, or natural talents, or even with an unchosen characteristic on the basis of which others despise them. Again, it is plainly possible for a person to identify with something that he has not chosen or to regret something consciously chosen. Even the cases of conscious choice that are supposed to create difficulties for equality of welfare, such as the development of refined tastes, are difficult to represent as a calculated gamble. Someone who decides not to insure against a risk she faces or who makes speculative investments is making a calculated gamble, and some people have thought that this image can be extended to the person who decides against taking a safety precaution. The person who decides that it is worthwhile to study opera is much harder to assimilate to the same image. The vocabulary of option luck is hard to square with the idea that people develop tastes because they believe them to be worthwhile: someone might decide to study a musical instrument while realizing that he is unlikely to excel at it or recover the costs of study.

Dworkin's third way of drawing a distinction, focusing on chosen ambitions as opposed to unchosen endowments, complicates matters further because when people make choices within a market economy, they always do so in a particular context that is itself the product of countless choices of other people. Those circumstances are the results of other choices, but they are not chosen by the person who simply takes them as given.[21] Yet the opportunity cost test demands that the costs associated with the aggregate market effects of other people's choices *not* be treated as outside individual responsibility.

Many philosophers who take Dworkin's analysis as their point of departure have honed in on these contrasts and advocated abandoning the identification test. G. A. Cohen, for example, says that Dworkin "has, in effect, performed for egalitarianism the considerable service of incorporating within it the most powerful idea in the arsenal of the anti-egalitarian right: the idea of choice and responsibility,"[22] but he goes on to advocate a different way of identifying what he describes as "Dworkin's cut"[23] between choices and circumstances. Despite differences in emphasis, the general thrust of Cohen's and other interventions is to treat the question of choice as a question about individual control. A person's choices are just those things over which he has control, whereas the circumstances are those things over which he has none. This approach has some intuitive plausibility, although as Cohen concedes it may require the resolution of difficult metaphysical questions about free will. On this view, the demands of equality and responsibility are distinct but consistent: everyone is presumptively entitled to an equal share, whether of welfare or resources. This presumptive entitlement does not apply, however, if someone willingly takes a risk. In that case, the risk-taker is responsible for the outcome, whether good or bad. Departures from strict equality are acceptable provided that they have been chosen because, as Cohen describes the luck-egalitarian position, the point of equality is to remove the effects of brute luck. Option luck can be left in place.

The luck-egalitarian position takes its inspiration from Dworkin's analysis but differs from it in important ways. Three of these are particularly significant. First, the fundamental way of reconciling equality and responsibility is different from Dworkin's. For the luck-egalitarian, responsibility provides a justified ground for departures from a background of equality.[24]

For Dworkin, by contrast, responsibility is supposed to be part of equality and only a political value in relation to it.

Luck-egalitarianism solves the problem of expensive tastes in the wrong way because responsibility enters as an extrinsic constraint, always in tension with the underlying idea of equality. It is not surprising that critics of luck-egalitarianism have charged that it is objectionably focused on choices, both by supposing that we must investigate every choice a person makes to see if she could have avoided it and by holding people to account for the full consequences of every choice they make or could have made.[25] By making responsibility an exception to equality, luck-egalitarianism is forced to suppose that questions of responsibility must be adjudicated on a case-by-case basis. Every expensive purchase must be assessed to see if it could have been avoided.

Second, the luck-egalitarian analysis of the difference between expensive needs and expensive tastes is fundamentally different from Dworkin's. For luck-egalitarians, the central question is how someone came to have a need or taste. If she acquired a need through risk-taking behavior, she gets no indemnification. If she acquired the taste through a process of socialization beyond her control, she is not responsible for it.

These first two differences have led luck-egalitarians to embrace a variety of broadly welfarist views. If responsibility is understood in terms of control and provides a principled ground for an exception to a background presumption of equality, then there is no special connection between resources and responsibility. Some have suggested that equality of welfare requires equalizing opportunity sets across different people's lifetimes, so that each person faces an array of choices that is equal in its expected welfare to that faced by others but leaves room for him to choose which actual paths to go down.[26] Others have advocated subsidies for those who develop expensive tastes without choosing them, but none for those who choose to develop them.[27]

On this view, responsibility is not central to the best conception of equality but rather carves out a principled exception to the demands of equal welfare: everyone is presumptively entitled to equal welfare, except where a departure from equal welfare is the result of the voluntary choice of the person who receives something other than an equal share.

Third, markets, understood as a way of measuring the relative scarcity and opportunity costs of particular choices, have no special place in the luck-egalitarian account. The challenges faced by planned economies may convince a luck-egalitarian to allow markets some significant role in social organization, but they have no normative status of their own. For equality of resources, markets are required if people are to accommodate their choices to the choices of others, by offering each other incentives, and responding to those incentives. Markets are the mechanism through which an egalitarian outcome is fixed rather than a tool for approximating an egalitarian outcome that could be specified apart from it. The only measure of one person's share of resources is the uses to which other people might choose to put them.

These three fundamental differences suggest that the debate between Dworkin and many of his egalitarian critics is not about where to make the "cut" between choices and circumstances at all, or even about what the appropriate metric of equality is. Both of these questions reflect a deeper issue about the importance of individual choice in relation to equality. For Dworkin, the requirement that the state treat its citizens with equal concern and respect applies against the background of the requirement that each citizen has a special responsibility for his or her own life. For the luck-egalitarian, by contrast, people do not have a responsibility for their lives as a whole but rather for the discrete decisions they make about particular matters.

Dworkin's way of framing the issue reflects his broader interpretive approach to political philosophy, which views ideas of liberty, equality, and responsibility as all interpretive concepts that must be understood in terms of substantive views about what is valuable. Luck-egalitarians are committed to a very different approach that supposes that the difference between choice and circumstance, or brute and option luck, or the things that a person is or is not responsible for are ultimately factual or perhaps metaphysical distinctions that are relevant to political philosophy but owe nothing to it.[28] The question of whether someone decided to develop a particular expensive taste presents itself as a question of fact. It may be extremely difficult or even impossible to answer such a question, but for the luck-egalitarian, social institutions must try to approximate such an answer.

For Dworkin, however, the question of which distinction is most basic must be an interpretive question. If the choice/circumstance distinction or the brute/option luck distinction were fundamental, then resources are an imperfect metric and markets are a hopeless mechanism for measuring choices. Equality of resources makes sense only if choice and responsibility are understood through the idea of identification. Identification, however, cannot be treated as a factual question about a person's mental state. Instead, it needs to be understood in terms of the idea that people must accommodate their choices to their fair share of social resources and so, indirectly, to the choices of others.

The basic idea is this: as people decide what matters to them in their lives, they also decide which aims to pursue. They always do that in the context of needing to decide which aims are realistic to pursue in the light of the resources they can expect to receive. The particular choices that citizens make are their responsibility because they are the accommodations that each person makes to the choices of others. Outside of an adequate distribution of resources and a forum in which people can use those resources as they see fit in the light of the options that others provide them with, there is no relationship between persons and outcomes such that it makes sense to say that someone should bear the cost of a particular choice. The requirement that each person bear the cost of his or her choices is a systematic implication of allowing each person to use his or her share this year as he or she sees fit, consistent with the claim of others to do the same with their shares. The distinctions between choice and circumstance, or talent and ambition, turn out to be implications of identification rather than fundamentally different distinctions.

On this holistic-interpretive account, liberty and equality are not values that operate disjunctively in the way they do for the luck-egalitarian. Cohen is right to credit Dworkin with incorporating ideas of freedom and responsibility into egalitarian thought, precisely because they have been *incorporated* rather than just added. They operate together because the relevant conception of responsibility applies only when people have liberties. Unless people are free to use their resources as they see fit, enter into cooperative arrangements with others, or try to convince others of the value of their ways of doing things, they cannot take responsibility for their particular choices. For the same reason, the aggregate effects of the choices of others are not treated as a circumstance beyond an individual citizen's responsibility, despite the fact that, in all but the most unusual cases, they will be entirely outside that person's control. Each person's special responsibility for his or her own life can be understood only in the light of the choices that others may get in exercising their own special responsibility.

The claim that people must take responsibility for their expensive tastes because those tastes are chosen thus turns out not to be a factual claim about the ease or difficulty with which people acquire particular tastes. The key idea is that justice demands that people accommodate their use of resources to their fair shares. In a recent essay, Dworkin endorses the Rawlsian idea of a "division of responsibility" between society and the individual: "I urge a division of responsibility between the community and its individual members so that the community is responsible for distributing the resources people need to make successful lives, and individuals for deciding what lives to try to make of those resources, that is, what lives to count as successful."[29] Control over any particular choice drops out of the analysis

Dworkin's account of individual responsibility thus contains a clear response to Nozick's challenge: equality of resources demands that people be able to use their resources as they see fit, and if a million people each wanted to spend a quarter to watch Wilt Chamberlain play basketball, they are free to do so because they are using their shares as they see fit. At the same time, Dworkin contends that his approach is fundamentally different from Rawls's in two ways. First, his focus on identification is supposed to present an alternative to Rawls's use of a social contract argument to "insulate political morality from ethical assumptions and controversies about the character of the good life." Dworkin's own view "makes no use of any social contract: it hopes to find whatever support its political claims may claim not in any unanimous agreement or consent, even hypothetical, but rather in the more general ethical values to which it appeals."[30] Second, Dworkin rejects Rawls's difference principle, which he characterizes as "partially endowment sensitive (luck and talent do determine who remains better off once the worst off group is made as well off as possible), but it is radically choice insensitive as well, because the worst off benefit, at the cost of others and to the greatest extent feasible, whether or not their own choices put them in their unfortunate position."[31] He suggests that his alternative hypothetical insurance approach makes much more turn on responsibility.

EXPENSIVE NEEDS AND INSURANCE

Interpreting the distinction between talent and ambition in terms of the systematic requirements of equality of resources provides a satisfying solution to the problem of expensive tastes, but it may seem to create a new problem about expensive needs. Even the most thoroughgoing defender of individual responsibility would deny that people are responsible for debilitating illnesses that befall them. The person who finds himself with an irresistible urge, such as an addiction, or an overwhelming need, such as illness, is being limited in his or her ability to pursue the things he or she thinks most valuable. Illness and disability are a problem not because those who suffer from them have low welfare, but because they face difficulties in doing things with their resources and so have a narrower range of choices than other people.[32]

Dworkin proposes to solve this problem through the mechanism of insurance. The core idea is that rather than redistributing health or bodily powers directly, the risk of illness or disability can be pooled. There are certain disasters against which people would insure themselves. Actual insurance markets protect against some, but not all of these, because actual insurance companies are aware of "pre-existing conditions." The person who already has an illness, or a genetic or other risk factor, for example, will have difficulty acquiring health insurance. Although private insurers offer long-term disability insurance, they will not offer income insurance to those people who are most likely to want or need it – the people who have reason to expect that their incomes will be low. Despite these familiar features of actual insurance markets, insurance provides a useful model for thinking about certain types of risks that could be exempted from the general requirement that people accommodate their choices to their shares of resources.

The insurance market has to be hypothetical because if people know their talents and abilities, the insurance market will suffer selection effects – people will not insure against outcomes that they know they will never have to face, and people who know that they will face those outcomes will be unable to afford the premiums because prudent insurers will charge them extra based on their risk factors. Because insurance is hypothetical, it is also mandatory – people cannot opt out of it once they discover their real risk factors.

The need to remove these factors makes the insurance scheme hypothetical in a sense that goes beyond the already hypothetical nature of the island auction. Equality of resources mandates that basic aspects of the auction, namely, the operation of markets and voluntary exchanges based on the actual choices of actual people, be preserved in a just society. The insurance argument, by contrast, focuses on what people would do under circumstances that could not be implemented by any set of institutions, such as making purchases without knowing their tastes.

Despite this hypothetical character, Dworkin frames the issue in terms of actual markets. The cost of insurance is always higher than the expected value of the payout because of resources that must be used to administer the scheme. The possibility of putting those resources to alternative uses creates opportunity costs. These extra costs are essential to any use of insurance to model the pooling of risks because all insurance schemes also consume resources and can be justified only if their actual cost can be justified.

Dworkin's solution is to ask what level of insurance people would purchase if they did not know the magnitude of the risk they face but only the average level of risk in their society. Assuming such a level of insurance could be set, it would be fair to include it in everyone's bundle of goods since all would have an interest in protecting themselves against catastrophic outcomes.

Dworkin suggests that people would insure themselves only against outcomes that they regard as truly disastrous, not against outcomes that they would regard as merely undesirable, because the cost of insuring against undesirable outcomes would be much too high. The premium for a policy that guaranteed the highest incomes in society would have to be higher than the highest incomes in society. No rational person would choose to spend their entire life paying off an insurance premium against an eventuality that they would not regard as disastrous. The same argument follows further down the income scale. Even insuring to an average level of income, Dworkin remarks, would require a prohibitively high premium again for an outcome that people would not regard as disastrous. The only insurance level that would be tolerable and prudent would be a protection against very low income.

In the same way, people would be willing to insure themselves against the prospect of having a severe disability. But the price of the premium might preclude them from insuring up to the average level of functioning in their society. The lower the maximum payout, the lower the premium will be, and so the more likely it is that everyone would be willing to pay it.

Even income insurance would need to focus on talents rather than ambitions. The underlying idea of equality of resources is that people are able to accommodate their choices to the distributive shares they receive. Insurance against unwillingness to develop talents would be a form of insurance against a person's own decisions. People who regarded themselves as responsible for their choices would not insure themselves against it. By contrast, they would insure against limited or unmarketable talents because they could not regard themselves as responsible for their talents. Such insurance would be limited, however, to protecting against the worst outcomes rather than guaranteeing the best ones.

Some critics have tried to use the insurance argument to generate an argument for equality of income on the grounds that rational people would insure up to average income – and would be willing to take the chance that, should they be very talented, they would be required to use their talents in ways that did not fit with their ambitions – to meet the premiums.[33] This objection, however, rests on the assimilation of Dworkin's position to the luck-egalitarian view he rejects. Dworkin's claim is not that people would buy insurance so as to remove the element of luck from their overall life prospects. Instead, they would insure against outcomes that compromised their ability to take responsibility for their own lives. They would not compromise that responsibility to protect themselves against the possibility that their conception of the good life would be expensive.

Moreover, a higher level of insurance is not just unattractive from the standpoint of its direct impact on each person's own tastes and ambitions. It is also unattractive because of its impact on the tastes and ambitions of talented people. The total stock of resources in society depends on the willingness of people to develop their talents. People may decline to develop their talents if the need to pay stiff insurance premiums would leave them with no more resources than they would have if they declined to develop them. The point is not that people are inherently lazy and so only willing to deploy their talents if they stand to gain materially. People might develop their talents in a wide variety of ways, and the prospect of additional resources – and thus of increased opportunities to do the other things a person considers valuable – may entice them to develop those talents in ways that accommodate the tastes of others. Without the prospect of incentives, people might instead choose to devote their energies to the direct pursuit of their other goals. Dworkin suggests that we may have to accept movie-star size salaries if we want an abundant supply of movies to enjoy.[34]

The point of this argument is not simply to make a secondary appeal to the self-interest of those selecting the level of mandatory coverage, but to reiterate the role of markets in defining equality of resources. If movies are not made because some object to the large incomes actors command, others will rightly complain that they are being denied the opportunity to use their resources to purchase things that matter to them. If people are free to decide whether to develop or apply their talents, and enter into voluntary transactions, then they must also be able to set the terms on which they will exercise their talents. But that is just to say that they must be free to offer each other, and accept from each other, material incentives.

The argument about the incentive effects of insurance thus has less to do with the dismal side of human nature than with the role of markets in defining equal resources. Insurance sets the background against which people engage in private transactions. It does not replace those transactions. The inequalities in material assets that arise out of the incentives that people offer to and accept from each other are acceptable from the standpoint of equality of resources and do not amount to any sort of concession to "human nature" or compromise so as to improve the level of those who received less. Instead, the argument goes in the opposite direction: it is not that people must be offered incentives because of the good consequences that accrue from their responding to them. People must be able to offer incentives to others because it is up to them to decide what to do with their fair share of resources. Those who respond to incentives must be free to do so because they are free to decide what their priorities are. In particular, they are free to decide whether to develop or deploy their talents in ways that others find useful or pleasing, or to decline to do so.

Compensating for illness and disability are not the only uses to which Dworkin puts his insurance mechanism. Equality of resources takes a special interest in disabilities not because of the welfare deficits they cause, but because of the ways they limit the choices a person may make. In a parallel though not identical fashion, Dworkin argues that people would also insure themselves against disastrously low incomes that result from a lack of talent but not against low incomes that result from a lack of effort. In a more concrete application of the same set of ideas, he argues that the appropriate level of publicly funded health insurance can be determined through the same hypothetical inquiry.

ASSESSMENT OF THE INSURANCE ARGUMENT

Dworkin's hypothetical insurance argument distinguishes expensive needs from expensive tastes and does not demand that unlimited resources be transferred to people whose condition is disastrous. Applied to talents, it provides an intuitively plausible result, that is, taxation to support needs rather than tastes. All of the particular claims that Dworkin makes about what people would regard as disastrous are plausible enough: a low income is disastrous, but lacking a high or even average one is not; being unemployable because of the combination of one's marketable skills and broader economic conditions is disastrous, but voluntary unemployment is not. It provides a useful way of thinking about various health and income support programs as forms of public insurance.

The difficulty with the insurance argument, however, is that it appears to presuppose the very distinction between need and taste that it was supposed to draw. The market figures in equality of resources as the realm of individual choice and responsibility, and market transactions must actually occur to have normative significance. I cannot wash your windows and then demand payment on the grounds that you would have hired me to do so if you had been asked, or if you had been more prudent, or if you knew your real interests, even if each of these things is true. The hypothetical insurance scheme, by contrast, figures as protection of the conditions of choice rather than actual choices.

Modeling social insurance as a private transaction that is continuous with the actual transactions required for equality of resources is doubly misleading. First, one of the central ideas of equality of resources is that distributive shares cannot even be compared apart from actual market interactions. The purchase of specified levels of insurance is not a private interaction at all. Second, the insurance is mandatory, not voluntary, and it is coercively enforced. Dworkin's argument is supposed to show that the market is legitimate as a measure of voluntary cooperation, but compulsory forms of cooperation do not fit a market model, and pretending that they do is more apt to mislead than illuminate.

This is not merely an expository difficulty. It goes to the heart of equality of resources, which contends that the role of markets is not merely to approximate a result that could have been achieved otherwise. Yet the insurance argument is exactly that type of argument: we set up social institutions to approximate the results that we would get if ideal people were able to purchase insurance under certain types of ideal conditions. Those ideal conditions are not marketlike conditions because people are not able to accommodate their decisions about choices to the choices of others.[35]

Underlying both of these differences between the market mechanism and the insurance mechanism in Dworkin's account is the tension between treating insurance as part of the market mechanism and Dworkin's broader strategy of appealing to the division of responsibility between society and individual citizens. Each citizen has a special responsibility for his or her own life, and that special responsibility can be exercised only against the background of protection against certain types of disastrous circumstances, because it is only within the context of protection against those circumstances that separate persons, with separate lives to live, are able to accommodate themselves to the choices of the others. On this more Rawlsian understanding, the responsibility of society as a whole is not an *indirect* way private citizens take up their special responsibility for their own lives, but they exercise it without knowing their particular ends or being able to accommodate themselves to others. It is fundamentally different because it is the background condition of free private interaction. On Dworkin's broader interpretive approach, this Rawlsian reading of the insurance argument must be the correct one because the only way that we can make talk about how much insurance people would buy directly relevant to their claims against society as a whole is by understanding the insurance argument – in all of its dimensions, including hypothetical pricing – through the broader demands of equality. Talk about how much insurance people would buy in various circumstances – whether income and disability insurance or, closer to our current world, health insurance – is not an empirical hypothesis about widespread preferences but a normative claim about the conditions in which people can be required to take responsibility for their lives and choices.[36]

Indeed, the insurance argument does not look so very different from Rawls's contract argument in favor of the difference principle, which demands that inequalities in the distribution of primary goods, including income and wealth, must work to the advantage of those receiving less, that is, must raise the absolute level of the expected shares for those who are worst off. Like the Rawlsian argument, the insurance argument concludes that government must guarantee people adequate resources and opportunities to guarantee that everyone can plan his or her life in the expectation of remaining a full member of society. Insurance protects people so that no matter how badly things go for a person, whether in terms of brute luck or their own choices, he or she will remain a full participant, able to set and pursue some conception of the good. It is inherently cautious in its concern for extreme outcomes and also supposes that people would not risk throwing away their freedom to raise their expected level of income.[37] And like the argument for the difference principle, the insurance argument is hypothetical, asking about the hypothetical choices of people who regard themselves as capable of taking responsibility for their actual ones.

If the insurance argument is interpreted in a way that makes it continuous with Rawls's argument for the difference principle, equality of resources becomes more attractive because it enables it to articulate the place of responsibility while avoiding the unpalatable implications of luck-egalitarianism. Dworkin has rightly distanced himself from luck-egalitarians, and he has rejected the idea that anyone who knowingly takes a risk forfeits any claim to public assistance. Dworkin has charged Rawls with failing to explain why the worst off deserve special consideration, without regard to how it is that they came to be worse off. Dworkin's own insurance argument provides the explanation that he thought was missing from Rawls: a government that treats its citizens with equal concern and respect must take responsibility for providing them with adequate liberties and opportunities, including protection against outcomes that are disastrous for their ability to take up their own responsibility for their own lives.

Notes

1. Ronald Dworkin, "Introduction: Does Equality Matter?" in *Sovereign Virtue: The Theory and Practice of Equality* (Cambridge, MA: Harvard University Press, 2000), 6.

2. Ronald Dworkin, "Justice and Rights," in *Taking Rights Seriously* (Cambridge, MA: Harvard University Press, 1977), 180.

3. Ronald Dworkin, "What is Equality? Part 3: The Place of Liberty," *Iowa Law Review* 73 (1987): 1–54, reprinted in *Sovereign Virtue*, 130.

4. Ronald Dworkin, "The Place of Liberty," 128.

5. Will Kymlicka, *Contemporary Political Philosophy* (New York: Oxford University Press, 1990), 4.

6. Dworkin, "The Place of Liberty," 131.

7. Ronald Dworkin, "What is Equality? Part 1: Equality of Welfare," *Philosophy & Public Affairs* 10, no. 3 (1981): 185–246, reprinted in *Sovereign Virtue*, 49.

8. Ronald Dworkin, "Is Wealth a Value?" in *A Matter of Principle* (Cambridge, MA: Harvard University Press, 1985), 237–66.

9. "Equality and Capability," in *Sovereign Virtue*, 289.

10. Ronald Dworkin, "*Sovereign Virtue* Revisited," *Ethics* 113 (October 2002): 107.

11. "Ronald Dworkin Replies" in *Dworkin and His Critics: With Replies by Dworkin*, ed. Justine Burley (Malden, MA: Blackwell Publishing, 2004), 349.

12. The intuitive idea is familiar. In *Leviathan*, Hobbes suggests that intelligence is distributed equally, because "there is not ordinarily a greater signe of the equall distribution of any thing, than that every man is contented with his share." Thomas Hobbes, *Leviathan*, rev. st. ed., ed. Richard Tuck (New York: Cambridge University Press, 1996), 87 [61].

13. Technically, this formulation is not correct because the initial allocation of clamshells is itself equal and can be known to be so without running the auction. Dworkin's point is that the idea of an equal distribution can only be aligned with the economic idea of efficiency through something like a market. Efficiency demands that resources go to their most highly valued use, that is, the use for which one is most willing to pay for them since an exchange between that person and any other holder of a particular resource would be beneficial to both. Markets enter in enabling people to use their resources to make what they regard as mutually advantageous exchanges. On this point, see Joseph Heath, "Dworkin's Auction," *Politics, Philosophy and Economics* 3, no. 3 (2004): 313–35.

14. Strictly speaking, this also requires qualification. The lack of envy does not establish that a distribution is equal. If I consume my resources or give them away, I have no grounds to complain that I have less than others, but that reflects the requirement that I take responsibility for my choices, not the fact that I have the same amount. Indeed, the thing I cannot complain about is the (simple) fact that I have less.

15. Dworkin, "The Place of Liberty," 149.

16. Dworkin, "The Place of Liberty," 147.

17. Despite his misgivings about economic analysis of law, Dworkin's use of the principle of correction commits him to one of its central and controversial claims: contracting is the ideal solution to problems of social coordination, and other areas of law need to be understood as attempts to approximate contractual results in cases of market failure. Dworkin develops this view in detail in his

discussion of tort in *Law's Empire* (Cambridge, MA: Harvard University Press, 1986), 295.

18. Dworkin, "The Place of Liberty," 157.

19. Ronald Dworkin, "Equality, Luck and Hierarchy," *Philosophy and Public Affairs* 31, no. 2 (March 2003): 192–3.

20. Dworkin also argues that equality of resources allows a further integration of individual choice and the demands of justice, on the grounds that it incorporates a formal conception of the good life, which he calls "the challenge model," according to which a life is valuable if freely chosen under just circumstances. On the challenge model, justice is one of the parameters of a good life, so that a life that is successful in other respects is compromised if achieved through an unjust distribution of resources. This integration makes Dworkin's liberalism "comprehensive," in its presupposition of a distinctive view about the nature of good lives, rather than "political" as Rawls intends his liberalism to be. For Rawls, political liberalism limits itself to questions about the coercive structure of society and presupposes no single view about what makes a life go well because citizens need not resolve those questions to live together on terms of freedom and equality. Although a full assessment of this issue will have to wait for another occasion, it is worth noting that the depth of this difference from Rawls depends on whether equality of resources presupposes the challenge model, so that anyone who did not endorse the challenge model would have to reject equality of resources, or whether, instead, connection goes only the other way, so that those who accept the challenge model must also accept equality of resources. If it is only the second, then Dworkin's liberalism also appears to be political. Rawls too could demonstrate that particular views about the good life are consistent with political liberalism. The whole point of his account is that no *particular* view is presupposed because citizens can have different conceptions.

21. This objection is raised in detail in Colin Macleod, *Liberalism, Justice, and Markets: A Critique of Liberal Equality* (New York: Oxford University Press, 1998).

22. G. A. Cohen, "On the Currency of Egalitarian Justice," *Philosophy and Public Affairs* 99, no. 4 (July 1989): 933.

23. Cohen, "Currency of Egalitarian Justice," 916.

24. G. A. Cohen, "Currency of Egalitarian Justice"; Cohen, "Expensive Taste Rides Again," in *Dworkin and His Critics: With Replies by Dworkin*, 3–29; Elizabeth Anderson, "What is the Point of Equality?" *Ethics* 109, no. 2 (Jan. 1999): 287–337; Susan Hurley, *Justice, Luck, and Knowledge* (Cambridge, MA: Harvard University Press, 2003); and Samuel Scheffler, "What is Egalitarianism?" *Philosophy and Public Affairs* 31, no. 1 (Winter 2003): 5–39.

25. As Samuel Scheffler puts it, according to luck-egalitarians, "people automatically forfeit any claim to assistance if it turns out that their urgent needs are the result of prudent or well-considered choices that simply turned out badly." Scheffler, "What is Egalitarianism?" 18–19.

26. Richard Arneson, "Liberalism, Distributive Subjectivism, and Equal Opportunity for Welfare," *Philosophy and Public Affairs* 19, no. 2 (Spring 1990): 158–94.

27. Cohen, "Expensive Taste Rides Again."

28. Dworkin uses this phrase to characterize Archimedean political philosophy in "Objectivity and Truth: You'd Better Believe It," *Philosophy and Public Affairs* 25, no. 2 (Spring 1996): 88.

29. "Ronald Dworkin Replies," in *Dworkin and His Critics*, 391 n 18. The general idea that individuals have different responsibilities than society does can be found in *Law's Empire*, 295. Rawls introduces the idea of a division of responsibility in his "Social Unity and Primary Goods," in *John Rawls: Collected Papers*, ed. Samuel Freeman (Cambridge, MA: Harvard University Press, 1999), 359–87, and incorporates it explicitly in *Political Liberalism*. "The ... account of primary goods includes what we may call a 'social division of responsibility': society, citizens as a collective body, accepts responsibility for maintaining the equal basic liberties and fair equality of opportunity, and for providing a fair share of the primary goods for all within this framework; while citizens as individuals and associations accept responsibility for revising and adjusting their ends and aspirations in view of the all-purpose means they can expect, given their present and foreseeable situation. This division of responsibility relies on the capacity of persons to assume responsibility for their ends and to moderate the claims they make on their social institutions accordingly." John Rawls, *Political Liberalism* (New York: Columbia University Press, 1993), 189.

30. Dworkin, "Introduction: Does Equality Matter?" 5.

31. Ronald Dworkin, "*Sovereign Virtue* Revisited," *Ethics* 113, no. 1 (October 2002): 122. Dworkin's reading is very different from Rawls's own account of his position. In "Social Unity and Primary Goods," Rawls introduces the idea of a "division of responsibility" between "the citizens considered as a collective body" and individual citizens. Rawls, "Social Unity and Primary Goods," 371. Rawls's basic idea is that when society has met its obligations, each citizen must adjust his or her choices to the expectations that have been so generated. In the much earlier "Reply to Alexander and Musgrave," Rawls notes that the idea that citizens have a special responsibility for their own lives is presupposed by the very idea of "primary goods" as a metric of distributive shares. Rawls, "Reply to Alexander and Musgrave," in *John Rawls: Collected Papers*, 232–53. Far from "rescinding" from talk about responsibility, then, Rawls makes it absolutely central.

32. Dworkin, "Equality, Luck and Hierarchy."

33. Dworkin's official response to this objection is not likely to satisfy his critics. He objects that insuring against limited talents would lead to what he calls "the slavery of the talented" as they devote themselves to using their talents in the most effective way so as to pay off their insurance premiums. Dworkin gives the example of a woman who despises acting but is forced into a career on the screen to support the extravagant insurance that everyone would purchase. Remarkably, some critics seem to contend that the slavery of the talented is not objectionable at all and that people should use their abilities so as to produce the net social product that will bring about equal incomes for all. Miriam Cohen Christofidis, "Talent, Slavery, and Envy," in *Dworkin and His Critics*, 30–44. The difficulty with the slavery of the talented is not, however, that it would lead to nightmarish results that are so reminiscent of familiar objections to utilitarianism. The real difficulty is that the slavery of the talented cannot even

arise within the context of equality of resources because the mere fact that someone has some ability does not turn it into a resource to be used to improve the prospects of others or, for that matter, for any other purpose. Something is a resource only if it enters into the market sphere in which people offer each other incentives. If I convince you to let me record your beautiful singing voice, your singing voice becomes a resource, relevant to the "envy test" and, in real life, potentially subject to taxation so as to provide for the insurance aspects of equality of resources. If you decline my incentives, however, and keep your voice to yourself, then it does not enter into the scheme of equality of resources. The talented may need to pay higher taxes to cover the insurance premiums, but they are not enslaved because they are never compelled to use their talents in any particular way.

34. Ronald Dworkin, "Equality of Resources," in *Sovereign Virtue*, 105.

35. On this point, see Joseph Heath, "The Benefits of Cooperation," *Philosophy and Public Affairs* 34 (forthcoming).

36. Dworkin seeks to distance the insurance argument from Rawls's argument on the grounds that his insurance arguments "have been designed to permit people as much knowledge as it is possible to allow them without defeating the point of the entire exercise entirely. In particular, they allow people enough self-knowledge as individuals to keep relatively intact their sense of their own personality, especially their theory of what is valuable in life, whereas it is central to the original position that this is exactly the knowledge that people lack." See "Equality of Resources," in *Sovereign Virtue*, 118. Despite this disclaimer, the purchasers of hypothetical insurance buy a standard package of insurance based on what Rawls calls their "higher order interest" in protecting their "two moral powers."

37. Rawls uses the phrase "strains of commitment" to give voice to this idea, albeit in the slightly different context of explaining why contractors in the original position could never take the risks that come with utilitarianism. See Rawls, *A Theory of Justice* (Cambridge, MA: Harvard University Press, 1971), 176ff.

4 | Rights, Responsibilities, and Reflections on the Sanctity of Life

BENJAMIN C. ZIPURSKY AND JAMES E. FLEMING

An intrinsic feature of Ronald Dworkin's jurisprudence is his insistence that there are no bright lines between legal and nonlegal discourse, between problems in political philosophy and those in constitutional theory, between political morality and law. For Dworkin, the need to articulate philosophical questions and to answer them grows out of practical issues that demand action of judges, legislators, lawyers, and citizens. He thus calls for doing "philosophy from the inside out."[1] Nowhere is this clearer than on the issues of abortion and the right to die, to which Dworkin has devoted an entire elegantly written and brilliantly argued book, *Life's Dominion*.

The practical decisions for which Dworkin seeks answers exist at all of these levels in both the abortion and the right-to-die arenas. For judges, there is the question of what constitutional boundaries should be articulated and enforced with regard to state and federal attempts to regulate abortion and physician-assisted suicide. For legislators, not only the constitutionality but also the wisdom, fairness, and advisability of restrictions, and the particular nature of these restrictions, need to be considered. Lawyers must think through these issues, of course, as well as the broader issues of what sort of counsel is appropriate to citizens and legislators and what sort of law ought and ought not to exist in these areas. And finally, for citizens, there are not only the gripping dilemmas of whether to have an abortion and whether to assist suicide, seek assisted suicide, or create a living will; there are also questions about how to talk about and resolve these issues in a mutually respectful way in a constitutional democracy that evidently views them as all-or-nothing matters. In his characteristically ambitious manner, Dworkin aims to provide guidance on all of these practical issues.

Life's Dominion is philosophical and practical in equal parts, however. Dworkin's most potent practical tool is philosophical analysis. In the abortion arena, his fundamental question is what is meant by the assertion that the life of a fetus is a locus of intrinsic value and therefore may not be sacrificed. Similarly, in the context of physician-assisted suicide, the fundamental question is what is meant by the assertion that human life, even the

109

life of a person who no longer wishes to live because of painful terminal illness, is intrinsically valuable and therefore may not be taken. The common
philosophical question Dworkin finds in these contexts is the question of
what it means to assert that life is of intrinsic value. The shades of meaning
of these assertions, the nature of intrinsic value of life, the connection of
these statements to the idea of rights against others and against the state,
and the place of such debates within a liberal political society and within
our constitutional framework are the objects of Dworkin's analysis.

To say that the life of a fetus or a terminally ill patient who wishes to die
is of intrinsic value and therefore may not be taken, according to Dworkin,
is to assert a view about *the sacredness of life*. Views about the sacredness of
life belong to a broader category that includes religious views. It is of vital
importance that a government not impose such views on an individual or
coerce an individual concerning them. As a matter of political morality and
a matter of constitutional law, Dworkin argues, individuals are entitled to
decide for themselves what it is that makes life sacred. Because the justifications of bans on abortion and physician-assisted suicide and euthanasia rely
on the state's taking a position on what makes life sacred, such bans violate
the entitlement to decide for oneself on what makes life sacred. Such bans
are therefore illegitimate, unjust, and unconstitutional. This is not to deny,
however, that the justifications of these actions presuppose responsible and
sober deliberation, or that the state may and should foster such deliberation.
Nor is it to deny the variety of significant concerns and interests that are
raised by both types of laws, and both types of rights claims. These clusters
of practical issues must be carefully put in place once we recognize the basic
parameters of the state's power and the individual's rights. Moreover, we
gain perspective on the softer-edged but equally important question of how
to establish mutual respect surrounding these divisive issues. The respect
we owe to others on these issues is akin to the respect we owe to others
on differences in theological, religious, and spiritual views. For that is ultimately what our differences of opinion on abortion and physician-assisted
suicide amount to.

This chapter consists of four parts. In Part I, we provide an exegesis of
Dworkin's moral and constitutional arguments for the right to abortion and
the right to die, bringing out the complex interconnections among these
arguments. Part II places Dworkin's positions against the backdrop of a critique of liberalism to which he was in part responding; Dworkin's defenses
of rights to abortion and physician-assisted suicide do not – contra critics
such as Michael Sandel – rely on a conception of liberalism as a doctrine
of neutrality or values-gatekeeping. Rather, they depend on a notion of

liberty of conscience and, Dworkin suggests, religious liberty. In Part III, we briefly explore some concerns about Dworkin's argument, both in political morality and constitutional law. Part IV concludes by suggesting that Dworkin's arguments from liberty of conscience would be on firmer ground if he were to cast them in terms of autonomy generally rather than in terms of religious liberty specifically.

I. AN EXEGESIS OF DWORKIN'S ARGUMENTS

A. Politics, Law, and Civics in Abortion and Euthanasia: The Cluster of Practical Problems

Like many of Dworkin's most renowned essays, *Life's Dominion* focuses on highly controversial political and moral issues that occupy the American political landscape and divide the American people. However, in his other work, such as that on segregation, affirmative action, gay rights, and pornography, Dworkin has typically taken up one side of the issue and fervently defended it against the other.[2] Indeed, Dworkin has attracted his share of admirers and detractors in part because his writing is imbued with an unparalleled confidence of style and a forthright claim both to have arrived at a position that is uniquely justifiable and to have shown the opposing positions to be dead wrong. Rhetorically and epistemically, Dworkin's prose bristles with a claim to have the right answer – a feature that is particularly conspicuous when he has selected issues on which many fervently disagree or at best agree to disagree.

Life's Dominion deviates from this pattern, at least superficially, for it aims to find for the abortion and euthanasia controversies a way that the two sides can "reason together" with an attitude of respect rather than "pale civility" (1). Furthermore, Dworkin aims for a "responsible legal settlement," "one that will not insult or demean any group, one that everyone can accept with full self-respect" (10–11). When the far right favored segregation or (along with some radical feminists) the banning of pornography, Dworkin did not seek to find a responsible legal settlement or a way to reason together; he aimed simply to prove that they were wrong. Something quite different is taking place in *Life's Dominion*.

The difference has two aspects, one pertaining to the appropriate legal and constitutional framework for analyzing these issues, and the other to the appropriate vocabulary for discussing them. Similarly, Dworkin's argument has two sorts of intended audience: the world of judges, legislators, attorneys general, and lawyers, on the one hand, and the world of debating citizens, on the other. On the legal level, Dworkin aims to defend a framework that recognizes an individual right against state criminalization of abortion and physician-assisted suicide but nevertheless recognizes a place for the state to protect the moral environment and to encourage individuals to reflect responsibly and conscientiously concerning how to respect the sacredness of life, including fetal life. On the level of civil discourse, Dworkin aims to show why mutual respect is the appropriate attitude for citizens to take toward those who differ with them on abortion and euthanasia. In this regard, *Life's Dominion* resonates deeply with the branch of liberalism that takes tolerance as the central liberal virtue, whereas much of Dworkin's other work has exalted the virtues of equality or integrity above all else.

It would be a mistake, however, to see in *Life's Dominion* a change in overall political philosophy, jurisprudence, or outlook. Rather, as Dworkin explicitly acknowledges, the aspirations of the book are driven in part by his perception of the practical problems that need to be resolved or settled. Foremost in his mind, it appears, is the intractability, intolerance, incivility, and lack of mutual respect that characterizes public discourse regarding abortion and euthanasia, and the all-or-nothing character of the constitutional and legal debates. For Dworkin, philosophical analysis is a tool for solving political, legal, and moral problems that confront us as a society. Here, the sense of extremism and intractability *is* a major part of the problem that confronts us.

The legal problems addressed by *Life's Dominion* are multiple, equally real, and very much alive. The book was written twenty years after the Supreme Court's decision in *Roe v. Wade* striking down Texas's criminalization of abortion as an invasion of the individual woman's right to choose whether to terminate a pregnancy.[3] During those two decades, there were vigorous attacks on *Roe* in the Court, Congress, state legislatures, presidential campaigns, Supreme Court nomination hearings, and hundreds of books and articles. While Dworkin was writing *Life's Dominion*, the United States Supreme Court was deliberating on *Planned Parenthood v. Casey*, and shortly before the publication of the book, the Court produced a fragmented reaffirmation of the central holding of *Roe*.[4] Similarly, the book was published just four years after the Court permitted Missouri to restrict the exercise of the right to refuse life-sustaining hydration and nutrition in *Cruzan*,[5] and four years before the Court declined to recognize a right to physician-assisted suicide in *Washington v. Glucksberg*.[6] To this day, state legislatures, Congress, courts, and political candidates continue to debate the dimensions of the legal rights to abortion and euthanasia.

Of course, there is a variety of questions about whether legislators should pass statutes constraining abortion or euthanasia, and if so, what these statutes should provide. However, Dworkin's principal focus is on the constitutional question of whether the state or federal governments *may*, constitutionally, criminalize abortion or physician-assisted suicide. And his answer to both questions is (with substantial qualifications) that they may not. In the end, then, Dworkin arrives at the quintessential liberal position on each of these questions: the controversial choice about whether to have an abortion or whether to end one's own life are decisions the individual is entitled to make, and the state may not substitute what it believes is the right decision for what the individual believes and decides. The challenge of *Life's Dominion* is not just in defending a position; it is in arriving at a position that generates a sound constitutional argument that takes seriously the utterly different position of the opposing side.

B. The Abortion Debate

1. Distinguishing two debates

An interesting aspect of *Life's Dominion* is Dworkin's claim to have discovered why the abortion debate has seemed so intractable: it is because the standard view is that the abortion debate is about whether a fetus is a person. Dworkin asks the standard question:

> Is a fetus a helpless unborn child with rights and interests of its own from the moment of conception? If so, then permitting abortion is permitting murder, and having an abortion is worse than abandoning an inconvenient infant to die. If not, then people who claim to be "pro-life" are either acting in deep error or are sadistic, puritanical bigots, eager not to save lives but to punish women for what they regard as a sexual sin (9–10).

He continues:

> Self-respecting people who give opposite answers to the question of whether a fetus is a person can no more compromise, or agree to live together allowing others to make their own decisions, than people can compromise about slavery or apartheid or rape. For someone who believes that abortion violates a person's most basic interests and most precious rights, a call for tolerance or compromise is like a call for people to make up their own minds about rape, or like a plea for second-class citizenship, rather than full slavery or full equality, as a fair compromise on the racial issue.

Dworkin argues:

> So long as the argument is put in those polarized terms, the two sides cannot
> reason together, because they have nothing to reason, or to be reasonable
> about. One side thinks that a human fetus is already a moral subject, an
> unborn child, from the moment of conception. The other thinks that a just-
> conceived fetus is merely a collection of cells under the command not of a
> brain but of only a genetic code, no more a child, yet, than a just-fertilized
> egg is a chicken. Neither side can offer any argument that the other must
> accept – there is no biological fact waiting to be discovered or crushing
> moral analogy waiting to be invented that can dispose of the matter. It is a
> question of primitive conviction, and the most we can ask, of each side, is not
> understanding of the other, or even respect, but just a pale civility, the kind
> of civility one might show an incomprehensible but dangerous Martian.

According to Dworkin, this typical understanding of the nature of the
debate confuses two different ideas. On the one hand, there is a possible
debate about *whether a fetus at the moment of conception is a rights-bearing
moral subject*. On the other hand, there is a question about *whether the life of
a fetus at the moment of conception is sacred* (24). Let us call these the "rights-
bearing" debate and the "sacredness of life" debate, respectively. When the
debate is put in terms of the sacredness of life, Dworkin argues, it is clearly
intractable, because questions of what is sacred, what makes it sacred, and
what is the nature of sacredness are in the realm of the deeply spiritual and
religious, and we cannot hope to get beyond such basic convictions. On the
other hand, one's answer to the sacredness of life issue is not necessarily
what is dispositive as to the permissibility of abortion. The claim that a
fetus has a "right to life" purports to be a position in the rights-bearing
debate.

To be sure, Dworkin argues, *if* a fetus is a rights-bearer, one cannot
simply leave a pregnant woman to decide as she wishes whether to have an
abortion (109). However, the intractability of the sacredness-of-life debate
does not apply to the rights-bearing debate. Indeed, Dworkin argues that
a fetus at the moment of conception is *not* a rights-bearer (15–24). Moreover, Dworkin implicitly maintains that the reasons he puts forward for the
assertion that a fetus at the moment of conception is *not* a rights-bearer are
compelling as reasons and should be regarded as compelling by the Roman
Catholic and the Christian Fundamentalist just as they are by Dworkin
himself (13–15). The Roman Catholic and the Christian Fundamentalist
have strong and understandable grounds for deeply opposing abortion: it
destroys something that they legitimately and not unreasonably believe to

be as sacred as any adult human life. But on his view this is a consideration within the sacredness-of-life debate, not within the rights-bearing debate.

Dworkin makes a companion argument within constitutional law. He contends that the rebuttal of *Roe*'s argument for a woman's right to an abortion based on a fetus's right to life fails because it works only if it is persuasive as a rights-bearing argument (107–13). Both because of the failure of that argument within the rights-bearing debate in moral and political philosophy, and because of its indefensibility as an argument with regard to who is a constitutional person, the argument fails to defeat the argument of *Roe*. Therefore, the battle waged from the premise that a fetus's right to life precludes a woman's right to choose is untenable. The question, within the rights-bearing debate, may be hotly contested, but it is not intractable or nonjusticiable, and Dworkin's answer ought to be accepted as a matter of moral philosophy and as a matter of constitutional law.

Dworkin's terms for encapsulating this confusion differ from those we have introduced. Rather than expressly distinguishing two debates, he distinguishes two reasons, or arguments, for the impermissibility of abortion. The first he calls a "derivative" reason: it is an argument that the impermissibility of abortion derives from a fetus's status as a rights-bearer at the moment of conception (11). The second he calls a "detached" reason: the impermissibility of abortion derives from the fact that a fetus at the moment of conception is a thing of intrinsic value, or sacred (11). Dworkin takes himself to have a refutation of the derivative reason – that a fetus is a rights-bearer – for he thinks he can demonstrate that its initial premise is false. On the other hand, he admits that the premise of the detached reason – that a fetus at the moment of conception is sacred – cannot be refuted. However, he believes that the detached reason is incapable of supporting an argument for criminalizing abortion. Indeed, on Dworkin's view, the detached reason turns out to support an argument for a woman's right to decide.

2. The argument against the derivative reason for criminalizing abortion

A. THE MORAL AND POLITICAL RIGHT-TO-LIFE ARGUMENT

Dworkin's all-important argument against the derivative reason for maintaining that abortion is wrong and should be criminalized is advanced within a more complex, interpretive argument in the book. He puts forward what he concedes is a highly contentious argument that those who purport to hold the derivative position that abortion is wrong are actually more charitably interpreted as adhering to the detached reason (13–24). There are at least three reasons counting in favor of this interpretation. One is that it renders more consistent the view that opinion polls indicate many Americans hold toward abortion: it is profoundly wrong but the choice whether to have an abortion should be left up to the individual (13–15). Another is that it offers a more historically and doctrinally consistent account of the Roman Catholic Church's opposition to abortion, which unites that view with its opposition to euthanasia and contraception (39–50). A third is that "it is hard to make sense of the idea that an early fetus has interests of its own, in particular an interest in not being destroyed, from the moment of its conception," (15) and the rights-bearing account depends on a fetus having interests of its own (11, 24). The third reason, offered putatively by Dworkin as a ground for interpreting anti-abortion advocates as not holding the position they claim to hold, is actually Dworkin's central argument that the derivative argument against the permissibility of abortion is unsound.

Does a fetus itself, at the moment of conception, have a *right* to life? Dworkin argues that it could have a "right" to life only if it had an interest in being alive. The clauses "human life begins at conception," "a fetus is a person from that moment," and "abortion is murder or homicide or an assault on the sanctity of human life" can be used in a manner that reflects an intention to refer to a fetus's own right, according to Dworkin (11).

> They can be used to make the claim that fetuses are creatures with interests of their own right from the start, including, preeminently, an interest in remaining alive, and that therefore they have the rights that all human beings have to protect these basic interests including a right not to be killed. Abortion is wrong in principle, according to this claim, because abortion violates someone's right not to be killed, just as killing an adult is normally wrong because it violates the adult's right not to be killed. I shall call this the *derivative* objection to abortion because it presupposes and is derived from rights and interests that it assumes all human beings, including fetuses, have (11).

Dworkin then argues, centrally, that "it makes no sense to suppose that something has interests of *its own* – as distinct from its being important what happens to it – unless it has, or has had, some form of consciousness: some mental as well as physical life" (16). A fetus's brain is not sufficiently developed to have any form of consciousness, he argues, until after midgestation (17). It follows that an immature fetus "cannot have interests and therefore cannot have an interest in surviving" (18). Therefore, on Dworkin's view, an immature fetus – certainly a fetus at the moment of conception – does not have "rights" and *a fortiori* does not have a right to life.

We will scrutinize this argument in greater detail later in this chapter. For the moment, two points about it merit attention. First, it is not, as it stands, intended as an argument for the permissibility of abortion. We have suggested that it should be understood as a refutation of a particular form of argument against the permissibility of abortion. Dworkin himself expressly puts it forward as part of an argument for interpreting "pro-life" arguments to have a meaning or an import different than they sometimes purport to have.

Second, Dworkin's status as a political philosopher and constitutional theorist was established on the basis of his revitalization of the notion of rights in American political and legal thought.[7] In the passages just summarized, Dworkin, the preeminent "rights" theorist, has addressed the most inflammatory issue phrased in "rights" language that has existed during his lifetime, and he has confidently disposed of his opponents' rights argument *as a genuine rights argument*. Apparently for strategic and rhetorical reasons, Dworkin has presented this argument as a preliminary clearing of the brush, but if he took his adversaries at their word, it would be the central issue in the book. Dworkin suggests that opponents of the right to abortion did not always use the language of rights and personhood and that their contemporary decision to use those concepts has had, for them, the salutary effect of appearing to make their arguments secular (39–45).

B. THE CONSTITUTIONAL RIGHT-TO-LIFE ARGUMENT

In addition to refuting a derivative argument for a fetus's right to life from within moral and political philosophy, Dworkin also dispatches the argument that a fetus is a "person" within the meaning of the United States Constitution (109–12). Dworkin correctly notes that Justice Blackmun's opinion of the Court in *Roe* rejected the idea that a fetus is a constitutional person,[8] and that few critics of *Roe* have challenged that contention. Dworkin adds that most critics of that decision have argued that the Constitution leaves states free to criminalize abortion or not as they wish, and that this view is inconsistent with a fetus being a constitutional person. Moreover, he notes that the history of abortion laws in the nineteenth century, when the Due Process and Equal Protection Clauses of the Fourteenth Amendment were ratified, displays a set of values inconsistent with the idea that a fetus is a constitutional person.

Dworkin is equally succinct in his refutation of the argument that states are entitled to treat a fetus as a constitutional person (113–16). To give states the power to declare new categories of constitutional persons is implicitly to give states the power to change the balance of rights and liberties envisioned in the Constitution for those whom it already considers to be persons. For example, if states declared corporations to count as constitutional persons and therefore to have the right to vote, it would thereby dilute the vote of ordinary citizens who are plainly viewed as constitutional persons. Thus, on Dworkin's view there is no good constitutional right-to-life argument.

3. The argument for a constitutional right against the criminalization of abortion

A. INDIVIDUAL RIGHTS AND STATE WRONGS

The argument against the derivative reason for the impermissibility of abortion leaves open the question of whether a state may criminalize abortion. It does not follow, from the fact that one particular justification for prohibiting abortion fails, that there is a right to have an abortion or a right against the criminalization of abortion. Such a conclusion would require stronger premises, such as an argument: (a) that there is an affirmative basis for treating the decision whether to have an abortion as a *right* – a special sort of protected interest or prerogative of personal decision – of a pregnant woman, or (b) that efforts to prohibit abortion invariably constitute impermissible state action by virtue of exemplifying an illegitimate ground of coercion or violating a condition of legitimate regulation. Dworkin constructs an argument that state prohibition of abortion based on a detached reason is impermissible, a version of (b). He also offers an argument that falls under (a). Below, we will suggest that Dworkin's argument (b) is more central to his analysis than some readers might have appreciated.

Dworkin begins his argument for a right to abortion by emphasizing the particularly strong interest a pregnant woman has in whether she may have an abortion and the undeniable importance to her of having the right to be the one to make the decision. Abortion is different from many other issues, he argues, because "the effect of coercion on particular people – pregnant women – is far greater. Making abortion criminal may destroy a woman's life" (154). Moreover, drawing together reproduction, contraception, and abortion cases, Dworkin argues that Justice Brennan was on solid ground in *Eisenstadt*[9] in concluding that "'[i]f the right of privacy means anything, it is the right of the *individual*, married or single, to be free from [unwarranted] government intrusion into matters so fundamentally affecting a person as the decision whether to bear or beget a child'"

(157–58). Dworkin characterizes this right in terms of a "principle of pro-creative autonomy" (157).[10]

The idea of an *especially strong interest in whether one bears a child* and *an especially weighty preference to be the decision maker on that issue*, however, cannot be all there is to Dworkin's view of the basis for the right to an abortion, for that would not account for his focus on the nature of the alleged sacredness of the life. Moreover, Dworkin has famously offered a general theory of rights that expressly denies that we should answer the question of what rights we have by asking what our fundamental or especially important interests are.[11] Of course, this leaves open the possibility that the existence of an especially important interest in being able to decide whether to have an abortion may be a necessary condition for the existence of a right. It simply means that the recognition of that interest cannot be all there is to the issue.

Indeed, for Dworkin, the right to abortion is best justified by focusing on what is impermissible, or wrong, about a state's attempt to criminalize abortion, not just by looking at why it is so important for a woman to be able to decide whether to have an abortion. For a state to criminalize abortion, on his view, is for it to adopt as an official position that the life of a fetus is sacred at the moment of conception. But the question of what makes life, or a life, sacred is itself an essentially religious issue: a fundamental issue in life about which individuals grope for answers, and on which individuals are most fundamentally spiritually committed. For a state to select an answer to that question and impose it through law, on Dworkin's view, is tantamount to telling citizens how they must think about what makes life sacred. This is to deny citizens the right to decide for themselves the most fundamental spiritual issues of life and death, and this, in turn, is a form of oppression. "[T]he constitutional question at stake is whether a state can impose on everyone an official interpretation of the inherent value of life" (159).

Three features of Dworkin's argument for the right to abortion are particularly noteworthy. First, it moves seamlessly between arguments of political morality about what is permissible from a normative point of view in the manner in which the government regulates individual conduct, on the one hand, and arguments of constitutional law about what the Constitution permits states to do and what individual rights it protects, on the other. Second, the argument hinges on a characterization of state prohibitions of abortion as impositions of an official view concerning the sanctity of life, impositions that deny an individual's prerogative to form her or his own view of the sanctity of life. Third, the argument contends that prohibitions on abortion constitute imposition of views on the sacredness of life and, as such, are instances of the same wrong that a state commits when it deprives persons of the opportunity to make their own decisions about which religious views to accept.

B. THE INTERCONNECTIONS BETWEEN THE MORAL AND LEGAL ARGUMENTS

Each of these three aspects of Dworkin's analysis plays a critical role in his account, and their interconnectedness is characteristically nuanced. Thus, for several fundamental premises in Dworkin's position, the status of certain normative propositions as principles entrenched in American constitutional law is pivotal. For example, he writes that "judicial decisions that have applied that general principle of privacy to reproduction, contraception, and abortion have been collected, through the common-law method of adjudication, into a distinct, more concrete principle that we may call the principle of procreative autonomy. It provides the best available justification for the Supreme Court's decisions about contraception" (158). In the light of Dworkin's jurisprudence, in the form most thoroughly developed in *Law's Empire*, the principle (among those that are well qualified from the point of view of "fit") that provides the best justification of existing decisions actually *is* the law.[12] The conclusion, which Dworkin explicitly draws, is that the principle of procreative autonomy is the law.

> The Supreme Court, in denying the state the specific power to make contraception criminal, presupposed the more general principle of procreative autonomy I am defending. That is important, as I have said, because almost no one believes that the Court's contraception decisions should now be overruled. The law's integrity demands that the principles necessary to support an authoritative set of judicial decisions must be accepted in other contexts as well. It might seem an appealing political compromise to apply the principle of procreative autonomy to contraception, which almost no one now thinks states can forbid, but not to abortion, which powerful constituencies violently oppose. But the point of integrity – the point of law itself – is exactly to rule out political compromises of that kind. We must be one nation of principle: our Constitution must represent conviction, not the tactical strategies of justices eager to satisfy as many political constituencies as possible (158).

Here, Dworkin is defending the right to an abortion in direct response to the argument of many people who believe that abortion is inexcusably destroying sacred human life – a belief that Dworkin himself concedes is perfectly reasonable, understandable, and central to their whole worldview – with a statement that *the law* forbids outlawing abortion. And he does so in a manner that, he believes, does not beg the question, for it is *what is already the law* (the Constitution) that forbids outlawing abortion. Because it is the Constitution, our higher law, it provides a legal, a political, and a moral reason for citizens and legislators to refrain from prohibiting abortion, and for citizens to take up an attitude of respect toward one another on this issue.

Dworkin also moves in the opposite direction. Indeed, the line of argument that involves the second and third points above actually moves from philosophical and moral analysis to legal argument. It is Dworkin's philosophical distinction between derivative and detached reasons for forbidding abortion, and his refutation of the alleged derivative reasons for prohibiting abortion from the moment of conception, that leads him to the view that it is a detached reason that animates the arguments of the anti-abortionists. This, in turn, leads him to a characterization of their position as an effort to legislate their "detached" reasons – to legislate a particular view of sacredness. And his essentially philosophical analysis of the nature of decisions about "sacredness," combined with his ethical analysis of the place of such decisions in a person's life, leads to his equation of such decisions with religious views. Finally, his analysis of such efforts to legislate on abortion as efforts to legislate religious views leads him to the legal claim that efforts to regulate abortion are violations of First Amendment religious freedom.

Our point in noting the two directions of Dworkin's arguments is not to charge him with inconsistency or question-begging. On the contrary, Dworkin is open about the lack of a hierarchy between legal and moral claims, and his denial of the autonomous nature of either legal or moral discourse is an earmark of his jurisprudential substance and methodology. In later sections of this chapter, however, we shall explore certain respects in which the seamless flow between legal and moral arguments in Dworkin's work may have unduly suppressed the contentiousness of some of his views.

C. THE ARGUMENT FROM SACREDNESS

Dworkin's argument that the prohibition of abortion is an instance of illegitimately coercing religious belief is a remarkably rich argument that relies, as just indicated, on a number of controversial premises. First, as already discussed, Dworkin argues that the anti-abortionists' position is based on the view that the life of a fetus is intrinsically valuable in a detached sense and that, therefore, the destruction of a fetus from the moment of conception is deplorable. Let us leave that discussion where it was. Second, he argues that views about what makes life valuable and what makes the wasting of human life deplorable are tantamount to views of what makes life sacred (71–84). Third, he suggests that there is a range of different views on what makes life sacred, and that this range falls on a spectrum, with one end emphasizing the significance of human creativity in producing things of value, and the other end emphasizing the role of nature or the divine in rendering things intrinsically valuable or sacred (89–94). Synthesizing these three points, Dworkin argues that the differences in opinion about the permissibility of abortion trace back to fundamentally different views about the degree to which it is the contribution of nature to life that makes life sacred and intrinsically valuable, and the degree to which it is the contribution of human agency that does so. More particularly, those who believe that abortion from the moment of conception is a deplorable waste of life hold a detached view, a commitment to the fundamental idea that nature's or the divine's contribution to life, as opposed to human agency, is principally what makes life valuable.

Next, Dworkin argues that views about the degree to which it is nature or the divine, as opposed to human agency (or vice versa), that makes life sacred are essentially religious views within the meaning of the religion clauses of the First Amendment to the United States Constitution (160–8). In *United States v. Seeger*,[13] Dworkin argues, the Court rejected a theistic criterion for the subject matter of religious beliefs (162–4). Yet on any plausible criterion of content for *religious* beliefs that does not make reference to theism, surely beliefs about what makes life inherently valuable – how much it is nature or the divine as opposed to human agency that makes human life valuable – should count as essentially religious. This contention is combined with the prior to reach the conclusion that the positions that motivate anti-abortion groups are essentially religious positions. It follows that, where anti-abortionists pass a law to effectuate their beliefs, they are in essence passing a law that deprives persons of the opportunity to decide for themselves on fundamentally religious questions about the meaning and value of life. This, according to Dworkin, is a violation of citizens' freedom to form their own religious beliefs. Now shifting expressly back to the law, Dworkin argues that this is a violation of a right enshrined in the First Amendment (164–6). The right to decide basic religious matters on one's own is, for Dworkin, a matter of autonomy, but it is rather different from the autonomy that is being asserted when a woman emphasizes her entitlement to say what happens to her own body. This right pertains to freedom from interference in thought and religious commitment (or liberty of conscience), not to dominion over one's own body (or "sovereignty" [54]). Although Dworkin himself does not expressly draw this distinction, one might say that a woman's right to abortion, on Dworkin's view, emerges from a fusion of these two aspects of autonomy.

C. The Right to Die

Dworkin argues that several structural features of the abortion debate are shared by the right-to-die debate (26–8). Indeed, *Life's Dominion* relies on the intuitively attractive proposal that there is much in common between these two enormously divisive issues that concern matters of life and death. And it offers startlingly provocative insights into the parallels between the two debates. Later in this chapter, we shall question certain aspects of the putative parallel. In this section, however, we largely will strive to present the most plausible version of the parallels and to apply the framework developed with regard to the abortion issue over onto the euthanasia issue.

1. The nature of the debate and the analogy to abortion

A singularly important problem in the euthanasia debate, according to Dworkin, is the conflation of two kinds of reasons for opposing physician-assisted suicide (190–6). One reason is that it is in the best interest of a patient to remain alive. This reason derives from a patient's own well-being and therefore can be called a derivative reason. On the other hand, and quite apart from the question of what is in a patient's own best interest, is the assertion that the destruction of a patient's life is itself the destruction of something intrinsically valuable, and therefore wrong. This is a detached reason for opposing physician-assisted suicide. Like the public abortion debate, the euthanasia debate has been mired by a confusion between these two kinds of reasons. And as with that debate, so here, becoming clear on the nature and the force of each of these putative reasons permits us to elucidate otherwise vexing issues regarding the morality and constitutionality of bans on euthanasia.

2. The argument for a derivative reason for permitting physician-assisted suicide

With regard to derivative reasons, there are at least two differences between the abortion and the euthanasia debates. Although Dworkin does not expressly draw these distinctions, it is helpful to do so. First, whereas the abortion issue largely concerns a dyadic question about membership – is a fetus at the moment of conception a member of the class of rights-holders or not? – the euthanasia debate is not largely dyadic or about membership; it is (in most of the cases Dworkin is concerned with) beyond contention that the suffering patient is a member of the class of rights-holders. Rather, the question is what is in the best interest of a patient, whom both sides treat as a rights-holder.

Second, the conservatives advocating a derivative reason against the permissibility of abortion were arguing that the rights and interests of a fetus demand that abortion be prohibited, and the liberals opposing the prohibition of abortion were denying that there was such a derivative reason. Now, there are *two* such debates in the euthanasia controversy, and one of them, but only one of them, parallels the above. Some conservatives contend that, although a patient is suffering from a painful terminal illness and expresses the wish to die, it is nevertheless in her best interest to remain alive; some liberals oppose this argument. However, there is also a reverse debate, which does not have an analogue in the abortion controversy. That is the liberal argument that there is a derivative reason for the patient to end her life rather than continuing it, and that such a reason provides an affirmative basis for a right to euthanasia; the conservative opposes this derivative reason. Dworkin addresses both of these types of derivative reasons in *Life's Dominion* (199–217).

Initially, it is worth noting that Dworkin's analytical framework actually provides a means of bolstering the argument against euthanasia with regard to a variety of individual claims (but not necessarily with regard to the law). In circumstances where a patient is enduring horrible suffering and experiencing no pleasure, and has little or no prospect of altering that situation, it can seem irrational to want to do anything else but die. However, many would argue that there is a derivative reason for staying alive in some such cases, and Dworkin interestingly supports that proposition. Dworkin argues at length for a distinction between experiential interests, on the one hand, and critical interests, on the other (201, 209–16). This is intended as a distinction within ethics and value theory; it does not relate to questions about how one ought to treat others but to questions about how one ought to live. Experiential interest is a subjective matter, not in the sense that everyone has their own view on it, but in the deeper sense that the value of what one is doing or has done is experiential value insofar as it is a matter of the quality of one's subjective experience of that aspect of one's life.

Thus, for example, the experiential value of a romantic relationship is, crudely put, a sum of all of the good and bad feelings one has had and continues to have in connection with that relationship. A hedonistic or utilitarian theorist of value would typically assert that a person's interests just are his or her experiential interests. Dworkin rejects this view, however. He contends that one has interests in how one's life goes that are not captured by the quality of the experiences one has. These are "critical interests," according to Dworkin, and they involve how well or badly various aspects of one's life has gone, how successful or unsuccessful it is as a life. Thus, to give an example inspired by Bernard Williams, a person's life has gone worse if his spouse has been cheating on him for decades, even if the spouse has succeeded in concealing her pervasive infidelity, perhaps especially so. The interest in not being cheated on is not exhausted by the interest in not having embarrassing and humiliating moments of suffering in which one learns that one has been cheated on – an experiential interest – or even in the diminution of the feeling of trust in a relationship. It is an interest in having led a life of mutual trust and candor, and this goes beyond experience to the objective reality of what one's life has in fact been. That is the sort of interest Dworkin is referring to by the phrase "critical interest."

On Dworkin's view, it is an open possibility that a person who is dying would lead a worse life if he simply killed himself immediately at the inception of the suffering in his illness rather than, say, taking the time to sort out his affairs and to allow himself, and his friends and family, to take in both the scope of his life and the tragedy of his impending death. That is not necessarily because the experience of winding down one's life would compensate for the experience of enormous suffering. It is because his life as a whole might display greater integrity, might hang together better. To this extent, Dworkin actually adds substance to the argument for a derivative reason against euthanasia, in some cases.

More important, however, Dworkin takes the position that one's critical interests sometimes lie in dying an earlier death than would occur if a dying patient were required simply to let the illness continue on indefinitely. Critical interests therefore sometimes provide a derivative reason for terminating life-sustaining treatment, for physician-assisted suicide, or for euthanasia. Dworkin in fact provides several moving and tragic examples where he takes this to be true (208–11). In such cases, the patients have very strong interests in being able to set the terms of their own death. Moreover, and in addition to the strength of this interest, there is a corresponding importance to the individual's prerogative to exert some control over the course of events concerning his or her own life: this is the importance of *autonomy*, not simply the weight of interests.

The upshot of this argument is that a consideration of derivative reasons against euthanasia does not lead to a defense for prohibiting euthanasia, just

as a consideration of the derivative reasons against abortion does not lead
to a defense for prohibiting abortion. With regard to the issue of abortion,
Dworkin contended that no derivative reason exists, at least not from the
moment of conception of a fetus, and moreover that the constitutional
structure does not permit us to regard fetuses at conception as persons. With
regard to euthanasia, Dworkin certainly recognizes the force of derivative
reasons against euthanasia, but he offers a powerful argument that there
are often derivative reasons for euthanasia.

3. The argument for a constitutional right against the criminalization of physician-assisted suicide

The nub of the analogy between the abortion and euthanasia controversies
lies in Dworkin's hermeneutical claim that the opponents of euthanasia
are relying largely on a detached reason rather than a derivative one. He
writes:

> The great moral issues of abortion and euthanasia, which bracket life in
> earnest, have a similar structure. Each involves decisions not just about the
> rights and interests of particular people, but about the intrinsic, cosmic
> importance of human life itself. In each case, opinions divide not because
> some people have contempt for values that others cherish, but, on the con-
> trary, because the values in question are at the center of everyone's lives, and
> no one can treat them as trivial enough to accept other people's orders about
> what they mean. Making someone die in a way that others approve, but he
> believes a horrifying contradiction of his life, is a devastating, odious form
> of tyranny (217).

As in the abortion context, the argument from the centrality of the
detached reason to the impermissibility of bans on euthanasia has several
steps. First, there is the hermeneutical claim that opponents of euthanasia and physician-assisted suicide are really best interpreted as relying on
a detached reason, an argument that because life itself is sacred it may
never be deliberately destroyed. Second, there is the claim that this sort of
sacredness view involves differing thoughts on the respective contributions
of nature and human agency. Third, there is the claim that this spectrum
is tantamount to a difference in religious belief. Fourth, there is the view
that to outlaw euthanasia is to impose a religious view on those whom
one is telling may not commit euthanasia. Now, moving back into the law
and drawing on the premise that the First Amendment forbids the imposition of beliefs of an essentially religious nature, Dworkin argues that the

prohibition of euthanasia and physician-assisted suicide violates the United States Constitution (238–40).

In the arena of abortion, Dworkin needs *Griswold*[14] – with its recognition of a privacy-based right to use contraception (and the reproductive rights that followed from it) – to generate what in constitutional law is the protected right of procreative autonomy (107, 157–60). In the arena of the right to die, at least with respect to physician-assisted suicide, he does not have the analogue to this. *Cruzan*'s "assumption" of a right of bodily integrity and a right to refuse life-sustaining treatment[15] is hardly as firm a support for the right to die as *Griswold*'s ringing endorsement of the right to use contraceptives was for the right of procreative autonomy. What is more, notwithstanding the *Casey* joint opinion's coupling of *Cruzan*'s right of bodily integrity with "*Griswold* liberty" to support reaffirming *Roe*[16] – which might imply that the two are equally firm and closely analogous – the joint opinion's own formulation of personal autonomy might provide greater support for a right to physician-assisted suicide than does *Cruzan*. *Glucksberg*, however, rejected the holding of the lower courts that *Casey* was "highly instructive" and "almost prescriptive" concerning the right to physician-assisted suicide.[17] In any case, even though Dworkin's arguments from integrity and principle, and for the virtues of coherence, have considerable force in constitutional law generally, they may have less force in an area like euthanasia, where our moral and factual understandings are still developing or in flux. Here, arguments for the virtues of incrementalism may have more force than they do in constitutional law generally.[18]

II. RIGHTS OF AUTONOMY WITHOUT NEUTRALITY

Among the most significant aspects of *Life's Dominion* is its avoidance of neutrality arguments. Whereas liberals are often derided for aspiration to forms of neutrality that are neither possible nor attractive, Dworkin's liberalism – and strikingly the liberalism of *Life's Dominion* – is plainly not rooted in neutrality. It is thus illuminating to understand Dworkin's versions of the arguments for the right to abortion and the right to die in relation to communitarian and civic republican criticisms of liberalism, notably those of Michael Sandel. Sandel argues that our democracy is engulfed by discontent because our public philosophy – "the political theory implicit in our practice, the assumptions about citizenship and freedom that inform our public life" – is impoverished and inadequate to the challenges of self-government.[19] That public philosophy, he contends, is a form of liberal political theory whose central idea is that, since citizens disagree about the best way to live, the government should be neutral and not affirm in law any particular conception of the good life. Instead, it should provide a framework of rights that respects persons as free and independent selves, capable of choosing their own values and ends. In searching for the "public philosophy implicit in our practice," Sandel focuses on constitutional law, "for it is here that the assumptions and commitments of the procedural republic" – its aspiration to neutrality and its conception of the freely choosing, "unencumbered self" – "most vividly appear."[20] He means especially the privacy and autonomy cases that Dworkin seeks to justify.

Sandel advances a famous formulation of the "neutrality" critique of liberal political and constitutional theory of the sort commonly associated with John Rawls and Dworkin. Dworkin's justifications for the rights to procreative autonomy and the right to die are not vulnerable to Sandel's critique. First, he rejects the requirement, in Sandel's formulation, that we "bracket[ ] moral and religious questions where politics is concerned."[21] Presumably, Sandel's formulation is aimed primarily at Rawls's idea of public reason: the requirement that political and legal decisions be justifiable on grounds that citizens generally can reasonably be expected to accept.[22] Rightly or wrongly, both critics and defenders of Rawls's idea of public reason have conceived it as a "gatekeeper" that keeps certain moral and religious convictions and arguments out of politics.[23]

Dworkin, in his Tanner Lectures on liberal equality, defends a liberal political philosophy on the basis of the "challenge model of ethics."[24] He states that liberalism, as commonly defended, apparently asks people to be detached and impartial in the political sphere, when they are, in fact, attached, passionate, and committed in their personal lives.[25] In contrast to this "discontinuity," he posits a continuity between what he calls the personal, including the realm of ethics, and the political.[26] He contemplates that people will bring their moral and religious convictions and arguments to bear in politics (a view that he certainly carries forward in *Life's Dominion*).

Put another way, Dworkin rejects the need for a "gatekeeper." In the first instance, as a general matter, he lets moral and religious convictions and arguments in. But in the final analysis, with respect to abortion and euthanasia, he argues that the First Amendment's protection of liberty of conscience prohibits government from imposing a particular moral or religious conception of how best to respect the intrinsic value of the sanctity of life. Instead, he argues, persons have the right to make the ultimate decision for themselves. This argument stands in place of a requirement of public reason (or bracketing or a gatekeeper).[27]

Dworkin does not make "autonomy arguments alone"[28] to justify the rights of procreative autonomy and the right to die. In *Life's Dominion*, he propounds a notably "moralized" liberalism, making moral arguments for these rights and defending the authority of government to moralize concerning persons' exercise of them. He writes that America's political heritage is characterized by "two sometimes competing traditions": "The first is the tradition of personal freedom. The second assigns government responsibility for guarding the public moral space in which all citizens live." The analysis continues: "A good part of constitutional law consists in reconciling these two ideas" (150).

Thus, Dworkin writes that the government may encourage women to "treat decisions about abortion as matters of moral importance" and may encourage women to take the decision responsibly, reflecting conscientiously on how best to respect the intrinsic value of the sanctity of life (150, 153). Indeed, it is telling against Sandel's critique that he fails to acknowledge Dworkin's praise of the *Casey* joint opinion for recognizing a proper role for government in encouraging responsibility when intrinsic values, such as respect for the sanctity of life, are at issue. At the same time, Dworkin argues that the constitutional right to procreative autonomy rests on a right to make essentially religious decisions for ourselves and that the state must respect a pregnant woman's right to make the ultimate decision: "If we aim at responsibility, we must leave citizens free, in the end, to decide as they think right, because that is what moral responsibility entails" (150). And he argues that the government may not impose a particular conception of how best to respect the sanctity of life with respect to abortion and euthanasia. To do so, he argues, would violate liberty of conscience and religious toleration (160–8).

Thus, Dworkin justifies the rights to procreative autonomy and the right to die without relying on a strong conception of neutrality. All in all, whatever force Sandel's neutrality critique may have with respect to other versions of liberalism, it is not well taken as against Dworkin's version. (We also would argue that it is not well taken as against Rawls's political philosophy and against the kind of Rawlsian constitutional theory that one of us has developed.[29])

Dworkin's argument is grounded, not in neutrality or in "autonomy rights alone," but in a deontology of state conduct. That is, as shown above, he advances a theory that derives from a conception of the permissible grounds for governmental decision. His concern is with respecting limits on the grounds for governmental decision and with avoiding governmental coercion concerning questions such as how best to respect the sanctity of life. More generally, his theory is a theory that limits the grounds on which a state may restrict or regulate our basic liberties, and he specifically denies that he is articulating a theory of rights that asks what our fundamental or especially important interests are and what freedoms are necessary to secure or further them.[30] For example, despite Dworkin's justification for a right of procreative autonomy, his theory differs importantly from a theory of autonomy rooted in a conception of the person and what is necessary for the development and exercise of moral powers, or the like. (In this respect, his theory differs from the Rawlsian theory of deliberative autonomy that one of us has propounded.[31])

This feature of Dworkin's theory in part accounts for why he contemplates a relatively larger space (than do most liberals) for governmental moralizing. On his view, there is a large space between complete, hands-off noninterference with liberty, individuality, autonomy, or choice (of the sort strong autonomy or individuality theorists advocate and Sandel criticizes) and coercion. Furthermore, government need not, and should not, be neutral in that large space. It may moralize, encourage responsibility, and the like, so long as it does not coerce the ultimate decision.[32]

III. THE LIBERTY OF CONSCIENCE ARGUMENT: SOME CONCERNS

Dworkin's argument from liberty of conscience is attractive and powerful. It provides gravity to the right to procreative autonomy and the right to die. It may be harder for conservatives, civic republicans, and communitarians to ridicule these rights, commonly justified in terms of autonomy, if they are grounded in liberty of conscience than if they are justified on the basis of the weight or importance of the interest for self-fulfillment, individuality, or the like. Dworkin also strives mightily at giving a sense to the common intuition that prohibition of abortion or euthanasia infringes religious freedom. Finally, Dworkin's argument is rhetorically moving: it is certain to rouse passion against coercion, oppression, and tyranny.

Yet Dworkin's argument for these rights on grounds of liberty of conscience runs into difficulties both as a matter of justification and as a matter of strategic politics. We begin with some difficulties of justification. First, there are doctrinal difficulties in the cases concerning religious freedom. Abner Greene has argued that "Dworkin has smuggled a broad autonomy argument into the religion clauses, which are best read as covering a narrower domain."[33] For, he argues, "Dworkin is wrong to assert that the

Supreme Court has 'decided' that religion for First Amendment purposes is not confined to some version of theistic belief"[34] but extends to include beliefs that are "sufficiently similar in content to plainly religious views" (155). The Supreme Court case on which Dworkin relies for this claim is *United States v. Seeger*.[35] The trouble, Greene argues, is that *Seeger* is a case of statutory interpretation, not constitutional interpretation.[36] That is, the case involved interpretation of the conscientious-objection provision of the military-draft statute, exempting from the military "persons who by reason of their religious training and belief are conscientiously opposed to participation in war in any form." It did not involve an authoritative constitutional interpretation of the First Amendment's religion clauses. This is not to say that *Seeger* is irrelevant to how we ought to think about what counts as religion under the First Amendment, just that it is considerably weaker authority for such a view than Dworkin would wish.

Beyond that, there may be not only constitutional but also philosophical problems with Dworkin's contention that beliefs about the intrinsic value of life are essentially religious in nature. To be sure, they certainly are controversial. But part of the point of Dworkin's book is to eschew "bracketing" issues because they are controversial.

Second – and we only gesture at what has become a very delicate issue of constitutional law – Dworkin does not reckon adequately with the differences between conduct and belief. To sanction persons for a racially motivated crime, or for an act of employment discrimination based on sexual orientation, for example, is not to violate their right to hold particular beliefs about race or sexual orientation. Nor is it to violate their First Amendment rights to express those beliefs. A fortiori, to sanction someone for engaging in conduct that the state has reasons to prohibit is not to sanction someone for the belief that such conduct is appropriate or permissible. Therefore, from its being a violation of religious freedom to prohibit someone from believing there is a right to die (or a right to have an abortion) or expressing that belief, it does not follow automatically that it is a violation of religious freedom to fail to recognize a right to die (or a right to have an abortion). Dworkin's free-exercise based arguments for the right to die and the right to an abortion may be, to this extent, more vulnerable than he indicates.

Beyond the level of theoretical justification, Dworkin's arguments appear to be, in part, efforts at a sort of political diplomacy that would provide each side with face-saving ways of recognizing both the rights to abortion and physician assisted-suicide, and the obligations to take seriously the moral responsibilities involved in exercising these rights. To the extent that these arguments have strategic aims to fortify what Dworkin believes are important liberties within a volatile political environment, it is an open question whether these fortification strategies are well calculated or will be effective. Dworkin's argument is narrower than it first appears, and it may be more readily averted than one might think. Because he casts the arguments for the right to abortion and the right to die in terms of autonomy, and because he notes or suggests similarities between his arguments and the autonomy arguments made in the Due Process liberty cases, one might readily assimilate his arguments to those autonomy arguments. But his argument is narrower: it emphasizes religious liberty, not autonomy generally, and it simply precludes government from imposing a conception of how best to respect the sanctity of life, not from pursuing conceptions of the good that violate autonomy generally. And so, his argument rules out of bounds a specific religious ground for denying abortion and euthanasia, but it does not protect these rights in order to secure the conditions necessary for the development and exercise of persons' moral powers, notwithstanding the grounds the state might offer to justify the denials. To that extent, his justification for these rights may be more easily averted or overridden. Because his focus is on limiting the grounds for governmental action rather than protecting autonomy in its own right, his justification may leave it open to the state to justify restricting or regulating the right to die on other grounds. That is, the state may be able to justify restricting the right to die if it can provide justifications besides promoting respect for the sanctity of life (or justifications that are pretexts for promoting respect for the sanctity of life). For example, in *Glucksberg*, the Supreme Court credited, as legitimate state interests, numerous grounds or concerns that the state had advanced to justify the prohibition on physician-assisted suicide, such as protecting the vulnerable from coercion.[37] None of these justifications explicitly invoked or obviously ran afoul of liberty of conscience. Therefore, those state justifications for prohibiting physician-assisted suicide may be able to elude Dworkin's arguments for a right to die that includes physician-assisted suicide.

IV. CONCLUDING REMARKS

Dworkin's arguments for the rights to abortion and physician-assisted suicide from liberty of conscience would be on firmer ground if he were to cast them in terms of autonomy generally rather than in terms of religious liberty specifically. Ironically, it may be that Dworkin's strategic aim of articulating a "textual home" (160) for these rights in the First Amendment's protection of religious liberty has obscured the force of his position, both legally and philosophically. As a legal matter, the broader Due Process right to autonomy is in fact where the United States Supreme Court has landed – at least on the abortion issue – and their religion clause interpretations have become increasingly cramped. But the larger point is that Dworkin's philosophical motivation for relating his concerns to freedom of religion should not be confused with an insistence on the claim that rights to abortion or physician-assisted suicide are based in a notion of freedom of religion. What is attractive to Dworkin is the idea that the autonomy in question is not the license to do what one wants; it is, he contends, a form of liberty of conscience that is correlative to the state's duty not to interfere with fundamental decisions on how one views the sanctity of life. But the state's obligation to respect a sphere of autonomy on such fundamental questions is not specifically an obligation to respect religious participation or religious belief. On the contrary, the obligation to respect religious commitments is more cogently understood as an implication of a broader obligation to respect liberty of conscience. Although it is surely a large burden to provide the justification of the claim that there is such an obligation – not based in neutrality, and not limited to religion – there are resources within classical liberal and constitutional theory, and within Dworkin's own work, to generate such a justification.

Dworkin thus lays out the basis for a powerful pair of arguments beginning with a state obligation to refrain from interfering with core domains of liberty of conscience and culminating in a right to abortion and a right to physician-assisted suicide. Neither argument is problem free as a matter of political theory or constitutional law, but both are direct, clear, cogent, and resonant with what are plainly fundamental tenets of liberal political and constitutional commitments. Moreover, Dworkin's analysis strikingly displays the parallelism of the arguments, both as an abstract matter and as they have been entrenched within a political/cultural clash.

ACKNOWLEDGMENTS

We would like to thank Abner Greene, Charles Kelbley, Linda McClain, and Arthur Ripstein for valuable conversations and comments, and Kristina Mentone and Devon Filas for helpful research assistance.

Notes

1. Ronald Dworkin, *Life's Dominion: An Argument about Abortion, Euthanasia, and Individual Freedom* (New York: Alfred A. Knopf, 1993), 28. Hereinafter, citations to this work will be indicated in text by giving page numbers within parentheses.

2. For segregation and affirmative action, see for example Ronald Dworkin, *Law's Empire* (Cambridge, MA: Harvard University Press, 1986), 379–99; Ronald Dworkin, *A Matter of Principle* (Cambridge, MA: Harvard University Press, 1985), 293–331. For gay rights, see for example Ronald Dworkin, *Sovereign Virtue: The Theory and Practice of Equality* (Cambridge, MA: Harvard University Press, 2000), 453–65. For pornography, see for example Ronald Dworkin, *Freedom's Law: The Moral Reading of the American Constitution* (Cambridge, MA: Harvard University Press, 1996), 214–43.

3. Roe v. Wade, 410 U.S. 113 (1973).

4. Planned Parenthood v. Casey, 505 U.S. 833 (1992).

5. Cruzan v. Director, Missouri Dept. of Health, 497 U.S. 261 (1989).

6. Washington v. Glucksberg, 521 U.S. 702 (1997).

7. Ronald Dworkin, *Taking Rights Seriously* (Cambridge, MA: Harvard University Press, 1977).

8. 410 U.S. at 162.

9. Eisenstadt v. Baird, 405 U.S. 438, 453 (1972).

10. As we discuss below, Dworkin's "principle of procreative autonomy" is not actually supposed to refer to an idea that relies on the importance of choice to an individual *abstracted from or independent of* the wrongfulness of the state's attempt to dictate an official position on this matter.

11. See for example Dworkin, *A Matter of Principle*, 65–6; Dworkin, *Taking Rights Seriously*, 272–3.

12. See Dworkin, *Law's Empire*, 225–58.

13. 380 U.S. 163 (1965).

14. Griswold v. Connecticut, 381 U.S. 479 (1965).

15. 497 U.S. at 279 (the Court assumed that there was a right to refuse life-sustaining treatment, but the holding of *Cruzan* was that even assuming such a right, states were permitted to condition the exercise of such a right on a showing by clear-and-convincing evidence of the patient's wish).

16. *Casey*, 505 U.S. at 857.

17. 521 U.S. at 726 (the Supreme Court in *Glucksberg* rejected the argument that there was a Fourteenth Amendment right to physician-assisted suicide).

18. This is not to say that we go all the way with Cass Sunstein and argue for judicial incrementalism or minimalism more generally with respect to issues about which there is moral disagreement. See Cass R. Sunstein, *One Case at a Time: Judicial Minimalism on the Supreme Court* (Cambridge, MA: Harvard University Press, 1999), 75–116.

19. Michael J. Sandel, *Democracy's Discontent: America in Search of a Public Philosophy* (Cambridge, MA: Harvard University Press, 1996), 4.

20. Ibid., 116.

21. Ibid., 18–19.

22. John Rawls, *Political Liberalism* (New York: Columbia University Press, 1993), 213–20, 223–30.

23. See Stephen Holmes, "The Gatekeeper," *New Republic*, Oct. 11, 1993, 39 (review of John Rawls, *Political Liberalism*).

24. Ronald Dworkin, "Foundations of Liberal Equality," in *The Tanner Lectures on Human Values*, vol. XI, ed. Grethe B. Peterson (Salt Lake City, UT: University of Utah Press, 1990), 1, 57–88. (Portions of Dworkin's Tanner Lectures are revised and reprinted in Dworkin, *Sovereign Virtue*, 237–84.)

25. Ibid., 12–16.

26. Ibid., 16–22.

27. Furthermore, Dworkin rejects the priority of the right over the good, a central tenet of the form of liberalism Sandel criticizes. Ibid.

28. Sandel, *Democracy's Discontent*, 106.

29. See James E. Fleming, *Securing Constitutional Democracy: The Case of Autonomy* (Chicago: University of Chicago Press, 2006); James E. Fleming and Linda C. McClain, "In Search of a Substantive Republic," *Texas Law Review*, 76 (1997): 509.

30. Dworkin, *A Matter of Principle*, 65–6; Dworkin, *Taking Rights Seriously*, 272–3.

31. See Fleming, *Securing Constitutional Democracy*, 62–74.

32. See Linda C. McClain, *The Place of Families: Fostering Capacity, Equality, and Responsibility* (Cambridge, MA: Harvard University Press, 2006), 43–8; Linda C. McClain, "Toleration, Autonomy, and Governmental Promotion of Good Lives: Beyond 'Empty' Toleration to Toleration as Respect," *Ohio State Law Journal* 59 (1998): 19, 91–100.

33. Abner S. Greene, "Uncommon Ground," *George Washington Law Review* 62 (1994): 646, 665.

34. Ibid., 663.

35. 380 U.S. 163 (1965).

36. Greene, "Uncommon Ground," 663–4.

37. 521 U.S. at 728–35. One of us believes that these reasons, coming from Rehnquist, were altogether disingenuous and that the *Glucksberg* decision was a constitutional travesty and a constitutional tragedy. See James E. Fleming, "Constitutional Tragedy in Dying: Or Whose Tragedy Is It, Anyway?" in *Constitutional Stupidities, Constitutional Tragedies*, ed. William N. Eskridge, Jr., and Sanford Levinson (New York: New York University Press, 1998), 162.

Hercules, Abraham Lincoln, the United States Constitution, and the Problem of Slavery

SANFORD LEVINSON

I. DWORKIN ON SLAVERY-ACCOMMODATING JUDGES

On December 5, 1975, Ronald Dworkin published in *The Times Literary Supplement*[1] a review of Robert M. Cover's now-classic *Justice Accused: Antislavery and the Judicial Process*.[2] Cover's central subjects were Northern judges, many of them professing to be antislavery, who nonetheless asserted that they were duty bound to enforce the iniquitous Fugitive Slave Laws of 1793 and 1850. Perhaps the most notable example was the 1842 decision in *Prigg v. Pennsylvania*,[3] written by Joseph Story, perhaps the most eminent member of the Court at that time in part because of his extrajudicial status both as the Dane Professor of Law at the newly founded Harvard Law School as well as the author of a three-volume treatise on the Constitution. In *Prigg*, Story described the Constitution as containing a "fundamental"[4] recognition of the rights of slaveowners, which meant not only that the Fugitive Slave Act passed by Congress in 1793 was perfectly constitutional but also, and just as ominously, that Pennsylvania's "liberty law," designed to accord suspected fugitives some basic rights of due process of law, was unconstitutional as an interference with the national rights granted slaveholders by the Constitution. Dworkin aptly wrote that "these statutes, particularly the [Fugitive Slave Act of 1850], offended ordinary notions of due process in several ways: the federal official was a mere commissioner who received a higher fee if the alleged slave was sent back than if he was not, there was no question of jury trial, and the defendant was not allowed to contest whether he was in fact a slave, that issue being left to be decided in the slave state after his return."

Dworkin's interest in Cover's book is easily explained. He has written, for example, of "individual rights [as] the zodiac sign under which" America was born, though he quickly conceded that the record of the United States "in recognizing and protecting these rights has been less than spectacular."[5] This being said, though, he has systematically commended, for what is now more than a quarter-century, a "moral reading" of American legal materials that pays full attention to the principles ostensibly underlying our institutions.[6] This would, presumably, reduce the gap between presumed aspirations and actual performance. Quite obviously, the worst example of that gap is slavery.

In assessing Cover (and the judges about whom he was writing), Dworkin might simply have focused on the substantive injustice of chattel slavery. Interestingly enough, though, one need not read his constitutional critique of the Fugitive Slave Laws as *necessarily* extending to the underlying institution itself.[7] Instead the emphasis appears to be on the propensity of the 1850 Act to generate "type-2" errors (i.e., false positives) rather than on the fact that even nonerroneous identifications of an accused runaway still involved collaboration in a great injustice. The relative "modesty" of Dworkin's critique serves to illustrate some important questions about Dworkin's overall jurisprudence as applied to the United States Constitution, the central topic of this chapter.

Although Dworkin generally praised Cover's "splendid" book, he criticized Cover for remaining basically in thrall to the classic distinction between positive law on the one hand, justified independently of substantive content entirely by reference to its pedigree in a particular decision-making process, be it legislative or that of a constitutional convention, and natural law on the other, which gives absolute priority to the actual substance of the ostensible law in question and declares invalid – that is, not "really" law – those commands that violate the norms of natural law. Natural law, of course, rests on a complex and highly controversial web of ontological and epistemological propositions. As Dworkin writes in *Law's Empire*, a natural lawyer has, at the end of the day, almost no interest in such conventional legal materials as "the constitution's text, the history of its enactment, prior decisions of the Supreme Court's interpreting it, and long-standing traditions of our political culture."[8] Instead, the natural lawyer views the Constitution as "only what the best theory of abstract justice and fairness would produce by way of ideal theory."[9]

In addition, though Dworkin did not press this particular point, in antebellum America natural law was simply too dangerous a theory for judges to embrace, given the widespread agreement, even by many Southerners, that slavery in fact violated the norms of natural justice.[10] Full adherence to natural law – including its natural-rights variant found in the Declaration of Independence – might well delegitimize the American political system insofar as it did indeed include legal recognition of the institution of chattel slavery. Instead, as Chief Justice John Marshall insisted in his opinion in *The Antelope*,[11] which includes a number of references to the injustice of slavery, the judge must act within the role constraints of the "jurist" and resist any temptation to occupy the role of the "moralist." For Marshall, the proper "jurist" must pay heed to "those principles of action which are sanctioned by the usages, the national acts, and the general assent, of that portion of the world of which he considers himself as a part, and to whose law the appeal is made. If we resort to this standard as the test of international law," he asserted, "the question . . . is decided in favor of the legality of the [slave] trade."[12]

We might well be interested in how Marshall's argument fits Dworkin's now-familiar "third theory of law" that, he suggested, *could* have been accepted by judges of the time and therefore would have allowed them to acknowledge at least some limited rights of (purported) slaves that would be "much more the responsibility of judges to protect," in distinct contrast to "the national policies of appeasement" of slaveowners that Cover discussed and Marshall appears to exemplify. As he would later elaborate at far greater length in such classic works as *Taking Rights Seriously* and *Law's Empire*, Dworkin pointed to "the theory that the law of a community consists not simply in the discrete statutes and rules that its officials enact but in the general principles of justice and fairness that these statutes and rules, taken together, presuppose by way of implicit justification." With regard to the American constitution, these presuppositions include "a conception of individual freedom antagonistic to slavery, a conception of procedural justice that condemned the procedures established by the Fugitive Slave Acts, and a conception of federalism inconsistent with the idea that the State of Massachusetts had no power to supervise the capture of men and women within its territory." Key to his argument is the denial that such principles were "simply the personal morality of a few judges"; instead, and crucially, they were "more central to the law than were the particular and transitory policies of the slavery compromise." As already suggested, Dworkin did not indicate in his one-page review whether the mistake of the judges was in not invalidating the Fugitive Slave Law in every jot or tittle, given the indefensibility of chattel slavery, or, rather, whether their error was more limited, reaching only to their willingness to uphold those parts of the law outlined above that so clearly violated norms of due process. The first, obviously, is a far more radical view than the second.

The well-known conservative philosopher Shirley Robin Letwin felt called on to criticize Dworkin's "third way" in a letter to the *TLS*.[13] She viewed Dworkin as engaging in a fundamental attack on "the rule of law." "While on the bench," she argued, "the judge has a *moral obligation* to uphold the law even when he dislikes it because otherwise there can be no rule of law."[14] She would have agreed fully with Marshall's "jurist-moralist" distinction articulated in *The Antelope*. Responding, Dworkin, I believe justifiably, accused Letwin of misunderstanding his argument.[15] In no way, after all, did he argue that mere "dislike" for a law justified a judge in refusing to enforce it. His point, he insisted, was that there really was no sufficiently "settled law" that determined that the cases be decided as the judges of the time in fact decided them. Instead, he wrote, "the constitutional and statutory provisions were so abstract and unclear, and the legal background so ambiguous, that there was no settled law to follow." Had he been writing later in his career, he would undoubtedly have emphasized that the judges in question were called on to "interpret" the law rather than to engage in anything that might count as mechanical application of settled law. That is, it was what he would famously call a "hard case," calling on the high arts of judicial craft. And this craft most definitely, he insisted, did not call on judges to impose "their own ideas of political policy or morality" but rather "to attempt to show that the morality they use to interpret the law is drawn from the legal system as a whole, and not from their personal convictions alone."[16] Dworkin has offered intricate analyses of the ways that particular interpretations of legal materials "fit" well with the deep morality underlying the system and thus serve to justify them. He turned Letwin's own expressed concerns on her, saying that his idea "limits rather than extends the discretion of judges"; they should indeed be constrained by "the legal system as a whole," which includes the background principles that he pointed to. If a judge's own notions do *not*, as a matter of empirical fact, "fit" well with these principles, then they most certainly cannot serve as the basis for legitimate decision.

It is a full three decades since Ronald Dworkin published this relatively short, albeit extremely rich, review, and one might wonder why I am beginning a consideration of Dworkin's constitutional jurisprudence with it. One answer I have already given: chattel slavery was the heart of what the great historian Don Fehrenbacher has labeled *The Slaveholding Republic*.[17] Even if one rejects, as does Fehrenbacher, the view of the abolitionist William Lloyd Garrison that the Constitution was a "Conspiracy with Death and an Agreement with Hell" from the very moment of its 1787 creation, it is hard – indeed impossible, once one reads Fehrenbacher's impressive, and dismaying, evidence – to avoid the conclusion that it had certainly become that by the time Garrison actually issued his charge in the 1830s, given the quite consistent propensity of decision makers (members of Congress, presidents, and judges) to offer pro- rather than antislavery readings of their duties.

There is a second reason, however, which is that this review represents the only significant attempt by Dworkin of which I am aware to confront chattel slavery within the overall context of his elaborate jurisprudential system. Not only has he never chosen to reprint the book review; more importantly, he has never returned to the subject, whatever his famous willingness to confront some of the most knotty problems presented in contemporary law and political theory, especially those involving the meaning of "equality" or, in his famous phrase, "equal concern and respect."[18] Although it is obviously true that formal slavery no longer is part of the American legal system, some of these contemporary issues, such as the legitimacy of racial preferences, are inextricably linked to that aspect of the American experience; even if there were no such linkage, though, the problem of how to respond, as a conscientious lawyer, to the presence of institutionalized slavery should remain of interest to anyone interested in problems of general jurisprudence. Moreover, of course, there remained in force until the early 1990s in South Africa a full-scale system of racial apartheid, administered in part by well-trained judges, a topic that generated an earnest and important debate that, to my knowledge, did not include any contributions by Dworkin.[19]

The question before us, then, is how a Dworkinian judge, including the famous Hercules, introduced to jurisprudence the same year as the Cover review in his classic article "Hard Cases,"[20] would respond to a panoply of problems surrounding chattel slavery. Hercules' task is nothing less than the "construct[ion of] a scheme of abstract and concrete principles that provides a coherent justification for all common law precedents and, so far as these are to be justified on principle, constitutional and statutory provisions as well."[21] Still, as noted earlier, this does not seem to be equal to a duty to adhere to what might be termed the "best morality," for that would transform Hercules from a "jurist" devoted to law, however complexly conceived, into an unabashed "moralist" who can, as a consequence, *always* achieve what I have elsewhere termed the "happy ending" of concluding that law requires (or prohibits) exactly what morality, best conceived, would require or prohibit.

Dworkin, however, resists the charge that he is in effect committed to a jurisprudence of happy endings. This is most clearly revealed in his introduction to his tellingly titled *Freedom's Law: The Moral Reading of the American Constitution.*[22] Thus, he notes "an objection that has been made to my arguments before, and that I anticipate will be made again . . . , that the results I claim for the moral reading, in particular constitutional cases, magically coincide with those I favor politically myself." Indeed, he cites "one commentator"[23] as suggesting "that my arguments always seem to have happy endings. Or, at any rate, liberal endings."[24] He offers a demurral.

He notes, for example, that although he personally supports "a theory of economic justice that would require substantial redistribution of wealth in rich political societies,"[25] he rejects views like those famously articulated in a 1969 *Harvard Law Review* article by Frank Michelman[26] that argued that the United States Constitution, best understood, *requires* at least a minimum-subsistence welfare state that, by definition, rests on compelled redistribution from rich to poor. In contrast to Michelman, "I have insisted that [legal] integrity would bar any attempt to argue from the abstract moral clauses of the Bill of Rights, or from any other part of the Constitution, to any such result."[27] To at least some extent, then, Dworkin remains an adherent, in however attenuated a way, to a classical doctrine of legal positivism, which is (some kind of) separation between law and morality. To be sure, he has devoted most of his career to reminding us, quite helpfully, of the extent to which moral judgments inevitably wend their way into the framework of our legal arguments. This being said, it is nonetheless true that not every (presumptively true) moral argument can dominate legal materials that reject the outcome required by morality.

The great tragedy of American history is slavery. Concomitantly, a test of any theory of law is how it responds to chattel slavery. Does it generate "happy," albeit quite possibly completely ahistorical, endings, or, on the contrary, does it embrace someone like Joseph Story (or John Marshall) as a true exemplar of the Herculean judge, whatever the tragic dimensions of accepting that role?

II. THE CONSTITUTIONAL ENTRENCHMENT OF CHATTEL SLAVERY

I have already introduced one central topic of this essay, the status of fugitive slave laws. Below, I shall treat two additional examples. The first is the Missouri Compromise that, in 1820, divided the new American territories added to the domain of the United States through the Louisiana Purchase into "free" and "slave" territories, depending on their presence north or south of latitude 36°30' north. This is a clear case of a "checkerboard" law that is in great tension with what Dworkin terms "legal integrity." My final example is the emancipation of slaves through presidential proclamation. First, however, I will fill in some of the historical details before returning, in Section III, to the thought of Ronald Dworkin. Consider the fact that "legal slave owners within such Union States as Kentucky and Missouri were permitted to recover their [fugitive] slaves until late in the [Civil War,] when the fugitive slave acts" were finally repealed on June 28, 1864.[28] To explain this, one might, of course, simply suggest that the slaveowners in these states had to be appeased, lest they throw their support to the Confederacy; such appeasement included responding to these slaveowners' expectations that their fugitives would continue to be subject to forced return. But it may be too facile to adopt the political explanation as conclusive. After all, Fehrenbacher notes that eleven Republicans in 1863 supported an amendment that would have kept in force the 1793 Act, "apparently agreeing with [the amendment's] author, John Sherman of Ohio, that certain southerners were still *entitled* to at least minimal protection of a right guaranteed by the Constitution."[29] There is, then, a second explanation for hesitation to repeal the act in toto, as well as explaining the peculiar fact that Lincoln's famous Emancipation Proclamation, issued on January 1, 1863, formally exempted from its force federally occupied lands in (partially) conquered Southern states as well as the Unionist slave states.[30] What might explain such actions?

Abraham Lincoln, who consistently opposed slavery on moral grounds throughout his career, appears to agree with Story's basic point that the protection of slaves as property was "fundamental" to the American polity. Consider a remarkable argument he made in the Lincoln-Douglas debate with regard to the Constitution and fugitive slave laws.[31] Thus, after quoting the text of Article IV, clause 2,[32] Lincoln states that it

> is powerless without specific legislation to enforce it. Now on what ground would a member of Congress who is opposed to slavery in the abstract [as Lincoln was] vote for a fugitive law, *as I would deem it my duty to do so?* Because there is a Constitutional right which needs legislation to enforce it. And although it is distasteful to me, I have sworn to support the Constitution, and having so sworn I cannot conceive that I do support it if I withheld from that right any necessary legislation to make it practical.[33]

Lincoln not only concedes Congress's power to pass such laws, itself a controversial proposition given the total lack of any such enumerated power in Article I, Section 8 of the Constitution; rather, Lincoln also appears to impose on members of Congress a constitutional duty – and not merely a permission – to support at least some fugitive slave laws, whatever one's private views as to the evil of slavery. It is, of course, not only judges who take solemn oaths to support the Constitution. *All* public officials, by terms of Article VI of the Constitution itself, are required to take such an oath, and one therefore should expect (or at least hope) that "conscientious legislators" and presidents will be as scrupulous as judges in fulfilling their solemn promises.

The second example mentioned above, slavery in the territories, was central to Lincoln's political career, for the Republican Party, in important ways an outgrowth of the Free Soil Party of the late 1840s, was committed to preventing the expansion of slavery beyond the states where it then existed. The key case, of course, was *Dred Scott*,[34] in which the Supreme Court in 1857 in effect declared unconstitutional the platform of the Republican Party insofar as it pledged passage of legislation that would indeed prohibit slavery in the territories of the United States. The specific topic of the case was the legitimacy of the Missouri Compromise of 1820 and its division of these vast new domains of the United States into "slave" and "free" territories. This legislation was, according to the majority, unconstitutional. Crucial for our purposes is the rationale articulated by Justice Catron in a concurring opinion. The Constitution, he said, "secures to the respective States and their citizens an entire EQUALITY of rights, privileges, and immunities."[35] As Taney wrote in his own opinion, Congress must act as a "trustee" for the entire citizenry, which meant that access to the territories must be guaranteed on equal terms to *all* citizens, including slaveholders. The consequence of the Compromise was, in effect, to deny access to slaveholders, who could not bring to the northern territories their slaves and, perhaps more importantly, their way of life that depended on the maintenance of a slave social order.[36] Lincoln famously opposed *Dred Scott* in the Lincoln-Douglas debates, declaring that he would, in effect, not feel bound, were he Illinois' senator, to cease efforts to halt slavery in the territories. At most, he would concede that the individual slave Dred Scott remained the legal property of his owner; but he would grant the case no force beyond that. *Dred Scott*, that is, in no way declared, in a phrase that would become influential in the mid-twentieth century, "the law of the land" with regard to the broader issue of slavery in the territories.

If Lincoln had built his entire political career around the proposition that Congress had the power to ban slavery in the territories, he had been careful to proclaim that he recognized fully the constitutional duty to protect the institution in the states where it already existed. As he put it in his first inaugural address, "I have no purpose, directly or indirectly, to interfere with the institution of slavery in the States where it exists. I believe that I have no lawful right to do so." Indeed, he reiterated his endorsement of the

1860 Republican platform, which had spoken of "the maintenance inviolate of the rights of the States, and especially the right of each State to order and control its own domestic institutions according to its own judgment exclusively."[37]

No one, at least as of 1861, was so bold to suggest that slavery could be threatened by unilateral presidential action. Two constitutional arguments are involved. One of them involves the limited power of the national government. The other is a classic separation-of-powers point: even if the national government is deemed to have certain powers, that does not in the least entail that the president can act without congressional authorization.

In any event, Lincoln *did* act, both to resist Southern secession and then, later, to issue the Emancipation Proclamation. Realizing that he had some duty to offer a legal justification, Lincoln cited "the power in me invested as Command-in-Chief of the Army and Navy of the United States in time of actual armed rebellion against authority and government of the United States," and he described the Proclamation "as a fit and necessary war measure for suppressing said rebellion." So, "by virtue of the power, and for the purpose aforesaid, I do order and declare that all persons held as slaves within said designated States, and parts of States, are, and henceforward shall be free." Finally, after noting that his act is "sincerely believed to be an act of justice, warranted by the Constitution, upon military necessity," he "invoke[d] the considerate judgment of mankind, and the gracious favor of Almighty God."

Lincoln did not write in a void. Indeed, he himself had earlier been very critical of capacious theories of war powers to liberate slaves. Consider, for example, a private letter, written in September 1861, to Illinois Senator Orville H. Browning, who had objected to Lincoln's having revoked almost instantly an order by General John C. Fremont (his predecessor as the Republican candidate for president in 1856), which had freed slaves belonging to Missouri rebels. Again, one can easily offer a completely political explanation for the revocation. But Lincoln proclaimed that what primarily motivated him were constitutional concerns:

> [Fremont's] proclamation ... is simply "dictatorship." It assumes that the general may do anything he pleases – confiscate the lands and free the slaves of loyal people, as well as of disloyal ones.[38] And going the whole figure I have no doubt would be more popular with some thoughtless people. ... But I cannot assume this reckless position. ... You speak of it as being the only means of saving the government. On the contrary it is itself the surrender of

the government. Can it be pretended that it is any longer the government of the U.S. – any government of Constitution and laws, – wherein a General, *or a President*, may make permanent rules of property by proclamation.

I do not say Congress might not with propriety pass a law, on the point.... What I object to, is, that *I as President*, shall expressly or implicitly seize and exercise the permanent legislative functions of the government.[39]

By the following May, Lincoln's views had modified somewhat. In revoking a similar proclamation by General David Hunter with regard to federally controlled areas in South Carolina, Georgia, and Florida, Lincoln now objected only that it went beyond *Hunter's* powers and left open the possibility that he, as Commander-in-Chief of the Army and Navy, would "reserve to myself" the decision whether "it shall have become a necessity indispensable to the maintenance of the government, to exercise such supposed power."[40]

But Lincoln, and his supporters, had to contend with former Supreme Court Justice Benjamin R. Curtis of Massachusetts, who had dissented in *Dred Scott* and thus established a certain measure of antislavery bona fides. Curtis had issued a pamphlet on "Executive Power"[41] following Lincoln's September 22, 1862, announcement that he intended to issue the Proclamation should the rebellious states not cease their campaign. In that pamphlet, Curtis castigated the theory of executive war power that Lincoln used to justify the potential act of emancipation. Emphasizing that the Proclamation reached *every* slave (and slaveowner) within the affected states, Curtis noted that "it is not, therefore, as a punishment of guilty persons that the commander-in-chief decrees the freedom of slaves. It is upon the slaves of loyal persons, or of those who, from their tender years, or other disability, cannot be either disloyal or otherwise, that the proclamation is to operate, if at all; and it is to operate to set them free, in spite of the valid laws of their States."[42]

Curtis emphasized as well that Lincoln's own theory of the war refused to recognize the legitimacy of secession, which meant, as a logical matter, that the states within the so-called Confederacy remained a part of the United States, with its citizens continuing to possess whatever constitutional rights attached to that status. Moreover, of course, Lincoln had consistently emphasized that he did not wish to disturb the traditional prerogatives of those states, which included the right to recognize the institution of slavery. Thus, said Curtis, "It has never been doubted that the power to abolish slavery within the States was not delegated to the United

States by the Constitution, but was reserved to the States. If the President, as commander-in-chief of the army and navy in time or war, may, by an executive decree, exercise this power to abolish slavery in the States" because of his belief that it will be conducive to overcoming "the enemy, what other power, reserved to the States or to the people, may not be exercised by the President, for the same reason ...?" Curtis wrote that "all the powers of the President are executive merely. He cannot make a law."[43]

Lincoln never offered a genuine response to Curtis or other critics, though, needless to say, others did. Thus, New Yorker Charles P. Kirkland quickly drafted and published an open letter, dated November 28, 1862, to former Justice Curtis.[44] He easily found Lincoln's proposed act to be within the internationally recognized laws of war by "depriv[ing] the rebels of their means of sustaining the rebellions" by being able to count on the labor of their slaves.[45] A similar defense was offered by another New York lawyer, Grosvenor P. Lowrey.[46] What is most interesting about Lowrey's defense was his adoption of what is, at bottom, an extra-constitutional argument.

> Where the Constitution itself is the subject of consideration, and the question is, shall it exist or cease, and the President finds his powers, as its military champion, challenged, the mind looks instinctively through the Constitution to that broader charter upon which it rests. And this it does, not for the purposes of finding a 'higher law' which shall contradict or thwart the Constitution (dangerous fallacy), but a higher law which shall sustain and be in agreement with it.[47]

So, Lowrey concluded, "First: Abraham Lincoln, as Commander-in-chief in time of war, embodies all the executive war powers of the nation. Second: These powers are extra-constitutional, having their origin in the nature of things."[48]

The most widely discussed defense of Lincoln's powers appears to have been offered by William Whiting, the Solicitor of the War Department, in a book on presidential war powers that went through no fewer than forty-three editions in eight years.[49] He devoted a full chapter to explaining why the President, "as commander-in-chief," possessed the power "to emancipate the slaves of any belligerent section of the country, if such a measure becomes necessary to save the government from destruction."[50] An important part of Whiting's argument was drawn from international law concerning the rights of belligerent parties. Indeed, Whiting argued,

> It is *only* the law of nations that can decide this question, because *the constitution*, having given authority to government to make war, *has placed no limit*

whatever to the war powers. There is, therefore, no legal control over the war powers except the law of nations, and no moral control except the usage of modern civilized belligerents.[51]

Once the President, then, decides that a measure is "necessary and proper," so to speak, to achieve victory, then he can order it, period.

Taken to an extreme, the views expressed by Whiting, Lowrey, and Kirkland seem to license presidential dictatorship during time of war. If one is going to be subjected to dictatorship, then surely Abraham Lincoln is far preferable to most candidates for the job. This does nothing to contradict the point that these views present an extraordinarily far-reaching reading of the presidential prerogative.

We seem, then, to have the following options with regard to assessing the constitutionality of the Emancipation Proclamation:

1) It was constitutional, but only because it was in fact so limited in its reach. Had Lincoln been more ambitious and ordered emancipation even in any territories controlled by the Union army, let alone any of the nonseceding slave states, or, perhaps, had he ordered emancipation earlier in his term of office, when Generals Fremont and Hunter were engaging in their own efforts, he would have violated his oath of office and, perhaps, merited impeachment rather than a Memorial. Lincoln, therefore, might not have been all that great an emancipator, but he was as great as the Constitution allowed him to be, which was, however, limited.

2) It was constitutional, because he indeed had basically unlimited power to do whatever he deemed instrumentally effective in waging a successful war to save the Union. Had he determined that nationwide emancipation would be efficacious to the goal, then he could have issued a far more sweeping Proclamation. After all, as Whiting noted, "the United States have in former times sanctioned the liberation of slaves even of loyal citizens, by military commanders, in time of war, without compensation."[52] Indeed, had he determined that simply confiscating slaveowner land, and redistributing it to slaves who had, say, joined the Union forces, that would have been perfectly proper as well. This means, then, that the limited reach of the Proclamation that *was* issued is a sign not of constitutional fidelity but rather of political will. Perhaps an equal way of putting this is to say that this notion completely collapses the notion of "law" into that of "prudence."

3) It was, alas, unconstitutional, though, at the end of the day, "no harm, no foul," because of the proposal by Congress, ratified by the States in 1865, to abolish slavery in the Thirteenth Amendment. As important, under this analysis, is Section Four of the Fourteenth Amendment, added to the Constitution in 1868, which explicitly states that "neither the United States nor any state shall assume or pay... any claim for the loss or emancipation of any slave; but all such debts, obligations and claims shall be held illegal and void." In the absence of such language, a careful lawyer – and, even more to the point, Herculean judge – imbued with respect for the Takings Clause of the Fifth Amendment might suggest that the United States would indeed have a duty to compensate at least some slaveowners, such as those who had remained loyal to the Union even while living in Confederate states, for the loss of their property. Indeed, whether for reasons of politics or constitutional fidelity, Lincoln had coupled proposals for emancipation and compensation until the Proclamation itself.[53]

4) One should mention a fourth possibility, which is to say that one is completely indifferent to the constitutionality of the Proclamation.[54] Benjamin Curtis included in his pamphlet a powerful denunciation of what he described as "[a] leading and influential newspaper" that, in support of Lincoln's announcement of his intentions, had written: "The Democrats talk about 'unconstitutional acts.' Nobody pretends this act is constitutional, and nobody cares whether it is or not."[55] Curtis then writes:

> Among all the causes of alarm which now distress the public mind, there are few more terrible... than the tendency to lawlessness which is manifesting itself in so many directions. No stronger evidence of this could be afforded than the open declaration of a respectable and widely circulated journal, that 'nobody cares' whether a great public act of the President of the United States is in conformity with or is subversive of the supreme law of the land...; that our public affairs have become so desperate, and our ability to retrieve them by the use of honest means is so distrusted, and our willingness to use other means so undoubted, that our great public servants may themselves break the fundamental law of the country, and become usurpers of vast powers not intrusted [sic] to them, in violation of their solemn oath of office; and 'nobody cares.'[56]

This fourth view is presumably alien to any traditional conception of constitutional fidelity, including most certainly Dworkin's, though it cannot, just for that reason, be ruled out as a possible response.

III. RETURNING TO DWORKIN

What, then, would a Dworkinian judge do when presented with these various controversies? As a matter of fact, we know what American judges did with regard to the Fugitive Slave Act and the Missouri Compromise, and the Emancipation Proclamation never received any judicial test. Would a Dworkinian judge be required to dissent with regard to the first two and to validate the last? Or, on the contrary, is it possible that even Hercules would have to collaborate with slavery?

"The most powerful arguments against slavery before the Civil War," Dworkin has written, "were framed in the language of dignity" and the horror of the "failure to recognize a slave's right to decide issues of value for himself or herself." Indeed, Dworkin states that "the most basic premise of our entire constitutional system – that our government shall be republican rather than despotic – embodies a commitment to that conception of dignity."[57] Moreover, it is worth noting that Dworkin, in describing Hercules' tasks, appears to presuppose a "constitution [that] sets out a general political scheme that is *sufficiently just* to be taken as settled for reasons of fairness."[58] Perhaps Hercules simply can't act within a system that fails this test. Interestingly enough, though, Dworkin has never suggested that the pre-Reconstruction Constitution does indeed fail, and he even does "not want to deny that realistic cases can be found that present true conflicts between legal and moral rights, if not in [contemporary] America, then those in despotic countries, Nazi Germany and at present South Africa, to which jurisprudence often turns."[59] So this suggests, at the very least, that even the most "despotic" countries might have constitutions that are just in *some* respects and that Hercules therefore might accept an appointment to the judiciary in *any* such country.

We know that the Dworkinian judge, wherever located, would be devoted to the Herculean enterprise of giving "moral" readings to the legal materials that s/he is working with. This being said, it is nonetheless true that Dworkin rejects natural law inasmuch as it is not the case that every (presumptively true) moral argument can dominate legal materials that reject the outcome required by morality. Thus, although Dworkin notes that "some of the American abolitionists" did indeed argue "that the Constitution itself was legally invalid because it embodied an unjust compromise that permitted slavery to continue, a compromise that was contrary to natural law" – and he notes as well that some twentieth-century legal philosophers, making similar arguments about the Nazi legal system concluded that it was "not law at all"[60] – he gives no indication that he agrees.

Recall that Dworkin, in responding to the view that he is committed to "happy endings," had offered the example of his rejection of a constitutionalized welfare state. Dworkin presumably agrees, for example, that the contemporary state is under no constitutional duty to save even one of its own citizens who is starving or freezing in a public park (or anywhere else),[61] whatever the moral abhorrence of that conclusion.[62] Does this conclusion depend on the view that because it is not truly comparable to slavery or to Nazi genocide, then it is really quite acceptable, even if "somewhat" abhorrent?[63] Or does it support a stronger argument, that even if someone argued that the ravages of being without resources in a market-oriented society were, in some ways, every bit as bad as chattel slavery,[64] one would still, nevertheless, be justified in rejecting claims to resources by the indigent because the overall constitution is "good enough" to merit adherence, even if, by stipulation, this was untrue of the post-1933 German constitution or of the pre-1994 South African constitution?

In any event, we now return to the central issue of this essay, the response of a Herculean judge to American chattel slavery. Recall that Dworkin initially criticized Cover for being insufficiently aware of how a judge, adopting the proper (non–natural-law) jurisprudential theory, could have been less supportive of slavery than the Northern judges who were Cover's subjects. Surely, one wants to say, that must be true at least in *some* respects: it would have cost a judge relatively little to say, for example, that there is a special injustice to rewarding federal magistrates with extra dollars for finding someone to be a runaway slave as against determining that the accusation was in fact not supported by sufficient evidence. But, of course, this would be a limited victory, however welcome it might be to the particular person helped by such a decision.

The strongest argument against the Fugitive Slave Clause, if one rejects reliance on a natural law argument, is simply that the Constitution establishes a "limited government of assigned powers" and that Congress is nowhere assigned a power to establish a federal procedure with regard to the return of fugitive slaves. If states are indeed obligated to return fugitives, it is up to them to accept their constitutional duties, and they are subject to criticism for not doing so. But this does not entail the ability of Congress to go beyond its carefully delimited powers. This argument is scarcely frivolous. As a matter of fact, *Prigg* goes far beyond Marshall's famous decision in *McCulloch v. Maryland*[65] in recognizing "implied" powers inasmuch as the so-called Fugitive Slave Clause is found not in Article I, which, generally speaking, deals with the powers granted Congress, but rather in Article IV, a "catchall" collection of clauses that, importantly, includes some specifications of congressional power in some of its clauses but *not* the Fugitive Slave Clause.

The Supreme Court was not unaware of this argument.[66] The basis for its rejection was less a principled overall theory of constitutional interpretation than a plea for national unity. Thus Justice Story admitted that "no uniform rule of interpretation can be applied" to "this part of the constitution."[67] What drives his opinion is his belief that the original 1787 inclusion of the Clause was essential to creating the Union and, concomitantly, that its enforcement was necessary to maintain it. "How," he asks, "are we to interpret the language of the clause?" He offers as "the true answer" the effectuation of its basic purposes, that is, preservation of a Union that indeed includes the institution of chattel slavery. "If, by one mode of interpretation, the right [to regain runaway slaves] must become shadowy and unsubstantial, and without any remedial power adequate to the end, and by another mode, it will attain its just end and secure its manifest purpose, it would seem, upon principles of reasoning, absolutely irresistible, that the latter ought to prevail."[68] Given that the "just end" of the Constitution is preservation of the Union, it rather easily follows that the Fugitive Slave Law should be upheld if one believes that it is, in fact, instrumental in that goal. Moreover, and just as importantly, it is hard to gainsay the proposition that the American legal system, as illustrated in *The Antelope*, amply recognized private ownership of and dominion over other human beings, so that slaveowners could certainly argue that they had a preexisting legal right that demanded recognition from judges, whatever their "personal" views with regard to slavery.

Should *Prigg* be given what Dworkin calls "gravitational weight" as a precedent in successor cases, at least prior to Reconstruction? Or, on the contrary, should it be treated as a "mistake."[69] After all, Dworkin readily concedes that the history of any court, in actuality, will include some inconsistency, so any working adjudicator is inevitably going to be have to figure out, when presented with presumptively inconsistent cases, which to honor, which, relatively speaking, to minimize. "If Hercules," for example, "discovers that some previous decision, whether a statute or a judicial decision, is now widely regretted within the pertinent branch of the profession, that fact in itself distinguishes that decision as vulnerable."[70] It is hard to say that *Prigg* could pass this particular test. There were, to be sure, many who "regretted" the decision, but they tended to be "outsider" lawyers linked with Abolitionism. Most "respectable" lawyers agreed with the anti-slavery Story that preservation of Union took precedence and that compromises with slavery simply had to be honored.

A second argument is considerably more interesting (and mysterious). "If [Hercules] believes, quite apart from any argument of consistency, that a particular statute or decision was wrong because unfair, within the community's own concept of fairness, then that belief is sufficient to distinguish the decision, and make it vulnerable."[71] Thus, if Hercules "can show by arguments of political morality that such a principle, apart from its popularity, is *unjust*, then the argument from fairness that supports that principle is overridden."[72] It is certainly not obvious that the Fugitive Slave Clause was unfair "within the community's own concept of fairness," given not only the brute fact of passage of the law by Congress but also its defense, as a sad necessity, by someone so acute as Abraham Lincoln. If one instead argues that such data are irrelevant because the Fugitive Slave Law was simply "unjust," period, then this seemingly takes us back to a pure natural law argument.

In any event, there is no reason to believe that Hercules would be disabled from serving as a judge in an antebellum federal court.[73] And we return to the question of whether Hercules would necessarily have been an interestingly different judge from, say, Joseph Story. Presumably both would agree that the best interpretation of the Constitution is the one that maximizes the "establishment of justice" congruent with maintaining the Union, since Dworkin has never endorsed the principle that legal justice should be done though the heavens fall. And this interpretive maxim led, perhaps properly, to *Prigg*. To reject *Prigg*, perhaps one has to accept another Garrisonian principle, "No Union With Slaveholders," and profess sublime indifference to whether the Union in fact survived.

The Fugitive Slave Law, then, presents one kind of challenge to a Herculean judge. The Missouri Compromise presents a distinctly different kind. In developing his all-important notion of legal "integrity," Dworkin offers the example of "checkerboard" legislation in which compromises with regard to especially controversial issues take the form, for example, of permitting abortions by pregnant women born in even-numbered years and prohibiting it to women born in odd-numbered years. Or racial discrimination could be prohibited in buses but permitted in restaurants.[74] And so on. Although Dworkin concedes that "we accept that shops or factories be forbidden in some zones and not others and that parking be prohibited on alternate sides of the same streets on alternative days," what is key is that these issues, he suggests, do not rise to the level of high principle. "We reject," he says, "a division between parties of opinion when matters of principle are at stake. We follow a different model: that each point of view must be allowed a voice in the process of deliberation but that the collective decision must nevertheless aim to settle on some coherent principle whose influence then extends to the natural limits of its authority."[75] Checkerboard ordinances have a distinctive defect: "They treat people differently when no principle can justify the distinction."

This, of course, captures almost perfectly the Missouri Compromise. Indeed, what establishes it as a "compromise" is that neither pro- nor antislavery legislators were able to prevail entirely. Instead, Congress agreed to allow settlers of those territories south of 36°30' to take their slaves from the slave states from which they came while prohibiting such settlement in the northern territories. It is as if a state allowed abortion in counties east or north of a given river while criminalizing it in counties west or south of the river.

Dworkin describes "checkerboard statutes [as] the most dramatic violations of the ideal of integrity," but he immediately concedes that "they are not unknown to our political history."[76] Indeed, the Constitution itself contained some "particularly hideous examples" derived from slavery, such as the three-fifths rule with regard to counting slaves a part of a state's population and forbidding Congress, prior to 1808, from passing legislation prohibiting the importation of slaves.[77] Such compromises were erased not only by the abolition of slavery in the Thirteenth Amendment but also, Dworkin suggests, with the addition of "the equal protection clause of the Fourteen Amendment," which "is now understood to outlaw internal compromises over important matters of principle."[78]

Putting to one side Dworkin's interpretation of the Fourteenth Amendment, one can still ask about the obligations of the Herculean judge *prior* to the Reconstruction Amendments. After all, Dworkin concedes that "hideous" compromises were accepted as the cost of attaining the original Constitution. Hercules would, presumably, have to reject the constitutionality of a law passed, say, in 1804 that attempted to end immediately the importation of slaves from abroad. Ironically, one could infer from these compromises the legitimacy of the equally "hideous" Missouri Compromise. But, presumably, a Herculean judge could believe that the number of "checkerboard" laws should be minimized, indeed absolutely limited to those enshrined in the original text. Otherwise, Congress should indeed be required to treat (at least) all American citizens equally. As was suggested by Justice Catron's capitalization of the word EQUALITY in his *Dred Scott* concurrence, that required the invalidation of the Missouri Compromise and of the limitation on the rights of slaveholders instantiated in the Compromise. After all, non-slaveowners were free to settle *any* territory, whereas slaveowners were limited to only part of the territory. What could be more "unequal" than that? Obviously the equality (or EQUALITY) condition could also be met by reinterpreting the Constitution to require (and not simply permit) the no-extension-of-slavery plank of the 1856 Republican platform. There is much to be said for this, though one must recognize the almost certain likelihood that any such decision would have triggered secession and civil war three years earlier, when a weak proslavery Northern Democratic President, James Buchanan, might well have accepted the peaceful dismemberment of the Union. If, though, one has little hesitation in accepting the legitimacy of *Prigg*, it is harder than one wishes to reject the equal legitimacy of *Dred Scott*.

Finally, in turning to the Emancipation Proclamation, it may be helpful to read Dworkin's response, during a 1997 conference at Fordham on "legal fidelity," to a question: might Hercules "be forced to the dreadfully unhappy conclusion that the Emancipation Proclamation was in fact unconstitutional?"[79] One argument offered for such a possibility was the Constitution's Third Amendment: "No Soldier shall, in time of peace be quartered in any house, without the consent of the Owner, nor in time of war, but in a manner to be prescribed by law." This supports the position that even in time of war the Constitution still controls, requiring prescription by law rather than allowing fiat decision making, however "reasonable" any such decisions might be.[80] And we have seen earlier in this paper how even Lincoln had severe doubts about the extent of his power, though he ultimately overcame them.

Dworkin responded as follows:

> In *Freedom's Law*, I denied that it would be a good translation of the Third Amendment itself to say it requires, or it is the source of, a general right of privacy. That seems to me an interpretive mistake. The linguistic intention, I think, was very different.
>
> But you are absolutely right, it doesn't follow from that that in asking the question, how do we make most sense of the document as a whole, we shouldn't recognize that here was an occasion in which it was asserted that the Constitution holds sway even in war time. Absolutely right. I call that gravitational force, meaning the fact that provision is there and did that thing, is pertinent to and maybe decisive of the correct interpretation of other more general clauses and issues. So, I agree.[81]

He noted that "the Emancipation Proclamation did not exempt loyal southerners,"[82] a point initially emphasized by former Justice Curtis in his critique of the Proclamation. Though the text is not clear, the context suggests that Dworkin/Hercules finds the application of the Proclamation to loyal Southerners at least somewhat problematic and therefore, possibly, unconstitutional.

How important is it to us how Hercules would answer the question? That is, does it discredit the Dworkinian enterprise if, perchance, it would indeed end up, at least on this occasion, accepting the view that respect for "legal integrity" would require collaboration with the vicious evil of chattel slavery? Or, on the contrary, does it enhance the jurisprudential seriousness of Dworkin's enterprise insofar as it underscores his willingness to view constitutional analysis, even when conducted by the most able judge imaginable, as at least on occasion the occasion for tragedy and not simply a comedy generating happy endings?

There is, of course, a certain paradox involved in the question. Generally speaking it counts in the favor of any particular approach that, overall, it leads to desirable results. Yet if it leads *only* to "happy endings," then one is tempted to a hermeneutics of suspicion insofar as one suspects that the approach is simply being manipulated to achieve desirable outcomes. One can avoid charges of manipulation if one announces that one's decision rule was "decide each case in a way that one believes will maximize overall social utility," but this, of course, tends to negate what most people think of as "law," which involves *some* notion of rule-following that, on occasion, requires "suboptimal" outcomes.[83] On the other hand, and just as obviously, an approach to legal interpretation that seems to generate "too many" heinous outcomes will almost inevitably discredit itself, save, perhaps, for the most benighted academic.

Dworkin, I think correctly, believes that it strengthens – in the sense of adding to its intellectual plausibility – his overall theoretical stance to acknowledge its incapacity always to generate "happy endings." But how satisfied should one be with a Dworkinian account if it turns out that Hercules would end up not only rejecting the constitutionalization of the welfare state, but also collaborating in significant ways with chattel slavery? Or, what may be just as important, how admiring can we be of the Dworkinian project if it leaves us genuinely uncertain as to Hercules' responses to such issues as the Fugitive Slave Law of 1793, *Dred Scott*, and Emancipation?

IV. CONCLUSION: OPTIMISM ABOUT THE RULE OF LAW

Whether or not his theory guaranteed "happy endings," Dworkin's theory of law, both to his critics and his admirers, seemed premised on a certain kind of optimism with regard to legal judgment (at least) in our own society.[84]

Basically, he reassures us that commitment to the rule of law, which includes the incorporation of background principles of the social order in the best efforts of the decision maker to make any given decision the "best that it can be," will not take (or leave) one too far wrong from a basically just state, even if gaps (perhaps inevitably) remain. The optimism is not that injustice (in a substantive sense) can be completely eradicated; rather it is that if judges recognize that principles are part of the law, the law will be able to produce a modicum of justice in a sufficient number of cases to justify even the legal losers maintaining loyalty to the overarching regime.

This optimistic view presupposes a certain substantive content to what can count as a principle. Most Dworkinian principles as discussed in his work certainly strike readers as "good." The suggestion that evil-doers should not be able to benefit from their foul deed leads few to cry out in outrage, for example. But imagine that someone, at least prior to 1865, announces that among the defining principles of the United States is not only that ours is a system that recognizes the rights of property owners[85] – a proposition that would undoubtedly be highly resonant even today – but also that among the objects subject to ownership are other human beings. This would mean, among other things, that the Constitution and other legal texts should be interpreted in a way that pays heed to *both* of these deep realities of the American polity. To put it another way, one might assert that slaveowners are entitled to at least the same amount of "concern and respect" as any other property owner.

Or, to take Rogers Smith's powerful and disturbing question, what if there is no singular "American political tradition" but rather conflicting traditions, including, in addition to the oft-proclaimed liberal one, at least one building on far more ascriptive views of politics that privilege being of a given race, gender, or religion?[86] One might, for example, read the Constitution's consistent assumption that political officials would all be male as less a simple reflection of grammatical conventions of the time than an assertion of principle that *only* males were fit to participate in the public world of politics.

Dworkin seems to suggest that principled decision making has substantive content, presumably the sort of principles that are justified by the best political morality. In that case you can distinguish between principled distinctions and unprincipled ones. But this obviously requires a robust notion of what can count as a genuine principle. To the extent that "an unjust principle can never be a (genuine) principle," this simply backs into natural law theory, but, as emphasized above, Dworkin seems estopped from making this move. If an unjust principle *can* be a (genuine) principle, though, then this seems suspiciously close to classical positivism, albeit a more sophisticated version than the one that Dworkin ascribes to H. L. A. Hart insofar as Hart and his followers are charged with ignoring the all-important role of background principles in giving life to legal judgment.

As a practical matter, the more (substantively) unjust the laws, the more arbitrary the legal rules seem, even if they seem to obey formal regularities. One avoids this problem only by denying that the legal system produces results that are *too* unjust. Consider in this context the assertion by Charles Fried, whose anti-utilitarian theory of law is similar in significant respects to Dworkin's, that "to assist others in understanding and realizing their legal rights is *always* morally worthy."[87] According to Fried, "The lawyer acts morally because he helps to preserve and express the autonomy of his client vis-à-vis- the legal system."[88] This means that one ought never denounce an attorney for representing a "repugnant client" because any such representation can be redescribed in the language of protecting legal rights and individual autonomy. But, all too obviously, the "autonomy" of the slaveowner requires the ruthless subordination of any autonomy of the slave. It is easy enough, of course, to recognize this point with regard to slaveowners (and those who represent them or rule in their favor). But one must recall the criticism directed at "wage slavery" with regard to similar, even if not identical, suppression of worker autonomy at the behest of the capitalist,[89] issues that remain central in the era of the modern state, especially as support for the "welfare state" appears to be waning in favor of embracing a more libertarian "market state."[90]

So we seem to have the following choices when presented with the possibility of repugnant principles (or clients who instantiate those principles). The first is to accept without blinking their constitutive status within the given legal system, even if, from a moral perspective, one bewails this positivist reality. In contrast, one can instead assert that there are, after all, substantive limits on what can count as acceptable principles underlying law. A third choice is to reply that what law (and background principles) allows is not *too* bad, that the accusation of "repugnance" is misplaced, better reserved for some other example that is "really" repugnant but, happily, not actually manifested in the legal system whose legitimacy one wishes, in the end, to preserve. Dworkin has never squarely faced, save for the extremely truncated review of Cover's book, what might be entailed in engaging in principled adjudication of the rights of slaveholders (or, concomitantly, a principled decision about determining who are "really" Jews and thus "eligible" to be sent to concentration camps and gas chambers).[91]

This essay has focused on the extent to which Dworkin tends to see the law through rose-colored glasses. But that metaphor has two different meanings. The first suggests he thinks that you can arrive at relatively just results using existing legal materials even if others might not think that the results can bear this weight. This is the accusation that he inevitably will reach "happy endings," a charge to which, as we have seen, Dworkin strongly demurs. The other, more troubling interpretation of the rose-colored-glasses metaphor is that the judge's (or Hercules') own notions about what is just or unjust, good or bad, are subtly altered by the legal decision maker's phenomenological need to restrict him/herself to existing legal materials and to avoid what well-trained lawyers would regard as "off the wall" arguments at that point in time. Dworkin does not pay adequate attention to the effect that the culture of legalism has on moral judgment – that is, what people are willing to say is just and unjust, or not too unjust.[92] He does not adequately address the need for legal decision makers to reduce cognitive dissonance either by seeing (valid) principles where there are no such principles or by seeing only moderate – and therefore acceptable – levels of injustice where there is really very serious injustice.

Today everyone regards slavery as extremely unjust; just as importantly, few see prudential reasons for appeasing those who would hold slaves. There is therefore little incentive to reduce cognitive dissonance by saying that it was not so bad, all things considered. This helps account for the fact that most analysts today would feel under enormous pressure to offer a constitutional justification for what Lincoln did in the Emancipation Proclamation rather than accept Justice Curtis's view that he ran roughshod over the vested rights of loyal slaveowners. On the other hand, where the morally just result remains strongly contested in the larger political community, it is easier to rely on legal formalism or prior precedent as a justification for reaching (what some analysts would describe as) unjust results. And this tough-mindedness demonstrates one's fealty to the Rule of Law and shows that one is not willing to simply make things up out of whole cloth. But one should recognized that this tough-minded adherence to the rule of law is made possible by a moral dissensus that allows mechanisms of cognitive dissonance to do their work.

As noted earlier, Dworkin himself appears to believe both that the United States, as a liberal polity, has a moral duty to provide minimum entitlements to the poor and that no such entitlements are in fact required by the United States Constitution. This particular separation between law and morality seems to rest, however, on the fact that many people in the relevant interpretive community of citizens, politicians, lawyers, and judges – that is, those people who are perceived, in the language of John Rawls, as having "reasonable" views, even if many members of the community are unpersuaded by them[93] – do *not* think that this is required by a just state.

Ironically, it is the fact that there is no consensus on what counts as either a happy or an unhappy ending that allows Dworkin to insist that this *is* an "unhappy" ending (from his perspective) required by law. If *everyone* within the relevant public agreed that the ending was unhappy, it would look much less plausible to say that the law could not reach the opposite result. Instead, we would surely have strong background principles that would amply justify the redistribution from well-off A's to indigent B's that is entailed in a welfare state. Instead, Hercules, by looking around and observing that perfectly respectable people believe that there is no "duty to rescue," can justify his own adoption of a tragic ending that indeed leaves the vulnerable unrescued.

Only today does the relevant interpretive community agree that absolute dominion over other human beings is not covered by the principle of "respect the rights of private property," whereas in the 1850s the relevant interpretive community was in a state of dissensus, with many respectable persons more than willing to accept such a linkage. Even Lincoln, as we have seen, went out of his way to pronounce his respect, as a well-trained lawyer, for the property rights of slaveowners in their own states and when they wished to regain slaves who had attempted to flee to "free" states. It appears, then, that one's ability to say that law permits a happy ending or requires, alas, an unhappy ending is not simply a function of detached legal or moral analysis but rather a function of social psychology. More precisely, it is a function of what other people in the relevant interpretive community think to be just and unjust and whether there is consensus or disagreement on those issues. Hercules is in effect always aware of the presence of other members of the interpretive community, whose eyes – one is tempted to evoke the Foucaultian "gaze" – are always on him, subtly shaping his ultimate behavior as an adjudicator, including, of course, the offering of arguments based on background principles that can legitimately be relied on by a legal decision maker. Hercules must be acutely sensitive to what is "on the wall" and "off the wall"; indeed, it is just this distinction that allows us to recognize the mere "personal" preferences of the judge in contrast to the implementation of deep social norms.

CODA

One hopes that this essay has helped to clarify how Dworkinian constitutional analysis works. Still, a certain frustration remains, for even after this quite extended examination, I continue to be completely uncertain whether Hercules would, or would not, have concurred with Justice Story in *Prigg* or agreed with Abraham Lincoln's strictures with regard to the constitutionally guaranteed status of slavery in the states wherein it already existed. One might conclude, then, with a plea that Dworkin return, after almost thirty years, to the issue of slavery and update his Cover review. But, as a matter of fact, that would probably only generate a further interpretive issue. Is Ronald Dworkin in fact the definitive source on what Hercules would in fact conclude, or is it possible that Dworkin himself might misapply "Dworkinian" jurisprudence? Might, then, Hercules' stance toward slavery simply be an "essentially contested" question, no more capable of being given final resolution by Ronald Dworkin than, indeed, by the author of the essay you have just concluded? And would this count as a strength or weakness of the approach to constitutional analysis that Dworkin has so assiduously developed over the past three decades?

ACKNOWLEDGMENTS

I am grateful to Jack Balkin, Brian Leiter, and Arthur Ripstein for their extremely helpful comments responding to earlier drafts of this essay.

Notes

1. See Ronald Dworkin, "The Law of the Slave-Catchers," *The Times Literary Supplement* (December 5, 1975): 1437.
2. Robert M. Cover, *Justice Accused: Antislavery and the Judicial Process* (New Haven: Yale University Press, 1975).
3. 41 U.S. (16 Pet.) 536 (1842).
4. 41 US., 611.
5. See Ronald Dworkin, "Political Judges and the Rule of Law," in *A Matter of Principle* (Cambridge, MA: Harvard University Press, 1985), 31.
6. See for example Ronald Dworkin, "Introduction: The Moral Reading and the Majoritarian Premise," in *Freedom's Law: The Moral Reading of the American Constitution* (Cambridge, MA: Harvard University Press, 1996), 2.
7. There can, of course, be no doubt that Dworkin finds slavery immoral. Indeed, for Dworkin it is a paradigm example of our capacity to identify "wrong" social practices: "We do have reasons for thinking that slavery is wrong and that the Greeks were therefore in error: we have all the moral reasons we would cite in a moral debate about the matter." Ronald Dworkin, "Objectivity and Truth: You'd Better Believe It," *Philosophy and Public Affairs* 25, no. 2 (Spring 1996): 87, 122, quoted in Brian Leiter, "Objectivity, Morality and Adjudication," in *Objectivity in Law and Morals*, ed. Brian Leiter (Cambridge, UK: Cambridge University Press, 2001), 89. Still, the major point with regard to those who reject the natural

lawyer's view of the relationship between law and morality is that agreement that some conduct X is wrong does not entail that a law commanding or protecting X is not to be regarded as law at all (and, therefore, exempt from enforcement by someone pledged to be faithful to law).

8. Ronald Dworkin, *Law's Empire* (Cambridge, MA: Harvard University Press, 1986), 378.

9. Dworkin, *Law's Empire*, 397.

10. See also Sanford Levinson, "Constitutional Rhetoric and the Ninth Amendment," *Chicago-Kent Law Review* 64 (1988): 131–61; and Sanford Levinson "Comment on Macedo," *Chicago-Kent Law Review* 64 (1988): 175–6; both reprinted in *The Rights Retained by the People: The History and Meaning of the Ninth Amendment*, vol. 2, ed. Randy E. Barnett (Fairfax, VA: George Mason University Press, 1993), 115–47, 161–2.

11. 25 U.S. (10 Wheat.) 66 (1825).

12. 25 U.S., 121.

13. See Shirley Robin Letwin, letter to the editor, *The Times Literary Supplement*, December 26, 1975.

14. Letwin, letter to the editor, (emphasis in original).

15. Ronald Dworkin, letter to the editor, *The Times Literary Supplement*, January 9, 1976.

16. As Dworkin would write in his essay "Hard Cases," "Hercules' theory of adjudication at no point provides for any choice between his own political convictions and those he takes to be the political convictions of the community at large. On the contrary, his theory identifies a particular conception of community morality as decisive of legal issues; that conception holds that community morality is the political morality presupposed by the laws and institutions of the community. He must, of course, rely on his own judgment as to what the principles of that morality are," but this is very different from a conscious rejection of that morality in favor of one's own political or moral preferences. See Ronald Dworkin, "Hard Cases," *Harvard Law Review* 88, no. 6 (April 1975): 1057–109, reprinted in Ronald Dworkin, *Taking Rights Seriously* (Cambridge, MA: Harvard University Press, 1977), 81–130.

17. Don E. Fehrenbacher, *The Slaveholding Republic: An Account of the United States Government's Relations to Slavery* (New York: Oxford University Press, 2001).

18. See for example Ronald Dworkin, *Sovereign Virtue: The Theory and Practice of Equality* (Cambridge, MA: Harvard University Press, 2000).

19. See for example the collection of articles brought together as "Should Judges Work in an Unjust Legal System? – A Debate Based on South Africa," *Bulletin of the Australian Society of Legal Philosophy* 12, no. 46–47 (October/December 1988): 176–232. A review of the indexes of Dworkin's books published over the past quarter century reveals no entry on "South Africa," nor does Stephen Guest's seemingly comprehensive bibliography of Dworkin's writing up to 1991 include anything whose title suggests any reference to the situation in South Africa. See Stephen Guest, *Ronald Dworkin* (Edinburgh: Edinburgh University Press, 1992), 309–13.

20. Dworkin, "Hard Cases," in *Taking Rights Seriously*.

21. Dworkin, "Hard Cases," in *Taking Rights Seriously*, 116.

22. Dworkin, "Introduction: The Moral Reading and the Majoritarian Premise."

23. He offers no specific example. See, though, Sanford Levinson, "Taking Law Seriously: Reflections on 'Thinking Like a Lawyer,'" *Stanford Law Review* 30, no. 5 (May 1978): 1071, 1090–1; Sanford Levinson, *Constitutional Faith* (Princeton: Princeton University Press, 1988), 88. See also William N. Eskridge, Jr., and Sanford Levinson, "Antigone and Creon," in *Constitutional Stupidities, Constitutional Tragedies*, ed. William N. Eskridge Jr., and Sanford Levinson (New York: NYU Press, 1998), 248.

24. Dworkin, "Introduction: The Moral Reading and the Majoritarian Premise," 36.

25. Dworkin, "Introduction: The Moral Reading and the Majoritarian Premise," 36, citing Ronald Dworkin, "What Is Equality? Part 1: Equality of Welfare," *Philosophy and Public Affairs* 10, no. 3 (Summer 1981): 185–246; and Ronald Dworkin, "What is Equality? Part 2: Equality of Resources," *Philosophy and Public Affairs* 10, no. 4 (Autumn 1981): 283–345.

26. See Frank Michelman, "The Supreme Court 1968 Term: On Protecting the Poor Through the Fourteenth Amendment," *Harvard Law Review* 83, no. 1 (November 1969): 7–282.

27. Dworkin, "Introduction: The Moral Reading and the Majoritarian Premise," 36.

28. James G. Randall, *Constitutional Problems Under Lincoln* (Urbana: University of Illinois Press, 1951), 356.

29. Fehrenbacher, *The Slaveholding Republic*, 250 (emphasis added). The amendment proved unavailing, though, and Radical Republicans were able to muster support for the bill repealing both of the Acts.

30. As the London *Spectator* put it with justified acerbity, the fundamental principle underlying the Proclamation appeared to be "not that a human being cannot justly own another, but that he cannot own him unless he is loyal to the United States." Quoted in James M. McPherson, *Ordeal by Fire: The Civil War and Reconstruction* (New York: Alfred A. Knopf, 1982), 298.

31. See Abraham Lincoln, *Speeches and Writings 1832–1858: Speeches, Letters, and Miscellaneous Writings: The Lincoln-Douglas Debates*, ed. Don Fehrenbacher (New York: Library of America, 1989), 620, 813 (emphasis added).

32. "No Person held to Service or Labour in one State, under the Laws thereof, escaping into another, shall, in Consequence of any Law or Regulation therein, be discharged from such Service or Labour, but shall be delivered up on Claim of the Party to whom such Service or Labour may be due." Many analysts have noted that there is no explicit mention of slaves in this clause. Frederick Douglass used this as the basis for an argument that it refers only to indentured servants "held to Service" by a contract voluntarily entered into.

33. Lincoln, "Debate of September 15, 1858," in *Speeches and Writings 1832–1858*, 620.

34. 60 U.S. (19 How.) 393 (1857).

35. 60 U.S., 529.

36. If a specific way of life associated with slavery had not been at stake, then, presumably, slaveowners would not have objected to selling their slaves in the states they were leaving before emigrating to the new (non-slave) territories.

37. The Address is available at http://www.yale.edu/lawweb/avalon/presiden/inaug/lincoln1.htm. If that were not sufficient reassurance of the slave states, he explicitly supported the so-called Corwin Amendment that had received the support of what was by then an overwhelmingly Northern Congress. That Amendment would in effect have guaranteed in perpetuity the maintenance of slavery in the states where it then existed by forbidding any future amendment "to the Constitution which will authorize or give to Congress the power to abolish or interfere, within any State, with the domestic institutions thereof, including that of persons held to labor or service by the laws of said State." Quoted in Mark Brandon, "The 'Original' Thirteenth Amendment and the Limits to Formal Constitutional Change," in *Responding to Imperfection: The Theory and Practice of Constitutional Amendment*, ed. Sanford Levinson (Princeton: Princeton University Press, 1995), 219.

38. Though note that Fremont seemed to limit his order to the slaves of rebels and not, therefore, of those who had remained loyal to the Union.

39. Abraham Lincoln, "Letter of September 22, 1861," in *Speeches and Writings 1859–1865: Speeches, Letters, and Miscellaneous Writings: Presidential Messages and Proclamations*, ed. Don Fehrenbacher (New York: Library of America, 1989), 268–9 (emphasis added). One should note the denial by Lincoln that the president can act without congressional authorization even as he acknowledges the possibility that Congress in fact had the power to legislate with regard to slavery. In form, then, this is a classic separation-of-powers argument. I note that this essay was written considerably before the administration of George W. Bush started citing Lincoln in making remarkably capacious arguments as to its "war powers" with regard to the "global war on terror." See Sanford Levinson, "Constitutional Norms in a State of Permanent Emergency," *Georgia Law Review* 40 (2006): 699; Sanford Levinson, "Response: The Deepening Crisis of American Constitutionalism," *Georgia Law Review* 40 (2006), 889.

40. Lincoln, "Proclamation [of May 19, 1862] Revoking Hunter's Emancipation Order," in *Speeches and Writings 1859–1865*, 318–19.

41. Benjamin R. Curtis, "Executive Power," in *Union Pamphlets of the Civil War, 1861–1865*, vol. 1, ed. Frank Freidel (Cambridge, MA: Belknap Press of Harvard University Press, 1967), 450. Curtis would end up as Andrew Johnson's leading counsel in his impeachment trial before the Senate in 1868. See *Union Pamphlets*, 450.

42. Curtis, "Executive Power," 459.

43. Although the *New York Times* supported the Proclamation, it would have preferred that it had been presented as a straightforward military order. "We think," it went on, "every dispassionate person must feel some doubt whether the Supreme Court will decide that the President has power to *repeal State laws*

on the subject of slavery, or to continue those laws in force according to the judgment of the military necessities of the moment." Editorial, *New York Times*, January 6, 1863, quoted in Carl Brent Swisher, *The Taney Court 1836–1864, The History of the Supreme Court of the United States*, vol. 5 (New York: McMillan Publishing Co., 1974) (italics in Swisher).

44. Charles P. Kirkland, "A Letter to the Hon. Benjamin R. Curtis,...in Review of his Recently Published Pamphlet on the 'Emancipation Proclamation' of the President" (New York: Latimer Bros. & Seymour Law Stationers, 1862). Available at http://www.hti.umich.edu/cgi/t/text/text-idx?c = moa&cc = moa&sid = 1&q1 = benjamin%20r.%20curtis&view = text&rgn = main&idno = ACR5107.0001.001.

45. Kirkland, "A Letter to the Hon. Benjamin R. Curtis," 10.

46. See Grosvenor P. Lowrey, "The Commander-in-Chief: A Defense upon Legal Grounds of the Proclamation of Emancipation; and an Answer to Ex-Judge Curtis' Pamphlet, Entitled 'Executive Power.' Second Edition, with Additional Notes," in *Union Pamphlets*, 474. Though this new edition was published in 1863, an earlier edition had been published in 1862.

47. Lowrey, "The Commander-in-Chief," 480–1.

48. Lowrey, "The Commander-in-Chief," 499. Especially interesting is Lowrey's insistence, *pace* Curtis, that Lincoln did not in fact abolish the institution of slavery. "The military power, acting through emancipation, does not pretend to destroy the legal right to own slaves, and is not, therefore, obnoxious to the charge of annulling or repealing state laws." Note the implication that it would in fact have violated the Constitution for Lincoln to have mandated the abolition of the legal institution of slavery per se.

49. See Robert B. McCoy, "Publisher's Preface" (unpaginated), a 1971 reprinting of William Whiting, *War Powers Under the Constitution of the United States*, 10th ed. (1864). Whiting had been named Special Counselor of the War Department in November 1862 before being promoted to the office of Solicitor upon the creation of that office in February 1863.

50. Whiting, *War Powers*, 66. Whiting made full use of early arguments that had been made by John Quincy Adams while a member of Congress following his presidency. As David Donald writes, "'By the laws of war,' [Adams] reminded his listeners, 'an invaded country has all its laws and municipal institutions swept by the board, and martial law takes the place of them.' In case of 'actual war, whether servile, civil, or foreign,' he grimly told Congress, the South's 'municipal institutions' would be entirely subject to these laws of war, which permitted the confiscation of enemy property, including slaves." David Herbert Donald, "Whig in the White House," in *Lincoln Reconsidered*, 3rd ed. (New York: Knopf Publishing Group, 2001), 145. Whiting quotes extensively from Adams at pp. 77–82.

51. Whiting, *War Powers*, 68–9 (emphasis added).

52. Whiting, *War Powers*, 82.

53. See for example Lincoln, "Message to Congress of March 6, 1862," in *Speeches and Writings 1859–1865*, 307; Lincoln, "Appeal to Border-State Representatives

for Compensated Emancipation, July 12, 1862," in *Speeches and Writings 1859–1865*, 340–2; Lincoln, "Annual Message to Congress," in *Speeches and Writings 1859–1865*, 412–14; Lincoln, "Message to the Senate and House of Representatives concerning a bill to provide slave states with compensation for end of slavery, February 5, 1865," in *Speeches and Writings 1859–1865*, 671. As this last example indicates, the Emancipation Proclamation in no way entailed shelving the analytically separable issue of compensation.

54. See Sanford Levinson, "Was the Emancipation Proclamation Constitutional? Do We/Should We Care What the Answer Is?" *University of Illinois Law Review* 2001, no. 4 (2001): 1135–58.

55. Curtis, "Executive Power," 470.

56. Curtis, "Executive Power," 470–1.

57. Ronald Dworkin, "What the Constitution Says," in *Freedom's Law*, 111.

58. Dworkin, "Hard Cases," in *Taking Rights Seriously*, 106 (emphasis added). David Lyons cites this and the following passage in his essay, "Moral Aspects of Legal Theory," *Midwest Studies in Philosophy* 7 (1982): 223–54; reprinted in *Dworkin and Contemporary Jurisprudence*, ed. Marshall Cohen (Latham, MD: Rowman and Littlefield, 1983), 68 n7. See also *Law's Empire*, 249–50, where Dworkin discusses how Hercules constructs the "best story" with regard to deciding how to fit a particular dispute into the overall narrative of a complex, sometimes contradictory, political-legal narrative:

Hercules' answer will depend on his convictions about the two constituent virtues of political morality we have considered: justice and fairness. It will depend, that is, not only on his beliefs about which of these principles is superior as a matter of abstract justice but also about which should be followed, as a matter of political fairness, in a community whose members have the moral convictions his fellow citizens have. In some cases the two kinds of judgment – the judgment of justice and that of fairness – will come together.... But the two judgments will sometimes pull in different directions. He may think that [a particular interpretation] is better on grounds of abstract justice, but know that this is a radical view not shared by any substantial portion of the public and unknown in the political and moral rhetoric of the times. He might then decide that the story in which the state insists on the view he thinks right, but against the wishes of the people as a whole, is a poorer story, on balance. He would be preferring fairness to justice in these circumstances, and that preference would reflect a high-order level of his own political convictions, namely his convictions about how a decent government committed to both fairness and justice should adjudicate between the two in this sort of case.

It should be obvious that there is some ambiguity in the notions of views "not shared by any substantial portion of the public" or "unknown in the political and moral rhetoric of the times." One can be fairly confident, as an empirical matter, that no one with the sociopolitical resources to become a judge will have views that are truly "not shared" by any fellow members of the society or that are "unknown" within the society. What one historian termed "anti-slavery constitutionalism" was certainly present in antebellum America. See William M. Wiecek, *The Sources of Antislavery Constitutionalism in America, 1760–1848* (Ithaca: Cornell University Press, 1977). Would this have been enough to license Hercules to adopt their theories (and, possibly, destroy the Union)?

59. Dworkin, *Law's Empire*, 326. This sentence, of course, presumably no longer applies to South Africa.

60. Dworkin, *Law's Empire*, 316.

61. Save for circumstances where the state itself is responsible for placing the person in a confined position, as is the case, for example, with prisoners or inmates of mental institutions; see *DeShaney v. Winnebago County Social Services Dept.*, 489 U.S. 189 (1989).

62. Interestingly enough, Dworkin has no discussion of *DeShaney* in *Freedom's Law* nor, so far as I am aware, has he systematically addressed the case and the issues it presents elsewhere in his copious writings.

63. See J. M. Balkin, "Agreements with Hell and Other Objects of Our Faith," *Fordham Law Review* 65, no. 4 (March 1997): 1703, 1731–7. In his discussion of "Evil legal systems," *Ronald Dworkin*, 82–5, Stephen Guest quotes H. L. A. Hart's acerbic comment that

    If all that can be said of the theory or set of principles underlying the system of explicit law is that it is morally the least odious of morally unacceptable principles that fit the explicit evil law this can provide no justification at all. To claim that it does would be like claiming that killing an innocent man without torturing him is morally justified to some degree because killing with torture would be morally worse. (*Ronald Dworkin*, 82–3, quoting Hart, "Legal Duty and Obligation," in *Essays on Bentham* [New York: Oxford University Press, 1982], 151).

64. See for example Stanley L. Engerman and Robert W. Fogel, *Time on the Cross: The Economics of American Negro Slavery* (Boston: Little Brown, 1974).

65. 17 U.S. 316 (1819).

66. 41 U.S. 539, 618.

67. 41 U.S., 610.

68. 41 U.S., 612.

69. Dworkin, "Hard Cases," in *Taking Rights Seriously*, 118.

70. Dworkin, "Hard Cases," in *Taking Rights Seriously*, 122.

71. Dworkin, "Hard Cases," in *Taking Rights Seriously*, 122.

72. Dworkin, "Hard Cases," in *Taking Rights Seriously*, 122–3 (emphasis added).

73. Whether Hercules could have served as a judge on, say, the South Carolina Supreme Court is a separate question.

74. See Dworkin, *Law's Empire*, 178.

75. Dworkin, *Law's Empire*, 179.

76. Dworkin, *Law's Empire*, 184.

77. Dworkin, *Law's Empire*, 184. One should note, incidentally, that the South would have been delighted to have counted slaves as "full" persons, indeed even as "double persons," at least when computing representation in Congress, since such a "full count" would have given the Southern states additional representation in a situation where, of course, slaves (like women) could not vote. It was

Northern state representatives who suggested that slaves should count not at all in computing the basis for representation. Arguments were neatly reversed with regard to determining population with regard to collecting "direct" taxes, one of the more obscure features of the original constitution that has turned out to have almost no importance (unlike the representation clause).

78. Dworkin, *Law's Empire*, 185.
79. Sanford Levinson, question, "Fidelity as Integrity: Colloquy," *Fordham Law Review* 65, no. 4 (March 1997): 1359.
80. Sanford Levinson, question, "Fidelity as Integrity," 1358.
81. Sanford Levinson, question, "Fidelity as Integrity," 1359.
82. Sanford Levinson, question, "Fidelity as Integrity," 1360.
83. See Frederick Schauer, *Playing by the Rules* (New York: Oxford University Press, 1991).
84. What follows substantially tracks extremely helpful comments by Jack Balkin in response to an earlier draft of this essay.
85. See for example U.S. Const. Amend. V.
86. See Rogers Smith, *Civic Ideals: Conflicting Visions of Citizenship in U.S. History* (New Haven: Yale University Press, 1997).
87. See Charles Fried, "The Lawyer as Friend: The Moral Foundations of the Lawyer-Client Relation," *Yale Law Journal* 85, no. 8 (July 1976): 1060, 1075 (emphasis added).
88. Fried, "The Lawyer as Friend," 1074.
89. See for example the most brilliant of all defenses of chattel slavery, George Fitzhugh, *Cannibals All, or, Slaves Without Masters* (1857). Indeed, one reason to integrate slavery into courses in both standard-form constitutional law and jurisprudence is to force us to examine, with far more precision than is ordinarily the case, exactly what constituted the injustice of slavery and whether it "really" was eliminated by the Thirteenth Amendment in 1865.
90. This argument is spelled out in Philip Bobbitt, *The Shield of Achilles* (New York: Alfred A. Knopf, 2002).
91. As to the latter, see Richard Weisberg, *Poethics and Other Strategies of Law and Literature* (New York: Columbia University Press, 1992), 136–58; Richard Weisberg, *Vichy Law and the Holocaust in France* (New York: New York University Press, 1996).
92. See Jack M. Balkin, "Understanding Legal Understanding: The Legal Subject and the Problem of Legal Coherence," *Yale Law Journal* 103, no. 1 (October 1993): 105, 168–9.
93. See for example John Rawls, "The Idea of Public Reason Revisited," in *The Law of Peoples* (Cambridge, MA: Harvard University Press, 2001), 129–80.

Bibliography

Introduction: Anti-Archimedeanism

Burley, Justine, ed. *Dworkin and His Critics*. Oxford: Blackwell Publishing, 2004.

Fish, Stanley. *Doing What Comes Naturally: Change, Rhetoric, and the Practice of Theory in Literary and Legal Studies*. Durham: Duke University Press, 1989.

Guest, Stephen. *Ronald Dworkin*. Stanford: Stanford University Press, 1991.

Hunt, Alan, ed. *Reading Dworkin Critically*. New York and Oxford: Berg, 1992.

Hurley, Susan. *Natural Reasons: Personality and Polity*. Oxford: Oxford University Press, 1989.

Perry, Stephen. "Interpretation and Methodology in Legal Theory," in *Law and Interpretation*, ed. A. Marmor (Oxford: Clarendon Press, 1995).

Posner, Richard A. "Conceptions of Legal 'Theory': A Response to Ronald Dworkin." *Arizona State Law Journal* 29 (1997): 377–88.

Raban, Ofer. "Dworkin's 'Best Light' Requirement and the Proper Methodology of Legal Theory." *Oxford Journal of Legal Studies* 23 (2003): 243–64.

Schlink, Bernhard. "Hercules in Germany?" *International Journal of Constitutional Law* 1 (2003): 610–20.

Westmoreland, Robert. "Dworkin and Legal Pragmatism." *Oxford Journal of Legal Studies* 11 (1991): 174–192.

Chapter 1. The "Hart–Dworkin" Debate: A Short for the Perplexed

Atkinson, Max. "Taking Dworkin Seriously." *Australasian Journal of Philosophy* 61 (1983): 27–39.

Balkin, J. M. "Taking Ideology Seriously: Ronald Dworkin and the CLS Critique." *UMKC Law Review* 55 (1987): 392–433.

Brubaker, Stanley C. "Reconsidering Dworkin's Case for Judicial Activism." *Journal of Politics* 46 (1984): 503–19.

Brubaker, Stanley C. "Taking Dworkin Seriously." *The Review of Politics* 47 (1985): 45–65.

Burton, Steven J. "Ronald Dworkin and Legal Positivism." *Iowa Law Review* 73 (1987): 109–29.

Cohen, Marshall, ed. *Ronald Dworkin and Contemporary Jurisprudence*. London: Duckworth, 1984.

Coleman, Jules. "Negative and Positive Positivism." *Journal of Legal Studies* 11 (1982): 139–64.

Coleman, Jules, ed. *Hart's Postscript*. Oxford: Oxford University Press, 2001.

Coleman, Jules. *The Practice of Principle*. Oxford: Oxford University Press, 2001.

Coleman, Jules, and Scott Shapiro, eds. *The Oxford Handbook of Jurisprudence and Legal Philosophy*. Oxford: Oxford University Press, 2001 (various chapters).

Corlett, J. Angelo. "Dworkin's Empire Strikes Back!" *Statute Law Review* 21 (2000): 43–56.

Culver, Keith. "Leaving the Hart-Dworkin Debate." *The University of Toronto Law Journal* 51 (2001): 367–98.

Donato, James. "Dworkin and Subjectivity in Legal Interpretation." *Stanford Law Review* 40 (1988): 1517–41.

Endicott, Timothy. "Herbert Hart and the Semantic Sting." *Legal Theory* 4 (1998): 283–300.

Endicott, Timothy. "Are There Any Rules?" *The Journal of Ethics* 5 (2001): 199–219.

Endicott, Timothy. "Raz on Gaps – The Suprising Part," in *Rights, Culture and Law*, ed. L. H. Meyer, S. L. Paulson, and T. W. Pogge (Oxford: Oxford University Press, 2003).

Galis, Leon. "The Real and Unrefuted Rights Thesis." *The Philosophical Review* 92 (1983): 197–221.

Grafstein, Robert. "Taking Dworkin to Hart: A Positivist Conception of Institutional Rules." *Political Theory* 11 (1983): 244–65.

Hart, H. L. A. "American Jurisprudence through English Eyes: The Nightmare and the Noble Dream," in *Essays in Jurisprudence and Philosophy* (Oxford: Clarendon Press, 1983).

Hart, H. L. A. "Legal Duty and Obligation," in *Essays on Bentham* (Oxford: Clarendon Press, 1982).

Hart, H. L. A. "Postscript" to *The Concept of Law*, 2nd ed. (Oxford: Clarendon Press, 1994), 239–44.

Hershovitz, Scott. *Exploring Law's Empire: The Jurisprudence of Ronald Dworkin*. Oxford: Oxford University Press, 2006.

Himma, Kenneth Einar. "Waluchow's Defense of Inclusive Positivism." *Legal Theory* 5 (1999): 101–16.

Kornhauser, Lewis A. "No Best Answer?" *University of Pennsylvania Law Review* 146 (1998): 1599–1637.

Kramer, Matthew H. "Also Among the Prophets: Some Rejoinders to Ronald Dworkin's Attacks on Legal Positivism." *Canadian Journal of Law and Jurisprudence: An International Journal of Legal Thought* 12 (1996): 53–82.

Kramer, Matthew H. *Law Without Trimmings: A Defense of Legal Positivism*. Oxford: Oxford University Press, 1999.

Kress, Ken, and Scott W. Anderson. "Dworkin in Transition." *The American Journal of Comparative Law* 37 (1989): 337–51.

Lyons, David. "Moral Aspects of Legal Theory." *Midwest Studies in Philosophy* 7 (1982): 223–54.

Lyons, David. "Principles, Positivism and Legal Theory." *Yale Law Journal* 87 (1977): 415–35.

Leiter, Brian. "Beyond the Hart–Dworkin Debate." *American Journal of Jurisprudence* 48 (2003): 17–51.

MacCallum, Jr., Gerald C. "Dworkin on Judicial Discretion: Comments." *The Journal of Philosophy* 60 (1963): 638–41.

MacCormick, D. N. "Dworkin as Pre-Benthamite." *The Philosophical Review* 87 (1978): 586–607.

Mackie, John. "The Third Theory of Law." *Philosophy and Public Affairs* 7 (1977): 3–16.

Mureinik, Etienne. "Dworkin and Apartheid," in *Law and Social Practice*, ed. H. Corder (Cape Town: Juta, 1988) 181.

Nino, Carlos S. "Dworkin and Legal Positivism." *Mind* 89 (1980): 519–43.

Pannick, David. "A Note on Dworkin and Precedent." *The Modern Law Review* 43 (1980): 36–44.

Raz, Joseph. "Authority, Law and Morality," in *Ethics in the Public Domain* (Oxford: Clarendon Press, 1994).

Raz, Joseph. *The Authority of Law*. Oxford: Clarendon Press, 1979.

Regan, Donald H. "Glosses on Dworkin: Rights, Principles, and Policies." *Michigan Law Review* 76 (1978): 1213–64.

Soper, E. Philip. "Legal Theory and the Obligation of a Judge: The Hart/Dworkin Dispute." *Michigan Law Review* 75 (1977): 473–519.

Waluchow, Wilfrid J. "Strong Discretion." *The Philosophical Quarterly* 33 (1983): 321–39.

Waluchow, Wilfrid J. *Inclusive Legal Positivism*. Oxford: Oxford University Press, 1995.

Woodman, Gordon. "Dworkin's 'Right Answer' Thesis and the Frustration of Legislative Intent: A Case-Study on the Leasehold Reform Act." *The Modern Law Review* 45 (1982): 121–38.

Woozley, A. D. "No Right Answer." *The Philosophical Quarterly* 29 (1979): 25–34.

Chapter 2. The Rule of Law as the Rule of Liberal Principle

Altman, Andrew. "Policy, Principle, and Incrementalism: Dworkin's Jurisprudence of Race." *The Journal of Ethics* 5 (2001): 241–62.

Lagerspetz, Eerik. "Ronald Dworkin on Communities and Obligations: A Critical Comment." *Ratio Juris: An International Journal of Jurisprudence and Philosophy of Law* 12 (1999): 108–15.

Mian, Emran. "The Value Of Community, Or How Burke Compromises Dworkin." *Legal Theory* 9 (2003): 125–56.

Neal, P. "Liberalism & Neutrality." *Polity* 17 (1985): 664–84.

Peerenboom, Randall P. "A *Coup d'Etat* in Law's Empire: Dworkin's Hercules Meets Atlas." *Law and Philosophy: An International Journal for Jurisprudence and Legal Philosophy* 9 (1990): 95–113.

Pildes, Richard. "Why Rights Are Not Trumps: Social Meanings, Expressive Harms, and Constitutionalism." *Journal of Legal Studies* 27, no. 2 (June 1998): 725–63.

Richardson, Genevra. "The Legal Regulation of Process," in *Administrative Law and Government Action*, ed. Genevra Richardson and Hazel Genn (Oxford: Clarendon Press, 1994).

Waldron, Jeremy. "The Circumstances of Integrity." *Legal Theory* 3 (1997): 1–22.

Waldron, Jeremy. "Pildes on Dworkin's Theory of Rights." *The Journal of Legal Studies* 29 (2000): 301–7.

Winston, Kenneth I. "Principles and Touchstones: The Dilemma of Dworkin's Liberalism." *Polity* 19 (1986): 42–55.

Wolfe, Christopher. "Liberalism and Paternalism: A Critique of Ronald Dworkin." *The Review of Politics* 56 (1994): 615–39.

Wolfe, Christopher. "The Egalitarian Liberalism of Ronald Dworkin," in *Liberalism at the Crossroads: An Introduction to Contemporary Liberal Political Theory and Its Critics* (2nd ed.), ed. Christopher Wolfe (Lanham: Rowman & Littlefield, 2003).

Chapter 3. Liberty and Equality

Anderson, Elizabeth. "What Is the Point of Equality?" *Ethics* 109, no. 2 (Jan. 1999): 287–337.

Armstrong, Chris. "Equality, Risk and Responsibility: Dworkin on the Insurance Market." *Economy and Society* 34 (2005): 451–73.

Arneson, Richard. "Equality and Equal Opportunity for Welfare." *Philosophical Studies* 56 (1989): 77–93.

Arneson, Richard. "Liberalism, Distributive Subjectivism, and Equal Opportunity for Welfare." *Philosophy and Public Affairs* 19 (1990): 158–94.

Arneson, Richard. "Egalitarianism and Responsibility." *Journal of Ethics* 3 (1999): 225–47.

Arneson, Richard. "Equal Opportunity for Welfare Defended and Recanted." *Journal of Political Philosophy* 7 (1999): 488–97.

Arneson, Richard. "Luck Egalitarianism and Prioritarianism." *Ethics* 110 (2000): 339–49.

Arneson, Richard. "Luck and Equality II." *Proceedings of the Aristotelian Society*, supp. vol. (2001): 73–90.

Bennett, John G. "Ethics and Markets." *Philosophy and Public Affairs* 14 (1985): 195–204.

Champeau, Serge. "Ronald Dworkin, le Libéralisme et l'Égalité." *Revue Philosophique de Louvain* 97 (1999): 550–80.

Christian, Arnsperger. "Reformulating Equality of Resources." *Economics and Philosophy* 13 (1997): 61–77.

Christofidis, Miriam Cohen. "Talent, Slavery and Envy in Dworkin's Equality of Resources." *Utilitas: A Journal of Utilitarian Studies* 16 (2004): 267–87.

Clayton, Matthew, and Andrew Williams, eds. *The Ideal of Equality*. New York: Macmillan and St. Martin's Press, 2000.

Clayton, Matthew. "Liberal Equality and Ethics." *Ethics* 113 (2002): 8–22.

Cohen, G. A. "On the Currency of Egalitarian Justice." *Ethics* 99 (1989): 906–44.

Ely, John Hart. "Professor Dworkin's External/Personal Preference Distinction." *Duke Law Journal* (1983): 959–86.

Fleirbaey, Marc. "Equality of Resources Revisited." *Ethics* 113 (2002): 82–105.

Halpin, Andrew. "Clamshells or Bedsteads?" *Oxford Journal of Legal Studies* 20 (2000): 353–66.

Heath, Joseph. "Dworkin's Auction." *Politics, Philosophy & Economics* 3 (2004): 313–35.

Hinton, Timothy. "Choice and Luck in Recent Egalitarian Thought." *Philosophical Papers* 31 (2002): 145–67.

Hurley, Susan. *Justice, Luck, and Knowledge*. Cambridge, MA: Harvard University Press, 2003.

Jacobson, Daniel. "Freedom of Speech Acts? A Response to Langton." *Philosophy and Public Affairs* 24 (1995): 64–79.

Kymlicka, Will. *Contemporary Political Philosophy*. New York: Oxford University Press, 1990.

Langton, Rae. "Whose Right? Ronald Dworkin, Women and Pornographers." *Philosophy and Public Affairs* 19 (1990): 311–59.

Lippert-Rasmussen, Kaspar. "Egalitarianism, Option Luck, and Responsibility." *Ethics* 111 (2001): 548–79.

Macleod, Colin M. "Liberal Neutrality Or Liberal Tolerance?" *Law and Philosophy* 16 (1997): 529–59.

Macleod, Colin M. *Liberalism, Justice and Markets*. Oxford: Oxford University Press, 2000.

Matravers, Matt. "Responsibility, Luck, and the 'Equality of What?' Debate." *Political Studies* 50 (2002): 558–72.

Narveson, Jan. "On Dworkinian Equality." *Social Philosophy and Policy* 1 (1983): 1–23.

Nordahl, Richard. "Ronald Dworkin and the Defense of Homosexual Rights." *Canadian Journal of Law and Jurisprudence* 8 (1995): 19–48.

Otsuka, Michael. "Luck, Insurance, and Equality." *Ethics* 113 (2002): 40–54.

Plaw, Avery. "Why Monist Critiques Feed Value Pluralism: Ronald Dworkin's Critique of Isaiah Berlin." *Social Theory and Practice* 30 (2004): 105–26.

Rakowski, Eric. *Equal Justice*. Oxford: Oxford University Press, 1995.

Rickard, Maurice. "Freedom, Equality, and the True Costs of Resources." *Dialogue: Canadian Philosophical Review* 37 (1998): 761–7.

Roemer, John. "Equality of Talent." *Economics and Philosophy* 1 (1985): 151–88.

Roemer, John. "A Pragmatic Theory of Responsibility for the Egalitarian Planner." *Philosophy and Public Affairs* 10 (1993): 146–66.

Roemer, John. *Theories of Distributive Justice*. Cambridge, MA: Harvard University Press, 1996.

Roemer, John. *Equality of Opportunity*. Cambridge, MA: Harvard University Press, 1998.

Rogerson, Kenneth F. "The Inequality of Markets." *Dialogue: Canadian Philosophical Review* 28 (1989): 553–67.

Sandbu, Martin E. "On Dworkin's Brute-Luck-Option-Luck Distinction and the Consistency of Brute-Luck Egalitarianism." *Politics, Philosophy & Economics* 3 (2004): 283–312.

Scheffler, Samuel. "What is Egalitarianism?" *Philosophy and Public Affairs* 31, no. 1 (Winter 2003): 5–39.

Scheffler, Samuel. "Equality as the Virtue of Sovereigns: A Reply to Ronald Dworkin." *Philosophy & Public Affairs* 31 (2003): 199–206.

Sherwin, Emily. "How Liberal Is Liberal Equality? A Comment on Ronald Dworkin's Tanner Lecture." *Legal Theory* 1 (1995): 227–50.

Vallentyne, Peter. "Brute Luck, Option Luck, and Equality of Initial Opportunities." *Ethics* 112 (2002): 529–57.

Van der Veen, Robert. "Equality of Talent Resources: Procedures or Outcomes?" *Ethics* 113 (2002): 55–81.

Varian, Hal R. "Dworkin on Equality of Resources." *Economics and Philosophy* 1 (1985): 110–25.

Wilkinson, T. M. "Against Dworkin's Endorsement Constraint." *Utilitas: A Journal of Utilitarian Studies* 15 (2003) 175–93.

Williams, Andrew. "Dworkin on Capability." *Ethics* 113 (2002): 23–39.

Williams, Andrew. "Equality for the Ambitious." *Philosophical Quarterly* 52 (2002): 377–89.

Chapter 4. Rights, Responsibilities, and Reflections on the Sanctity of Life

Baird, Robert M. "Dworkin, Abortion, Religious Liberty, and the Spirit of Enlightenment." *Journal of Church and State* 37 (1995): 753–71.

Barclay, Linda. "Rights, Intrinsic Values and the Politics of Abortion." *Utilitas: A Journal of Utilitarian Studies* 11 (1999): 215–29.

Belshaw, C. "Abortion, Value and the Sanctity of Life." *Bioethics* 11 (1997): 130–50.

David, Gregory B. "Dworkin, Precedent, Confidence, and Roe v. Wade." *University of Pennsylvania Law Review* 152 (2004): 1221–53.

Kamm, F. M. "Abortion and the Value of Life. Ronald Dworkin: *Life's Dominion*" *Columbia Law Review* 95 (1995): 160–222.

Kamm, F. M. "Ronald Dworkin on Abortion and Assisted Suicide." *The Journal of Ethics* 5 (2001): 221–40.

Mitchell, David. "The Importance of Being Important: Euthanasia and Critical Interests in Dworkin's Life's Dominion." *Utilitas: A Journal of Utilitarian Studies* 7 (1995): 301–14.

Naticchia, Chris. "Ronald Dworkin's Life's Dominion." *Journal of Law and Politics* 10 (1997): 339–67.

O'Day, Ken. "Intrinsic Value and Investment." *Utilitas: A Journal of Utilitarian Studies* 11 (1999): 194–214.

Rakowski, Eric. "Ronald Dworkin, Reverence for Life, and the Limits of State Power." *Utilitas: A Journal of Utilitarian Studies* 13 (2001): 33–64.

Scanlon, T. M. "Partisan for Life." *New York Review of Books* (July 15, 1993), 40 (13): 45–50.

Stroud, Sarah. "Dworkin and Casey on Abortion." *Philosophy and Public Affairs* 25 (1996): 140–70.

Tomasi, John. "Liberalism, Sanctity, and the Prohibition of Abortion." *The Journal of Philosophy* 94 (1997): 491–513.

Chapter 5. Hercules, Abraham Lincoln, the United States Constitution, and the Problem of Slavery

Aronovitch, Hilliard. "A Liberal Reading of the American Constitution." *Canadian Journal of Law and Jurisprudence: An International Journal of Legal Thought* 10 (1997): 521–35.

Chaskalson, Arthur. "From Wickedness to Equality: The Moral Transformation of South African Law." *International Journal of Constitutional Law* 1 (2003): 590–609.

Eisele, Thomas D. "Taking Our Actual Constitution Seriously." *Michigan Law Review* 95 (1997): 1799–1838.

Levinson, Sanford. "Taking Law Seriously: Reflections on 'Thinking Like a Lawyer.'" *Stanford Law Review* 30, no. 5 (May 1978): 1071, 1090–1.

Levinson, Sanford. *Constitutional Faith*. Princeton: Princeton University Press, 1988.

McCaffery, Edward J. "Ronald Dworkin, Inside-Out." *California Law Review* 85 (1997): 1043–86.

Neeley, G. Steven. "Dworkin, Vague Constitutional Clauses, and the Eighth Amendment's Admonition Against Cruel and Unusual Punishment." *Contemporary Philosophy* 16 (1994): 18–27.

Pildes, Richard H. "Dworkin's Two Conceptions of Rights." *The Journal of Legal Studies* 29 (2000): 309–15.

Posner, Richard A. "Dworkin, Polemics, and the Clinton Impeachment Controversy." *Northwestern University Law Review* 94 (2000): 1023–47.

Sebok, Anthony. "Judging the Fugitive Slave Acts." *Yale Law Journal* 100 (1991): 1835–1854.

Sebok, Anthony J. *Legal Positivism in American Jurisprudence*. Cambridge, UK: Cambridge University Press, 1998.

Zagrebelsky, Gustavo. "Ronald Dworkin's Principle Based Constitutionalism: An Italian Point of View." *International Journal of Constitutional Law* 1 (2003): 621–50.

Index